To My Friends,
Mark and Sue

Ruminations

❦

"This is the inspiring story of one man's journey across half the world to make a successful life in America."

—**Congressman Bill Pascrell, Jr.**

"Phenomenal! Candid, humorous, yet at the same time touching and nostalgic memoirs by an acclaimed psychiatrist. A must-read for all South Asian immigrants and their progeny."

—**Amarjot S. Narula, MD**
President, New Jersey Psychiatric Association

"Controversial views on American health care, with which many physicians will disagree. Overall, *Ruminations* is riveting, compelling, and hard to put down."

—**Raj Gupta, MD**
President, Medical Society of New Jersey

"Lucid, absorbing, and easy to read. Almost any immigrant to any country will relate to Dr. Dang's early experiences in America. His comparison of the social and cultural systems in the United States and India offers an intriguing perspective, and his ability to laugh at himself adds to the book's appeal."

—**Shiv Khera**
International bestselling author of *You Can Win*

Ruminations

Memoirs of a
Psychiatrist from India

❧

Jagdish "Jack" Dang, MD

Trafford Publishing

Order this book online at www.trafford.com/08-1022
or email orders@trafford.com

Most Trafford titles are also available at major online book retailers.

© Copyright 2008 Jagdish "Jack" Dang, MD.
jackdangmd@yahoo.com
Edited by Janet Frick
Designed by Saija Autrand

Note for Librarians: A cataloguing record for this book is available from Library and Archives Canada at www.collectionscanada.ca/amicus/index-e.html

Printed in Victoria, BC, Canada.

ISBN: 978-1-4251-8512-1

We at Trafford believe that it is the responsibility of us all, as both individuals and corporations, to make choices that are environmentally and socially sound. You, in turn, are supporting this responsible conduct each time you purchase a Trafford book, or make use of our publishing services. To find out how you are helping, please visit www.trafford.com/responsiblepublishing.html

Our mission is to efficiently provide the world's finest, most comprehensive book publishing service, enabling every author to experience success. To find out how to publish your book, your way, and have it available worldwide, visit us online at www.trafford.com/10510

www.trafford.com

North America & international
toll-free: 1 888 232 4444 (USA & Canada)
phone: 250 383 6864 ♦ fax: 250 383 6804
email: info@trafford.com

The United Kingdom & Europe
phone: +44 (0)1865 487 395 ♦ local rate: 0845 230 9601
facsimile: +44 (0)1865 481 507 ♦ email: info.uk@trafford.com

10 9 8 7 6 5 4 3 2 1

Contents

Contents

Introduction

Let me introduce myself. I am a physician in my late sixties who is board certified in psychiatry and geriatric psychiatry. My practice extends over a period of forty years and includes work as a clinician, an administrator, a faculty member of a medical school, chairman of the department of psychiatry in a hospital, and director of psychiatry at several major nursing homes. I have helped determine the policies of hospitals and medical societies, and cringe when thinking of some policies that never change.

I was born in the northwest part of undivided India, and when that part became Pakistan after the partition in 1947, my family became refugees and moved to India; I was seven at the time. I had polio at age three. I came to the United States in 1966 and have visited India about every two to three years since then. I have seen a socialist and indigent India and the emerging capitalist, high-flying, high-tech India, ready to compete with the largest economies of the world. I have witnessed an explosion of population, pollution, corruption—and miraculous technological, financial, and medical advances. I have traveled a great deal in the United States and in some other countries. I have witnessed poverty and hunger and have seen affluence and power. I have known discrimination of many kinds and seen it work both against me and in my favor. I have also seen slavery in various forms. I have participated in community-service organizations and in ethnic and religious groups, and have read and written a great deal. I have been a voice on hospital boards and medical, psychiatric, and alumni associations. I have received many awards, including some that were rarely obtainable for an Indian in America back then. In 2003 I was named a distinguished life fellow of the American Psychiatric Association.

I have been happily married for almost forty years, and I have two well-settled children, five grandchildren, and a host of other very loving and concerned family members and friends. I have experienced more happiness and fun in life than any human being can expect to have, and have also seen a lot of misery. I have seen misery in families, in hospitals, and in extended-care facilities. I have known unethical health-care workers and administrators and deals being made behind the scenes in medical and psychiatric societies and institutions. I believe that our American health-care system is broken, and it is because of greed—the greed of doctors, hospitals, nursing homes, HMOs, lawyers, politicians, drug and appliance makers, and the advent of Medicare and Medicaid.

Our social systems, both Indian and American, leave a lot to be desired. I do not have enough answers. But I ruminate. Here is a collection of some of those ruminations.

⚜

Somebody once asked a popular Bollywood (Bombay Hollywood) actor-turned-politician when he was going to write his autobiography. He said something like, "If I write everything truthfully, the families of all those women I have had affairs with will fall apart." At my peril, I have tried to write the names, places, and events as I remember them. However, I had to change a few names.

I have written what I feel and I see, guided by my own opinions and assumptions, not those of others. Some of what I have written is provocative and explosive, and is going to touch the sensitivities of people, both Indian and American. We Indians are very sensitive to our culture and society being criticized, even when in our hearts we know it is true; why expose our vulnerabilities? We quickly become defensive and have all kinds of excuses: "it does not happen anymore; it happens only in remote villages; only low-caste people do it," and so on. My reflections and thoughts are not based on universal facts; experiences like mine don't necessarily happen all over India. It is a very large country, where different areas and classes of people have different customs. Also, of course, India has changed a great deal over the years. I have written about what happened then, to me. Similarly, my experiences in America are not universal; they do not necessarily happen to every Indian here, physician or not. They don't happen to all immigrants, either. Every immigrant is an individual, and each one has different aspirations, feelings, experiences, findings, and actions.

Perhaps this book will bring back memories, good and bad. Some of my family members and friends will feel that I have exaggerated some facts. What I have written is how I see and remember. When analyzing events and relationships, we sometimes see and hear what we want to see and hear. I have probably done that too. I may be seeing the glass half empty when actually it is half full, or the other way around. But some other people will also think that there is no water in the glass at all. The glass is definitely not full when you consider social systems, whether in India or in America. My apologies to anyone who is hurt or offended by my frankness.

Fifty, sixty years is a long time. Just before I left India, I lived in a small, one-story, two-bedroom house with eight other people; the nine of us shared one or two bicycles. During my subsequent visits, first there were one or two motor scooters, then one or two or three cars—even though only four people live in the same house, now built to three stories. That was the industrial change in India. Now about the social changes in America: when I came here, you could not go into a moderate restaurant without a tie and a jacket; now many fine restaurants will let you eat as long as you wear a polo shirt. Also, in the 1960s you could not imagine that half the children here in public schools today would be from single-parent homes.

I have poured out my heart, my feelings, my thoughts. I have tried to recreate times, places, and persons as I remember them. I am not a researcher, an academician, or a preacher. I am an ordinary man who has had some debilitating doubts and struggles, fought my frailties and demons, and found moments of ultimate joy, energy, and excitement. Most of my story is about quiet challenges, mundane happenings, and everyday living, but you will probably find some details amusing and others disturbing, occasionally even shocking. You may learn things you didn't know about medicine, psychiatry, mental patients, Indians, short people, bald people—and especially, how the cultures of India and the United States have changed during my lifetime and interacted with each other.

I hope my story may have something for everyone, immigrant or not. With recent interest in immigrants, Middle Eastern and Indian cultures, outsourcing, mental health, and the explosion of Indian doctors in America—not to mention the crisis in American health care—I believe that many readers will relate to something in my ruminations. I have enjoyed putting them on paper. Writing is a wonderful catharsis. You might want to try it yourself sometime!

PART ONE

Son and Grandson

1

My Date of Birth…
Which Date of Birth?

I was born sometime in 1940 or 1941. I don't know the exact date or even the year, as vital statistics were not kept in India then, and there was no such thing as a birth certificate. It was in a town called Lyallpur in the district of Punjab in the northwestern part of undivided India. That town is now in Pakistan and is called Faisalabad; they changed the name of the town when King Faisal of Saudi Arabia visited Lyallpur and gave Pakistan a large financial donation. I have been told that the town is now Pakistan's third largest city and a major business center, full of hustle and bustle. Even in 1940 it was a key business center. It had the only cloth-manufacturing plant in Punjab, and merchants from all over the state came to do business there. It had a clock tower as the central feature, with eight avenues emerging from around it like eight petals of a blooming flower. Urdu poets used to write *ghazals* (lyric poems) inspired by that clock tower, and legends were written describing its beauty. The tower was an architectural gift from the English to India during the colonial rule.

There were big celebrations when I was born. I know that because there are always celebrations in India when a son is born. And when the first child is a son, there is an even bigger celebration! A son is considered a great blessing: he carries the family name, and he and his family stay with the parents and supposedly take care of them in their old age. On the other hand, a daughter is a sort of burden. She is not a permanent part of the family; you bring her up, educate her (education of a daughter in those days meant teaching to cook, sew, knit, sing religious songs, and so on), and when the time comes you give her away to take the name of another family. In addition, as soon as a daughter is born, you have to start worrying about the dowry her in-laws will demand (or hint at) at the time of her wedding.

My sixteen-year-old mother gave birth to me in the house of my father's parents, with the help of a midwife and other women in the house, especially my grandmother. This was expected, as my mother was considered part of my father's family, and they all lived together in a joint family system. There were my grandparents, their oldest child (my father), their four other children, my mother, and me. When I was about two years old, a daughter was born to my grandmother. Now she had six children: three boys and three girls. Two more of her sons had died during infancy. The thinking was that the more children you had, the better off you were going to be in your old age; the sons could earn money and support you. Also, infant mortality was rampant and life expectancy was short, so the more children, the better. A couple who had a dozen children was considered very lucky and even got a grant from the government. Of course, no thought was given to how you would support or feed your growing family. That attitude is one of the reasons for India's overpopulation. Only recently is the attitude changing a bit, and there is some family planning now.

⚜

My date of birth is an imaginary date that my father came up with when he took me to school to register for the first grade. He mused something like this: "The weather was somewhat chilly when my son was born, so it must have been September, and it was probably the year 1940. Three is a lucky number, so let's say the third of September, 1940." My grandmother, when prodded years later, said that according to her calculations by the Hindu calendar, I was born on May 1, probably 1941. You can take your pick. My children call me twice a year to say "Happy Fake Birthday, Dad," or "Happy Real Birthday, Dad." I stick to September 3, because that is the date written on my passport and other legal documents. Me, always trying to be politically correct. My wife has two birthdays, too. She, however, likes to celebrate her "real" birthday.

My name was suggested by a Hindu priest in a religious ceremony held on the thirteenth day after birth, similar to a christening. The priest held a long prayer session, punctuated by a description of the stars that were connecting or interacting at the time of my birth. He also produced astrological charts predicting major events for my life. (I wish I had those charts today and could compare them to my real-life events.) A large number of relatives

11

and friends were invited and fed, and sweets were distributed. After naming me, the priest allowed me to wear clothes for the first time. Until then, I was allowed to be wrapped only in small blankets or sheets. Whether that custom is meant to prevent disease or to ward off bad spirits, I am not sure.

My full name is Jagdish Chander Dang, which means "son of God of this universe." All the names in India were long and tedious and had something to do with God—God of this and God of that. We Hindus have many gods, millions, so there is no dearth of names. In some parts of India the names are very long and include part of your father's name, the name of your village, and your caste. I never liked my long name and kept shortening it as time went on. I so much disliked long names that I gave very short names to my children. My daughter actually complained to me once about having the shortest name in her class.

⁂

My grandparents never went to school, and my grandfather, like most average Indians, was very much against any formal education. He had a store where he sold cloth, and he wanted his oldest son totally involved in that business. However, my father was keen on going to school, and his mother sent him to school and hid this fact from her husband. She was always for education, and always said regretfully, "If I had been born a man I would have gone to college, and we would never be poor." My mother repeated the same sentiments. (Rumor had it that she dropped out after third grade, but she boasted that she went up to fifth.) My father finished high school and made state ranking. To celebrate the feat, the principal of the school sent a band to the house. When my grandfather saw the band in front of our house, he felt that my father had humiliated the family name by going to school. He sent the band away and punished my father. My father was the first high school graduate in the whole extended family. He did most of the reading and writing for all of them; the others would apply a thumbprint whenever documents had to be signed.

We were a close-knit joint family, as most families were. I called my father's sisters *Didi* ("Sister") and his brothers *Bhapa* ("Brother," in Punjabi). I still do. The notion was that calling them "Aunt" or "Uncle" was too indifferent, and "Brother" and "Sister" brought you closer. There were funny and confusing inconsistencies in doing this. For example, I called my uncle Khushiram "Brother" but his wife "Aunt."

In Lyallpur we lived in a modest two-story townhouse with two large bedrooms, a living room, and a kitchen, all on the second floor. The lower floor was dark and was used for the storage of goods for our store. We had electricity, but food was cooked on an open hearth on coal or wood. We had running water. There was a large hallway between the bedrooms and the living room, and most of the floor of the hallway was a metal grille. Similarly, much of the roof over the hallway was a metal grille, sort of an open skylight. Houses in India have flat roofs, and in summer we took cots up to the roof and slept there. In one corner of the roof was a latrine with no running water. A lower-caste woman came to clean the latrine every day.

The house next door belonged to my grandfather's brother. We shared a common roof, with a five-foot-high wall separating the two houses. It was originally one house that had been divided into two when the wives of the two brothers did not get along. We found that hard to understand, because the two brothers were very close: they owned the store together, they ate together, and they sat on the cot outside the store all day, laughing and joking and making fun of everybody, including their wives. They did little work; the hired help minded the store. The wives, on the other hand, hated each other until the end. My grandmother, like everybody else in the community, was very superstitious. All her life she thought that I had contracted polio because her sister-in-law had put some kind of curse on us. There was enough reason for jealousy. After all, one woman had several children, including sons, and now had a grandson, while the other was a *banjh* for a long time—a childless woman. Both families were brought up with this continuous paranoia about each other. My grandmother used to say that when I was born there were wailing sounds heard from next door, and a clay doll was thrown to us over the roof.

We were a middle-class family. My father, being the oldest boy in the two families, often took the train to Bombay to buy merchandise at wholesale prices and brought it to Lyallpur for sale in the store. He was always considered a good businessman, but in reality he never succeeded in any business he endeavored to start up. His financial failures were attributed to various factors: too honest, too stupid, too lazy, unlucky, and so on. The apple does not fall far from the tree; I often think of these same reasons for not making as much money in my life as I could have.

My grandfather and grandmother never got along. Nobody had ever seen them being civil to each other. They did not talk to each other for days, and when they did, it was essentially fighting and arguing (mostly about his brother and brother's family). We often wondered how they had all those children together. My grandmother had a club like a baseball bat, which she used to beat laundry. She also used that bat freely on her children, especially on her sons, and gave them black-and-blue marks. It was a common practice; the corporal punishment of boys was believed necessary to keep them disciplined, although my grandmother went a bit overboard.

Women did not go out of the house much. A number of peddlers with wooden carts came to the street and shouted the goods they were selling: vegetables, milk and *kulfi* (ice cream), snacks (fresh-roasted peanuts, roasted whole sweet potatoes, candy, fried and salted lentils, peanut brittle), glass bangles, and so on. The woman of the house would stand at the upper balcony, talk to the salesman, haggle about the prices, and lower money in a basket tied to a rope; then the seller would put the goods and change in the basket. This was repeated several times a day. This custom could have been adopted from the Muslim majority where we lived, and their culture of keeping women in the seclusion of *purdah* (the veil).

2

The Child Bride,
Her Brothers, and Fireworks

Even though Indian children are not supposed to think, feel, or talk too much about their maternal roots, to me it was as important a facet of my life as any. My mother was fourteen years old and my father about seventeen when they got married. This is how it happened:

It is 1938. An elderly distant relative is visiting the Ahuja household in Gojra, thirty miles from Lyallpur, and eating lunch. He is sitting cross-legged on a clean carpet. He is served his lunch on a large metal plate with several metal bowls of vegetable curries, lentil soup, and yogurt. There is a tall metal glass of sweet yogurt shake, called *lassi*. For dessert, he is given a bowl of rice pudding and some carrot *halva* (cake). The host is fanning him lightly, as it is hot and there are flies around. The visitor sees a girl, my future mother, pass by shyly.

"Is that your daughter?"

"Yes, Uncle."

"She is beautiful. How old is she?"

"Fourteen. I am worried about her."

"You should be. Do you have a boy in mind?"

"Not yet. She is in your hands now; you have to help us. She has gone to third grade in school, knows cooking and knitting and sewing." (Even if she had gone to fifth grade, her father would be hesitant to say so because that in itself might be unacceptable, "too modern a girl for my son," who may be totally illiterate).

"I have a boy in mind. Good family. Distant relatives. Handsome boy. I think he even went to high school. The family has a good cloth business in Lyallpur. If I take the proposal to them, they can't refuse. Consider it done."

"Thank you so much, Uncle."

My mother's father goes inside the house and gives the good news to his wife. They start a quiet celebration with sweets. It is almost a done deal.

The relative goes to the Dang house and has a similar lunch. My grandmother, then a beautiful thirty-five-year-old woman, is fanning him lightly. He brings up the "proposal" from thirty miles away, unwittingly exaggerating a bit. My father's family feels as lucky as my mother's and starts celebrating.

That's how marriages were decided. Remember "marriages are made in heaven"?

The wedding happened with pomp and show: several hundred people, train ride, bands, decorated horse for the groom, lots of feasts, dowry, religious ceremonies, and the bride changing her name and family from her parents' to her in-laws'.

The Ahujas had a small grocery store and were considered "a good family"—same caste as the Dangs, good reputation in the community. They had four sons and one daughter. She was the apple of their eye, but she was still the daughter, not the son. The oldest brother, Kundanlal, was married and had an infant son. He died shortly after my mother got married. His wife did not remarry. A widow getting remarried was unheard of then and could even lead to a riot; even today it is rare. She lived to the ripe age of almost ninety and brought up her son in adverse conditions. They lived for years in a joint family with brothers-in-law and their wives and children—totally dependent on them, doing menial chores in the house, taking regular verbal abuse. Then her son married and she got continuous abuse from her daughter-in-law in the next multigenerational family. I never saw her smile and often saw her crying.

That was the life of most widows there. A widow was supposed to wear white clothes all her life—a symbol of mourning, and indirectly, a reason for ridicule and sympathy from others. Divorces were almost unknown in the past, but a divorced woman was treated even worse than a widow. (Divorce is a recent phenomenon in India; they call it a Western curse.)

A widow or a divorced woman coming to see a new bride was considered a bad omen. In fact, until recently a widow was considered unlucky for the family. She could not participate in joyous family functions for fear that she would bring bad luck. She could not laugh or show pleasure of any kind, or even go to a temple during any major events. She would do household chores, eat leftovers at the end of the day, and sleep on the floor or a low cot. She was verbally abused on a regular basis and was considered fortunate if she did not get physically abused or worse. If a woman was raped, she was considered "impure" and was not allowed to go into a temple to pray. Now that Indian society is better educated, these conditions have improved slightly, but I was quite disturbed by the treatment of women and other social customs in India. I am sure this had a lot to do with my choice of career, my decision to stay in America, and for all practical purposes how I have run my whole life.

❧✦☙

The Ahujas were not richer than the Dangs, but they were good to us, especially to me. They were always giving us gifts, which was not unexpected. When parents married off a daughter, they gave her gifts or a dowry. In addition, every time the daughter visited her parents, they were supposed to give her gifts, large or small, to take back to "her" house. If the daughter-in-law brought back a huge bounty from her parents' house, the family would spread it out in the living room and invite close relatives and friends to see the "honor" she brought home. If she did not bring much in the way of offerings, she got verbal abuse from her in-laws. Although the tradition is a bit more refined now (more subtle, less open), it is still very much in practice to this day. Despite the government's efforts—dowry is legally banned in India—this curse for the girl's family has not been eradicated.

I remember good times as a child whenever I visited the

Ahujas in Gojra. Every time my mother and I came back from visiting my uncles in Gojra, my grandmother invited family and friends and showed them the goodies that were given to us. In later years my family told me that the Ahujas were just a "show-off" family. Jealousy and rivalry between the in-laws was a normal thing; sometimes it became intense. In any case, I loved the affection and presents bestowed on me when I vacationed in my maternal family's house.

Gift-giving rules were almost extreme when it came to families connected by marriage. For example, if you visited your daughter's house, in addition to bringing gifts you were not supposed to accept any gifts in return. You were not supposed to eat there, or even accept a glass of water. If you came from a long distance and you had to eat there, the food came from a neighbor's house or you paid her in-laws a reasonable sum for that food. Even today, after being in America for more than forty years, and having been more or less Americanized, every time I go to visit my daughter and son-in-law, a fleeting thought crosses my mind that I should be taking gifts and should somehow be reimbursing them for the food I eat there.

Because the parents gave gifts to the daughters during their lifetime, and the daughters were generally believed to "belong" to their in-laws, they had no share in the inheritance from their parents; all of that went to the sons.

The house in Gojra was small, but I loved it. I don't remember my grandparents and my oldest uncle, Kundanlal, there, but the other three uncles and my cousin from the oldest uncle (only a

few years older than I) were great company. They did everything
to spoil me. I went to the movies with them and participated in
petty mischief. It was a ritual for my mother, as for every daughter-
in-law, to visit her family every few months, and it was also a ritual
for her in-laws to quietly resent it.

Diwali is a major Hindu festival, the festival of lights, which
represents our New Year. We decorate and string up lights around
the house, exchange gifts, feast, distribute sweets, pray, indulge in
gambling, and (my favorite!) light fireworks in the streets. My
Gojra uncles bought bundles of fireworks and we would set them
off in the streets until very late at night. These were some of the
happiest memories of my childhood. When we eventually moved
to India after the India-Pakistan partition, I remember celebrating *Diwali* with the Ahujas again and enjoying a lot of fireworks.
The Dangs did not have much in the way of celebrations or fireworks, and they actually resented the Ahujas for that.

We almost always spent *Diwali* in Gojra, mainly because two
days after *Diwali* comes *Bhaiya Dooj*, a brother-sister day, when
sisters are supposed to visit their brothers. Two occasions, *Bhaiya
Dooj* and *Rakhi,* are celebrations of brother-sister love. Brothers
and sisters visit each other, share a meal, and embrace, and the
brother gives gifts to the sister and promises to protect her in the
future. One reason could be that because women did not get any
inheritance, in case of divorce or their husband's death, their only
protection was their brothers. Even children celebrate the day; the
little girls are happy to get gifts and money, and their brothers cry
that they don't. I didn't have a sister until I was twenty-one, so my

cousins and aunts substituted. My aunts from India still to this day send a sacred thread to me by mail twice a year, and I send them a small check as a token of remembrance.

After the partition, my mother's oldest living brother, Krishanlal, struggled to get settled but was not successful. He even partnered with my father for another of his failed businesses. Because my uncle Krishanlal was now the oldest male in the family, he had the responsibility for taking care of his two younger brothers and his wife and children, so one day he took off for South India to look for more lucrative work. He was maligned by the community for deserting the family "for reason of greed." He struggled badly for a few years, started a grain business, and came back to Delhi a rich man. He never looked back after that, started importing grain from the South, and increased his wealth exponentially. During this time his only sister and her family, including me, were struggling to survive. He was always willing to help us, but my father took exception to his boasting, his showing off, and his wealth, and generally refused to accept any financial help from him. During all the years I lived in India with my family, and beyond, the relationship between the two families stayed cordial but restrained. After I got married, my wife loved them and they loved her, so during our trips to India we were able to reduce the strain between the two families, if temporarily.

When we visit India, we are almost as much in touch with our Ahuja cousins as with our Dang cousins.

3

Polio: Blaming Family, Visiting Shrines

I was about three years old when I contracted polio. My mother and I were returning from a visit to her brothers in Gojra when I was somehow exposed to the poliovirus and became paralyzed. The paralysis got better, but my right leg stayed weak. I did not learn to walk again until I was at least four, and I developed a limp. When I look back, I believe many of my life's events have been directly or indirectly affected by my polio.

My grandmother blamed my mother and her family for not really looking after me well, thus causing my polio. To her dying day, she never excused them. And, of course, she blamed her sister-in-law also for casting the spell. (Whenever a mishap occurred in our family, my grandmother blamed those two.) She was heartbroken, as I was the oldest son of her oldest son and I was listless, lying paralyzed and limp.

Because she thought my mother was too young and incapable of taking care of me, my grandmother took over my care. She took me to doctors: indigenous doctors called *hakims,* Hindu pundits,

Muslim mullahs, even shamans, quacks. Faith healers were popular, and people—even Hindus—who needed something from God went to the gravesites of religious Muslims, or imams. These gravesites were called *dargahs* and attracted thousands of needy people. My grandmother and I were always visiting these *dargahs*. She got me medicines, herbs, ointments, massages. She worked at me day and night, and it was because of her efforts, I have been told, that I started getting better and the residual paralysis was minimal. She thought cold was bad for me and was always covering me with three blankets at night. Instead of sleeping with my mother, I was sleeping with my grandmother. I also believe that she nursed me; it was a common practice then. I have vague memories of waking up in the middle of the night and finding my grandmother massaging my right leg with oils and potions. It was very annoying at that time. I always wore long pants, never shorts like most kids wore in school. This made me look different from other kids, but it was necessary to hide the discrepancy between the two legs. My right leg became about half the girth of my left, and about half an inch shorter; those traits remain to this day. I have never owned a pair of shorts.

Because of my grandmother's obsession with my leg, I ended up traveling a lot. Whenever she heard about a special doctor or priest or shaman, she would take me there without regard for distance or inconvenience. She would take me by train, bus, bullock cart—even on foot, with me on her back. If she could not do it, she asked my father to do so. He was the only other person involved with my treatment, as I remember. He took me to

Lahore a few times because that was the center of good health care then, and it was far, about seventy miles from Lyallpur. I remember once standing in line for hours to see a doctor, a white man, a specialist visiting from England.

When I was in medical school and visited home, the first thing my grandmother would ask me was to raise the legs of my pants so she could compare the two legs to see if my right had become fatter or stronger than before. When I was leaving for America, she asked me to see the specialists about my leg as soon as I reached here—after all, the best doctors were in the United States—and to write to her immediately when my polio was all better.

Soon after coming to the United States I did see a specialist, who took X-rays, examined me thoroughly, and in a grave voice announced that the bones in my polio-affected leg were very bad, ossified and brittle. He thought I would be walking with a cane within five to seven years and might need a wheelchair in less than fifteen years. That was forty years ago; to this day I am walking and running without any assistance, without any pain. I have had many such forecasts from several top specialists. With help from some supernatural power, I have proved them wrong. We doctors are often proved wrong.

Many years later when my wife and I were visiting India, my grandmother was bedridden. She called my wife to her, asked her to sit on the bed, hugged her, and said, "I am on my deathbed, but I have one last wish. I wanted to take Jagdish to a *dargah* when partition happened thirty years ago, and that *dargah* is now in Pakistan. I understand that they let people go to Pakistan now, especially if you are American citizens. I want you to take him there; I am sure his leg will get better." Of course, I was not even going to consider it, knowing all about polio and its sequel.

When I was about nine or ten, I often visited my grand-mother's brother Kanshiram Sapra in Ghaziabad, about fifteen miles from Delhi. He was a flamboyant man who was loud, jovial, and always joking around. He had an open house, a welcoming house, with food and music and comfort. He used to call me the Limping Prince; I did not mind. "Here is my Limping Prince. Come here and sit with your best uncle. Let's get him some food . . . I know he likes *roti* (pita bread) with a heap of butter on it." He would address whoever was in the room. "He is a topper in his class." "Sister, come here," addressing my grandmother. "Your limping grandson will someday attend college. I am telling you, he will be a guiding light for your family. You should feed him a lot of butter to increase his brain." I loved this uncle. Poonam, my wife, knew about him too; he was related to her through her aunt. After I got married, I told Poonam that I had always dreamed of having a house like his—cheerful, welcoming, hospitable, and full of people, music, and food. Poonam did not disappoint me; our house has always been like that. By the way, my uncle Kanshiram also had two wives simultaneously; it was allowed then, though it was unusual. I couldn't have had that, especially with Poonam around!

Even though I limped during all of my childhood, it did not bother me much. It should have—it was pretty obvious and kids used to tease me—but somehow I was able to block it out of my consciousness, so it did not cripple me mentally. I know it bothered a lot of people who were near and dear to me. But I could walk long distances, and I never had pain. Anyone walking with me would invariably ask if I was hurting, or if I wanted them to walk more slowly. Also, I was sometimes offered a seat if I was standing in a bus, which was embarrassing. When I wrote home that I had bought a car, my father wrote back, "I don't know for sure, but I believe you need a strong right foot to drive, so how are you able to drive?"

Actually, polio gave me advantages at times. I started school later than the usual age of five years. I have been told that I excelled in my classes from the very beginning—maybe that was because I was older than most of my classmates. Gym classes were mandatory in school, but I would get excused while the other kids grumbled. One year I got student aid on the basis of my "handicap." When I went for oral exams in medical school, I used to hope the examiner would see me walk and notice my limp. That way he would forget about everything else and ask me all the questions about poliomyelitis. Sometimes my wish came true: the detailed knowledge of this illness came in handy in many oral exams. I had thoroughly read the anatomy, physiology, radiology, and medicine of polio. When I came to the United States and went for a physical exam for the army draft, I tried using polio as an excuse to get out. Unfortunately, this strategy did not work. The doctor giving me the physical exam was blunt: "If you are a doctor and you are breathing, you are 1A." However, by the time I got in line, even the 1A's were not being called and the draft was almost over.

I used to fall occasionally—no warning, just fall while walking. I would quickly get up, look around to see if anybody was watching, brush myself off, and continue walking. I fell a couple of times while working in hospitals and nursing homes too, but the events were quietly ignored. I am especially frightened of walking in snow or ice. I have a perpetual fear that if I ever broke any of the bones in my right leg, the fracture would never heal. I have been told that the bones there have no marrow and because of calcification their healing power is gone. I have been told that by people who know. Sometimes my right leg becomes ice cold, especially at night. There is no special occasion when that happens. It is because the peripheral blood vessels constrict. After a while the leg becomes warm by itself. Doctors have reassured me that this is a totally harmless phenomenon.

About five years ago my leg started getting weaker—a big warning sign of post-polio syndrome. About forty years after polio, whatever damage was left from the affliction starts getting worse and the deterioration is swift and severe. In my case it happened more than sixty years later, and the progression has been slow. I asked several physicians about it, and each one offered a different solution. One said I needed to do regular exercise; another asked me to buy an exercise bike, which I did, and I started working out. Another wanted me to start yoga, and I followed his advice as well.

Then I heard of a nationally recognized post-polio-syndrome center right in my backyard, in Englewood, New Jersey. I was evaluated extensively by a physiatrist, a psychologist, and a host of other team members. They gave a gloomy prognosis: my only hope was to slow down physically, socially, and mentally. I was told it was common for polio survivors to become overachievers and very active. I was at that time involved in about fifteen organizations: medical and psychiatric societies, the hospital, my temple, ethnic societies, and community service organizations. I was also practicing psychiatry full-time and running around between hospitals and nursing homes, as well as teaching. I was writing articles and editing papers. I was told that my salvation was possible only if I stopped all of that abruptly. I heard it like a death sentence. I was not ready to do it. I reduced some of my extracurricular activities and ignored the rest of their advice. I could not understand why some specialists were advising more exercise and others less, for the same condition.

The polio bothers me more now than ever before, since my leg is getting weaker and my limp is getting more pronounced. However, now I am old, and at least it's perfectly normal to see an old person walk funny and have minor falls here and there. People often ask me if I am retiring soon. After having seen me around for forty years, maybe they consider this a normal question, but perhaps it is triggered by my accentuated limp. I very seldom feel tired after a full day's work, and when I do, I wonder if it is my age or if the prophecy of the Englewood psychologist is coming true.

I was in my fifties when one day my father, with tears in his eyes, said, "We had been told by doctors that you would stop walking at a young age and would be dependent on others for total support for most of your life." He went on to say how strange it felt that I was not only supporting myself but also supporting the whole extended family in numerous ways. "How wrong the doctors were fifty years ago," he said.

Yes, we doctors are often proved wrong.

4

India Partitioned:
Narrow Escape from Massacre

In 1947, when I was about seven years old, the British left India and divided the country in two: a Muslim Pakistan and a secular India. There was extensive ethnic cleansing. We Hindus were forced to leave Pakistan or face maiming, raping, and killing. Similarly, many Muslims fled India for what was now Pakistan, fearing for their lives. Hindus and Muslims who had lived together peacefully for generations were now bloodthirsty enemies. Life-long friends became mortal adversaries; neighbors were out to kill neighbors. Blackouts and curfews were common. Women were not allowed to walk out of the house. Sometimes you heard gun-shots; at other times you imagined gunshots. Crowds of attackers were known to invade and ransack houses, looting anything they could carry. Stories traveled through villages and towns—some true, others exaggerated or fabricated. Somebody in every house-hold always kept guard at night in case "they" came. We were in a state of siege. Large clubs, knives, and guns were stacked in the house. Women were given quick-acting poison pills to carry with them always, tied to their usual *dopatta* (scarf). They had instructions to swallow the pill if attacked or confronted with molestation.

Preparations were being made to leave Lyallpur at a moment's notice. Valuables were thrown into small, handy metal suitcases. We had a large, old-fashioned PIE radio (medium-wave and short-wave reception), a gift from my mother's family to my father's family. Either that was the only radio in the whole neighborhood or our house was bigger than others, because the family and neighbors would collect in our house and gather around the radio. It was not desirable to have any lights on or too much sound to draw attention, so the volume of the radio was kept very low and everybody strained to hear the latest in the kill-or-be-killed saga. (I remember similar scenes during World War II when the British forbade anybody to listen to the short-wave radio; people would collect around the radio and—because of their hatred of British oppression—give quiet high fives when the Japanese or Germans were winning.)

The family approached my father to explore ways of getting out of Pakistan. He was the only educated, well-traveled, street-smart person in the family that now gathered in our house, including uncles, aunts, grandparents, children, and some extended family members. After much thought and planning, he flew to Delhi with his middle sister, Kanta, who was a couple of years older than I. There he rented a small airplane with a pilot to take him to Lyallpur and bring the family to Amritsar, about eighty miles away and now in India—an expensive proposition. Meanwhile, the word came that the Muslims were at the doorstep and we must leave NOW. There were no means of communication. We all picked up our belongings and left for uncharted territory on foot. A caravan of forty to fifty men, women, and children, we walked to a village—any village—away from the dangerous city, hoping to meet up with my father eventually. We needed water, food, and shelter. We had some idea of the direction of the airport but had to divert our route several times when we heard that "they" were nearby. I could not walk much in that hot desert sun and wind, so my uncle Khushiram carried me on his back, and a suitcase in his hand, during at least part of the trek.

When my father returned with the chartered plane, he found his house padlocked and nobody there to tell him where everybody had vanished. He still had Kanta with him. The streets were empty; it was a scene from a ghost town, with no transport available. He eventually found a horse and buggy to take him and his sister around; he decided it was a necessary risk even though the driver was a Muslim. My father went from one village to another, asking people the whereabouts of his family. There were several caravans wandering, and we were just one of them. Time was of the essence and he kept following his hunches.

On his way to finding us, my father was stopped by four masked men with guns. He and his sister were ready to die, but the men turned out to be small-time bandits, maybe not even Muslims. They wanted money and his gold watch, which he gladly parted with, and they went away, still toting guns. What they did not know was that in the inner pocket of his jacket he had bundles of money meant for the airplane pilot. If they had considered why a man was wearing a jacket in that hot sun and taken that money, we could never have come to India in that plane and would probably not have made it out of Pakistan alive.

When he finally found us, he was not sure whether the plane was still waiting for him at the airport. We were able to rent a number of buggies with horses and started toward the airport. The scene at the airport was unforgettable: hundreds and hundreds of people vying for a plane ride to India, desperately offering money to the pilot, an Englishman. But he waited for my father; he had the down payment and did not want to betray us. A big fight ensued among the family members: who would go in the plane and who would stay back? There was room for only about twenty, and we were at least thirty-five. My father and the airplane pilot were roughed up a little. In the end, the pilot took all of us in that little plane with the promise of more money upon arrival. I have been told that the relatives who went on the plane and promised my father that they would share the expenses reneged in the end and he had to shell out the whole plane fare. Also, because the plane could not carry all their belongings, some relatives had to leave their suitcases behind and later blamed my father for their poverty. But there are so many stories concerning our journey to India and this is one of them; it is hard to separate the true from the fabricated.

We heard that after our departure, the airport was blockaded and hundreds of people were massacred. Very few people survived in the village where my father had tracked us down. In addition to the heat and starvation, there were gangs of people out for blood and money. Many villages became slaughterhouses.

What happened to the house and the store we left behind? I have no idea, but I have heard that any Muslim in Pakistan was permitted to break the lock of a Hindu house and claim himself to be the owner once the house was left behind by *kafirs*. All non-Muslims were *kafirs*, infidels, not worthy of existence. It was *jihad*, a victory for their religion.

The small plane arrived safely in Amritsar, India. The city was a scene from a World War II movie, littered with tents, refugee camps, throngs of people wandering around in circles in a confused state. Many people had lost much; others thought they had. Some had truly lost everybody and everything.

My mother's family also arrived safely after going from one village to another, switching various caravans, and facing a whole different set of crises. They had their own stories, but we were told very little about their ordeal.

⚜

More than five decades later, 9/11 happened in America. Many people from New Jersey were killed. My staff at Barnert Hospital in Paterson, New Jersey, did some volunteer work counseling and helping their family members. Dr. Philip Feldman, our psychologist, and I held a group session for doctors in the hospital. More than fifty doctors attended. Our medical staff resembled the

United Nations. We had a large number of South Asian and Middle Eastern doctors, in addition to doctors belonging to various other ethnicities and religions. Of course, we had whites, African Americans, and Hispanics. A lot of emotions were unearthed and verbalized. It came out that many physicians had witnessed atrocities and death as terrible as or worse than 9/11. One Ugandan doctor talked about having seen his three brothers die in the sectarian riots in his country. I talked about the partition of India, probably for the first time. That brought back a lot of repressed memories . . . and dreams and nightmares.

⤬

I do not remember too many people in India talking about the partition or the hardships. A few years ago my daughter got interested in the subject and asked my father-in-law to tell her his experiences. He kept postponing the discussion until one day she nailed him down and he could not say no to his granddaughter. He was talking and she was writing her journal. He told her how he went into a burning building to save a neighbor, how he had to ride his bicycle to the school of his younger brother to bring him home and on the way he was attacked and there was bloodshed all around them, and that once the whole extended family was holed up in a mansion when marauders came, and death and fire were everywhere. After about an hour of his story he started pacing, and later he broke down completely, remembering what had happened more than fifty years ago.

Nita's journal stayed incomplete.

5

Starting Over as Refugees

After the partition of India in 1947, about 15 million people became refugees both in India and in Pakistan. Because Pakistan was based on religious orientation, Muslims there had a sort of tacit approval to throw out all other religious faiths. If they did not leave they would be killed, raped, or converted, and their property would be confiscated. However, the new India was a secular state, and Muslims were continuously assured of their safety. Mahatma Gandhi, the Father of the Indian Nation, went on a fast till death to stop the massacre of Muslims in India. It was an everyday story that trains were arriving in Amritsar, India, from Lahore, now in Pakistan, full of thousands of dead Hindus with their throats slashed. Years later, my wife's grandmother told her that she had witnessed a whole well full of bodies of young women of the village who had jumped to their death to avoid being molested. It was also said that when the marauders came they raped every woman in sight, young and old, and whoever was left behind by fleeing men was converted to Islam.

A not-so-distant relative of ours was the chieftain in his village in the undivided India. He was also the local doctor. And the judge. And a man of considerable wisdom and wealth, known throughout the surrounding villages. Like so many other people who thought their country could not be divided on the basis of religion, he was a staunch supporter of Hindu-Muslim unity. He had always treated his subjects equitably. "I treat all Hindus and Muslims like my own sons. They won't kill me." In spite of the desperate advice from his family to the contrary, he slept out in the open one night, in front of his house. They found his throat cut the next morning.

When we were living in a very small cramped apartment in Delhi, his son, about sixteen at the time, dashed into the apartment one evening, short of breath, with bloodstains on his shirt, and announced, "I have killed two of 'them'; I just slashed their throats." A pall fell on the people in the room. One elderly man got up angrily, whisked him out of the room, and mumbled something like, "Young blood, revenge, never using good judgment! Go and change that damn shirt!" I was a small kid and was not supposed to see this scene. To this day, every time I see this man or any member of his family, I think of that evening. I don't know about Pakistan, but in India it was a crime to kill any Muslim, although I heard stories of trains full of Muslims, killed in retaliation by Hindus, dispatched to Lahore anonymously. The best estimates are that 2 million people, both Hindus and Muslims, were killed during the partition.

⁂

Refugee camps were set up in border towns in India, and we were given shelter, food, and clothing. We were given ration cards to enable us to buy food, fuel, blankets, and clothing at a reduced rate. We were offered monetary help in several ways. It could even be called a warm welcome by the new Indian government.

A number of families were separated in the exodus. Thousands of people were roaming around from one refugee camp to another, looking for their lost relatives. Many wandered the streets in a daze. Many had seen their relatives attacked but hoped they had survived, and kept asking for them. Our extended family had the advantage that we were more or less together because despite the chaos at the airport, we had all arrived on the same plane. My grandfather was lost for a while (probably searching for his brother's children and relatives, as my grandmother would say). My uncle Khushiram, who did most of the physical work, was lost temporarily because he was being shipped from one place to another, looking for relatives. Sooner or later, most families were reunited and started thinking of rebuilding their lives. My mother was expecting her second child during the crisis. My brother Harish was born a few weeks after the partition of India.

Nightmares about what people had witnessed or imagined were common. One person or another would scream in the middle of the night, "They are coming, they are coming!" My grandmother screamed in her sleep for years. Decades later, when India was a fully integrated society and I was going to medical school, she admonished me not to make friends with "them."

About 10 percent of my class was Muslim and, as far as I know, they were not treated any differently from the rest of us.

We moved from Amritsar to Delhi after a couple of detours. My father's friends helped us procure a small house. It was a hut-like structure; the government was building rows and rows of such houses for refugees. Our colony was called Rajinder Nagar, named after the first president of independent India, who came to inaugurate the colony. There is a commemorative stone about a block from the house where I grew up. Prime Minister Jawaharlal Nehru came too, with great fanfare. His daughter, Indira, was with him, the future prime minister. My grandmother always talked about how she broke the cordon of ropes and stood next to my grandmother during the lecture ceremonies.

⚜

A philanthropist named Girdhari Lal Salwan started a makeshift school in tents, and soon these tents were filled with students of all ages, all grades. By this time I was eight and in third grade. Later these tents gave way to temporary brick buildings, which mushroomed into the huge, full-fledged Salwan School, a brick-and-mortar middle and high school with a chain-link fence and sprawling gardens separating the girls' school from the boys'. (Gender segregation in schools is still a common practice in India.)

I was a geek even then, one of the few people who enjoyed school. I was also good in my studies. But the most poignant memory of my primary and middle school is having my hands flogged practically every day for coming late to school. (Was it really that often, or was it so traumatic that my palms still hurt when I think of it?) Punishment for arriving late was a regular practice, no questions asked. About a hundred children came late every morning. They were rounded up and asked to stand in a line. The principal would come with a thin, strong stick and a stern face. You would spread your hands, palms up, in front of him, and he would strike you with the stick twice on each hand. You quietly went to your class and repeated the exercise again the next day if you were late again. Corporal punishment was common and considered essential to studying. You were also flogged for not doing your homework and for doing mischief in class. I usually escaped this punishment because I always did my homework, got good grades, and was the teacher's pet. In most of the classes I was what they called a monitor, the eyes and ears of the teacher. I would be the one to tell the teacher who did not do his homework, who was the most mischievous, and so on. Because I was physically a weakling, this came in handy with getting favors from the bullies.

Most of our teaching was done in Hindi, and we started learning basic English in fourth grade. Mathematics was an important subject and good handwriting was essential. Memorizing was more important than learning. School had two shifts: seven a.m. to noon, and one p.m. to six p.m. Very strict discipline was kept, and parents were called to school on any infringement of it. Almost all parents were cognizant of homework and taught their children after school. When I see the intensity and passion displayed by parents in the United States during their children's

Little League games, other sports practices, and dance recitals, I think of same kind of fervor there in India for education.

Men went looking for jobs or training. My father started small businesses; none of them did well. My uncle Khushiram learned typing and got a job; in addition he taught students typing. My aunt Shashi sewed clothes for neighbors for a pittance, and we did little things to get whatever money we could, including making envelopes from old newspapers and selling them. By the time I was in eighth grade I was teaching younger kids from the block. I would get two rupees (then worth about forty cents) for a whole month of teaching a child every evening for two to three hours.

As a child I always wanted to be a writer or a teacher. However, my family convinced me not to go into either profession by threatening that I would starve to death. I believe that every Indian parent still professes that.

⚜

I loved reading. I read, read, and read. I would read anything I could get my hands on—my books, those of my uncle Puran (about seven years older than I), and any newspapers that I could get hold of, anything. Candy in those days came wrapped in a piece of newspaper; I would read that paper before I ate the candy. Unfortunately, the only library in Rajinder Nagar did not allow children to go in. I could not afford to buy books, but there was a corner store that rented novels. I would rent a Hindi novel a day when I could afford it. When my aunt Shashi was going to college for her BA in Hindi and I was in sixth grade, I would read her books. I didn't understand much but read nonetheless. By sixth or seventh grade I was trying to read my uncle Puran's physics and chemistry books, and wondering what that gibberish meant.

And I loved writing. Any writing except for schoolwork was prohibited in those days, at least in my house. Every household, especially every refugee household, concentrated on one and only one thing: formal education. Hobbies were discouraged. So I had to sneak around to write. There were no creative writing classes, no encouragement to do anything creative. Just one direction: study for your final exam. There used to be a kids' page in the Sunday Hindi newspaper, which unfortunately we did not get delivered. I would beg, borrow, and steal to get the paper to read its kids' page. And almost every week I would write a poem or a small article and scrounge up money for postage to mail it to the paper. Slowly my poems and articles started getting published. Mind you, each one was the brainchild of an eight- or nine-year-old and totally ridiculous, but I was so, so happy to see my name in print. And because I was doing well in school and it was not costing the family any money, my writing was tolerated, and eventually even subtly encouraged by them.

⁕

Life was different back then. We cooked on coals and used kerosene lamps for reading; houses were electrified later—and even then, power failures were normal. There was a common water source on the street for the whole block. You stood in line with your bucket in your hand; sometimes the lines were long.

Fights broke out when somebody tried to cut in line. You took your daily bath with a bucket and a mug, always in cold water. Almost fifteen years later when I visited the house of a friend from medical school, I found out that some aristocrats had been bathing with hot water every day. I don't remember taking hot-water baths until I came to the United States. We did not have the concept of toilet tissue; we washed off feces with water. There was no sewage system; human waste was collected every morning and taken by trucks to be dumped God knows where.

There was a custom of going "out" to move your bowels (sometimes even if you had a lavatory in the house). You took a mug of water and went out to a farm or a hill or into the woods, usually before dawn so as not to be seen by others, and moved your bowels in the open fields. Then you came home and washed your hands with soap and water. Even now, with India flying high, I believe it is a common practice in more rural areas. When you travel by train and look out the window in the early morning, you can see hundreds of people relieving themselves. Indian trains have toilets where all the human waste goes onto the train tracks. Most Indians walk around barefoot or wear open sandals. Unfortunately, microscopic hookworm eggs hatch in soil contaminated by infected human waste; the scarcely visible larvae then penetrate human skin and lodge in the intestinal system to produce iron-deficiency anemia and other illnesses. This is a major cause of widespread anemia in India.

People were quite religious. Temples, *gurdwaras* (for Sikhs), and mosques flourished. My grandmother was very religious. She woke up at three or four every morning, took her bath in cold water, and said her prayers. My father went through a number of religious rituals, too. They were strict vegetarians, as vegetarianism is considered a pillar of Hinduism by some. Most of my family was vegetarian. My grandfather and uncle Khushiram would eat goat meat about once a month, and they tried to make me eat meat too. My grandmother encouraged me to eat meat because somebody had told her that it would help my leg. Cooking meat was a major production in my house. Meat was expensive, but my grandfather would make some excuse to the family (usually my health) and buy some. Since he could not use the regular kitchen or utensils to cook it, he would cook it in the courtyard in special pots and we would eat it there. It became a day of celebration, and usually a male cousin or a friend joined us in the feast. A Jewish kosher kitchen reminds me of my kitchen in Rajinder Nagar.

We wore home-stitched clothes and home-knitted sweaters. My aunt Shashi was almost a professional in stitching, knitting, and crocheting. Later, when she got married, we had our clothes stitched by local tailors. Ready-made clothing for common people is a relatively new phenomenon in India. When I was about to leave for America, something special had to be done, so my uncle Khushiram took me to Connaught Place, Delhi's well-known commercial and business center, where we entered a store selling ready-made clothes. After some haggling we bought our family's first ready-made shirt for thirty rupees (about six dollars). I still remember the price because my uncle grumbled a lot and cursed the store manager all the way home for charging thirty rupees for what would have cost four rupees if stitched by a tailor.

⚜

As time passed, Rajinder Nagar changed. The small houses were torn down and huge structures were built on those lots. Central water, a sewer system, and electricity came. Good roads, temples, small schools, and medical dispensaries were constructed. I remember the markets and the meeting places. Bus transportation became the primary means of travel, along with the famous, sprawling network of Indian Railways. We refugees were not refugees anymore. Modernization in Delhi and other big Indian cities had begun.

6

Peanuts, Lies, and
Precarious Health

As a child I was always sick. If it was not typhoid, it was pneumonia or double pneumonia or malaria. And nosebleeds, all the time. Gastrointestinal problems. Anemia. You name the body system, I had problems. I was always coughing. Always going to the doctors (with my grandmother); thank God, routine health care was free. I believe I was mildly allergic to peanuts, but I liked peanuts and peanut brittle, and these were the only treats I could afford to buy with my tiny allowance. So I was always coughing: a dry, hacking cough. And my grandmother would yell at me, accusing me of again eating peanuts, and I would lie again and again. I still like peanuts and peanut brittle, but I am over that allergy.

When I went to medical school, all those illnesses went away. I would read about the diseases and remember that, yes, I had that one too. I believe my immune system was shot when I was a child. I also believe that some of my problems were psychosomatic, as I had no other outlet to unleash my frustrations. I was a sensitive, invisible child unable to handle normal, everyday problems.

Dust in the street might have triggered the dry, hacking cough from molds, spores, or dirt. As kids we played in the streets, which were dusty and filthy. Men often urinated in the street, standing against the wall of their neighbor's house, and their neighbors would return the favor. Drainage was poor. Every time it rained, there were puddles of water everywhere in the street. We played a lot of invented games with homemade hockey sticks, cricket bats, and wickets. And we played marbles, hide-and-seek, and ball games. I guess I was more sensitive to the pollution and spores than most of the other kids.

Once, when I was around eight, a stray dog in the street started following me. I got scared and started running. I was no match for the speed of the dog, who mauled me, biting me on my leg and back. I was laid up for weeks, getting treatment and the attention of everybody around me.

⁂

I got glasses when I was barely ten. Back then children did not wear glasses, and it was considered a major handicap. Schoolmates teased you, and distant relatives would make remarks about "the unhealthy child." A girl who wore glasses might not get a good match. Actually it was unknown for unmarried girls to have glasses, unless they were completely blind, and in that case they were unmarriageable anyway. Even in my case, many relatives would tell my grandmother, in my presence, how hard it would be to find a wife for a "handicapped child who limps and wears glasses." On the other hand, with glasses I could follow instructions on the blackboard better and had an edge up on my studies. With a constant nosebleed and ear discharge I visited the ear, nose, and throat specialist so often that he became a friend of my father and stopped charging us after a while.

In those days, doctors told you to stop eating solid food if you were sick. Only liquids; everybody emphasized drinking milk. But who could afford much milk? The doctors also suggested eating fruits and glucose, and drinking fruit juices. We could not afford much of any of these things, but somehow whatever we could afford I was provided. By the time I was in my third year at Maulana Azad Medical College, the professor of pediatrics, Dr. P. N. Taneja, was reminding us every day, "Please, when you go out as doctors, try to eradicate the myth of starving children who are sick. Tell mothers to feed their children when they have a fever." He was also telling us about the common unhealthy practices of people, such as walking barefoot, and breast-feeding children until five or six years old, thus effectively starving them. It was not until the late 1960s that I heard that doctors in India were finally allowing people to eat solid foods when feverish. The reason for my being so skinny (and short) was not so much my sickness as the starvation diet that I was always on. Glucose was being sold in fancy cans for sick people. That was scandalous. The professor reminded us that a spoonful of granulated sugar was probably better than a spoonful of glucose, at one-fiftieth the price.

❦

Because I was falling a lot, when I was fifteen an orthopedic surgeon suggested that I should have an ankle operation to effectively immobilize the ankle. I had that done and was laid up for weeks with a hard plaster cast, missing very important tenth-grade schooling. I don't know how but I excelled even during those final exams. Those poliomyelitis viruses must have expanded my brain a little while damaging my peripheral nerves.

I remember an incident after my hospitalization for ankle surgery. The hospital was very far from our home, and not too many people came to visit me there. Every second or third night my uncle Khushiram would ride his bicycle all those miles and come to see me. One day they told me I was being discharged. There were no means of communication and I was not sure if my uncle was coming to see me that evening. Even if he came, it would be difficult to ride behind him on his bicycle all the way home with that hard cast. (Many bicycles in India have extra seats on the bar between the handle and the main seat, and over the back wheel, so passengers can sit in front of and behind the person pedaling.) I was tired of being in the hospital and I don't know exactly what I was thinking: I decided to leave the hospital alone, by bus, even though I knew that they would have kept me there for a couple more days if nobody came to take me home.

I have done many stupid things in my life, but this probably tops them all. The attendant took me in the wheelchair out of the hospital to the bus stop and left me there. He expected a tip; I barely had money for bus fare. People at the bus stop were very helpful and I boarded the bus, despite a full-length hard cast on my right leg from toe to hip, and no crutches. The bus dropped me about two miles from my home. I hired a three-wheeled motor scooter (like a small taxi), knowing that I had no money with me and that when I got home my grandmother and aunts might not have enough to give to the scooter driver. I reached home un-eventfully but then got yelled at by every family member, and I was the laughingstock of the whole neighborhood as they watched me walk into the house with the help of two people. That evening my uncle rode his bicycle from his office to the hospital, only to find that I had left on my own, and I got yelled at some more.

∞❧∞

One additional illness that I have had all my life is primary insomnia. I have never really had a good night's sleep. If I were to calculate my sleep time for my whole life so far, it would probably come to about five hours a night of restless sleep, full of dreams, and I could tell you in the morning the approximate number of cars that passed by my house during the night. I used to blame it on habits formed from the rigorous schedule of internship and residency and being awoken several times during the night when I was on call. Later I thought it was caffeine in the tea and coffee that I drank during the day and sometimes in the evening. Stress and worries? All said and done, now I believe it is just insomnia, cause unknown.

51

I have never taken any medication for insomnia, have never needed to. I do sometimes steal twenty minutes from my routine during the afternoon to take a short nap. Some weekends I do sleep eight or more hours a night, but it is not really the kind of restful sleep I would like my patients to have. However, it has never bothered me.

I have used my insomnia to great advantage. I never feel tired during the day even if I slept for four hours or less the night before. I have read countless novels, magazines, and medical books at night, and have also written hundreds of personal letters, personal thoughts, and newsletter columns during those waking hours.

※

Because of all the illnesses I had, I never thought I would reach a ripe old age; in my youth that meant fifty years old. That fear has stayed with me throughout life. I bought the maximum possible life insurance when men of my age didn't even care about life insurance. I was surprised when I reached fifty, fifty-five, sixty, and even sixty-five. Just recently I have come to think that maybe I will reach the "overripe" old age of seventy or seventy-five, and that I should plan for a few years of retirement!

In fact I have seldom been sick as an adult: not even the usual headaches and arthritic pains for my age. I guess my immune system must have improved as I grew older. Between my work and all my volunteer activities, I have been physically and mentally very active. I never sat still until recently. I was always walking from one patient to the other, one floor to the other, and I would park in the farthest parking spot in the doctors' parking lot. I also enjoyed driving and never went to just one institution in one day.

Once my inhibitions passed, I did not look back. Until a few years ago when I started cutting back on my numerous activities, neither my polio, my short height, my protruding belly, my bald head, nor my foreign looks have ever stopped me. Poonam was very helpful in supporting my extracurricular activities, and with her quick wit and great interpersonal approach, she enjoyed them too. She went to my black-tie dinners and participated in the conversations—singing, dancing, and even accepting awards and honors as the first lady in spite of her extreme stage fright. She has never let me feel handicapped.

PART TWO

Student and Nephew

7

The "Biology Line": Chasing Buses, Not Girls

As mentioned earlier, my father had one failed business after another: cloth, grain, dry cleaning. And he moved from one city to another: Delhi, Hissar, Gurgaon. I stayed with my grandparents. It was not uncommon for grandparents to keep the oldest son of the oldest son, but my grandmother was special; she would not part with me. She never thought my mother was competent to take care of a sickly child. (Do most mothers-in-law think so?)

There were other reasons too. My father could not afford to send me to school. Wherever he moved, there were probably no schools, or at least none of higher learning. True, my grandfather did not work (lazy, my grandmother would say); my uncle Khushiram had a meager salary, and there were many mouths to feed. We were poor, but at least we were in Delhi and we had a house—the small but comfortable two-bedroom house that the government had built for the refugees after the partition. (It did not get any makeover until after I came to the United States.) My uncle Khushiram had barely finished high school, but with his typing skills he landed a clerical job in the Delhi office of the World Health Organization. By Rajinder Nagar standards, it was considered a good job. He was taking care of his parents, his younger brother Puran, his three younger sisters, and me. We entertained guests, too; sometimes cousins needed to stay in the city for months for business or schooling. He never made me feel that I was an outsider or a burden on the family. In winter most times those two bedrooms were so crowded at night that you had to walk over the cots if you wanted to go out. In summer we slept outdoors in the courtyard. Most of the houses in Rajinder Nagar were allotted to the refugees, and most of the households had a similar situation. When my uncle Khushiram got married, my aunt Ved moved in, but when his sisters and brother got married, they moved out.

Even though my uncle Khushiram made the major decisions for the family and was the only wage earner, his wife—"Ved Aunty," as I called her—was the lady of the house. She could very well have disrupted the milieu of the family. She was only a few years older than I; she could easily have overruled my uncle and my grandmother and thrown me out. She did not. Willingly or unwillingly, she cooperated. Years later I realized that she took on the role of my third mother—she was as much my mother as the other two (my mother and grandmother) and kept me there, an outsider, for so many years. (Even after years of psychiatric training and practice, I still struggle to understand the psyche of a man with three mothers!)

The "Biology Line": Chasing Buses, Not Girls

⊱❦⊰

My mother had five children, including me, as well as several mis-carriages. She never got any recognition from the Dang family, was considered inadequate, and was always financially strapped. My father had a habit of getting loans from family and friends. It was said that he would borrow to help others even when there was no food in the house for his own family. While others loved him, his family members, young and old, would malign him, especially the women: his mother, wife, sisters, everybody. There were always arguments and fights in the house. But to me, he was just a good man. He always stayed happy and jovial. Behind that facade he must have been troubled, though. Years later, Dr. Ruth Ehrenberg, my assistant superintendent at Metropolitan State Hospital, used to say, "Too good is no good. Always remember that, Jack." She was hinting at me, though it could have easily applied to my father.

I would visit my parents during summer vacations. Most of my life I was really a guest in that house. My father never lost his sense of humor and cheery disposition in spite of all the adversities. I have consciously tried to keep that attitude in my life. I can never forget his first attic apartment in an abandoned house, in Gurgaon, then a suburb of Delhi and now a sprawling high-tech city. There was one room, where my parents and siblings lived and where they entertained me during my vacations. The water source was on the first floor, an old-fashioned well where we got water with ropes and buckets. The room served as the bedroom, the kitchen, the bathroom, everything. I forgot to mention a very useful roof, large and flat, with a latrine on one side. We thought we were happy. Then one day the owner of the house, a distant relative, came and asked my parents to leave.

My father's next apartment was a one-room house. It had a big courtyard, which came in handy, and the courtyard had a well. The roof was flat, and when I came during the summers, my father would rig up a temporary light fixture on the roof and we played cards all night. Playing cards was considered bad, symbolic of gambling, and we became talk of the colony. "How can a father teach his children gambling and laughing and screaming, and having fun?" "Why doesn't he teach them reading and writing and math?" "Doesn't he have any sense of imparting discipline, responsibility, and social values to his children?" But we had fun, and I enjoyed going there any chance I got. I wish those same townsfolk could now see what highly educated and disciplined professionals all his sons have become. My father never let us feel that we were poor. He was criticized in my uncle's house (my house) for that behavior because we were never upbeat there.

❦

I made good grades in middle school and had to decide what courses to take in high school. We had no direction, but a distant, educated cousin of my mother suggested that I should go into the biology line. That was the foundation of my medical career. With my grades I could have taken any "line"—engineering, social sciences, whatever. Did anybody ask me about it? No. Even if any relatives had, I would probably have had no opinion and would have gone along with their decision.

The nearest high school for biology was far enough that I would have to take a bus. And that cost money. With my father's youngest brother Puran going to Calcutta for engineering, how were we going to afford it? But my uncle Khushiram took the responsibility upon his shoulders, and the decision was made. I rode the public bus to high school and studied biology and the sciences.

Taking public buses was a real challenge, and I did that for nine years. Buses were late and overcrowded. The line of people waiting for the bus disintegrated into a free-for-all as the bus came near. You had to run after the moving bus, and if you were lucky you got hold of the pole at the door of the bus (with a bag containing books and lunch in the other hand) and were dragged for a few feet before you got in. If your hand slipped, you just fell on the road and the bus kept going. There were almost as many people squeezed into the aisle and the doorway as sitting. It was survival of the fittest, twice a day, and most students went through with it. Every now and then I would walk the few miles in the hot sun to save the bus fare of twelve paise (about two cents). Once a relative saw me walking and told my uncle Khushiram. He got mad at me, probably not for walking but for besmirching the family name (by making it appear that I was being made to walk to school every day).

I took my lunch to school. I don't remember ever going to the school cafeteria in all those high school days; I couldn't afford it.

I made very few friends and did not participate in any sports. My English teacher was very tough on me and always reminded me that his other Dang student, my uncle Puran, six years before me, had been better than I. This teacher would taunt me in front of the class. The physics teacher, on the other hand, was quite fond of me. During practicals he came to me, praised me, talked about my uncle warmly, and told me that I would earn distinction in physics. He was right. Actually, my distinctions in physics and mathematics saved the day for me, and my grades in high school were so good that I got admitted to the premedical program in the choicest college in Delhi: Hans Raj College.

I might mention here that the government of India had so many scholarships available to refugees, to poor people, to good students, that all my education—including medical school—was free. I even got scholarships covering the books and the bus fare. But we were never sure I would keep the scholarship next year. So any decisions for higher education had to be made keeping in mind the possibility that we might end up in a big financial hole. My uncle Khushiram and my grandmother kept pushing the envelope for me.

✧❀✧

My premedical year was hard for me. (Which year wasn't?) It was the best college, only men, cream of the crop, so to speak. Tough competition. Very far from home. Very bad bus connections. No shelter for the bus stop outside the college. If it rained, I was soaking wet by the time I reached home. So many times I promised myself, "If ever I have enough money, I will donate to build a bus shelter here!" Now that I can afford to build a few bus shelters, I have never visited the college or the area nearby to fulfill my promise.

By the time I reached home, I was so tired that I could not concentrate on my studies. And studies you had to do. Plenty of homework. Others I don't remember, but the chemistry professor gave so much work, so many chemical formulas to write, that almost every night I fell asleep on the books until my grandmother came, cursed the teacher, and tucked me into bed. Every teacher reminded us that in a very short time we were going to have final exams, and even a single extra point could mean the difference between admission or no admission to medical school. Either you were good or not, and I was in between.

We did not hear about any romances during the premedical years. Once in a while you heard a rumor that a student was being expelled for having brought in a female to the all-male college. Maybe the rumors were started by the authorities to scare us away from any hanky-panky. Most other colleges were coed, although there were a couple of colleges for women only. I had fallen "in love" with so many girls that I would see in my daily routine, in the neighborhood, on the bus, in the nearby colleges, on the street. In reality, I never even shook hands with a girl. I dreamed of them and thought about them. Most of the kids did just that. Love and romance were postponed until we were fully educated, had a good job, and were married.

The only entertainment we had was the movies. I saw enough

of them, although I believe I saw fewer than most other kids. (We were considered "kids" until we were married.) I idealized some of the heroes and tried to mimic them. My favorite was Raj Kapoor. He was usually portrayed as "poor me," a skinny, homeless guy with a dry sense of humor. He fell in love with a girl, sang songs, lost her because of his poverty and stupid ways, cried a lot, and in the end got his girl. Our other entertainment was the radio, the same PIE radio that my mother had brought from her father's house as a gift when I was born. (I always wonder how come my family brought that bulky radio to India in those terrible times of partition, killings, and caravans.) Radio was government controlled and gave news and boring classical music most of the time. Film songs were considered a vice and were broadcast only a couple of hours a week. The elders did not officially sanction listening to radio at the cost of studies.

꧁꧂

I was short and looked emaciated throughout high school and premedical school. Years later, when I applied for a government medical career job with the Union Public Service Commission (UPSC) in India and was selected, I was later rejected because I failed their physical fitness exam. The minimum weight requirement was one hundred pounds, and I was only ninety-nine. Yes, I was already a doctor, and weighed only ninety-nine pounds, when I came to the United States. Thank God, the American Embassy did not have the same requirement for giving visas!

8

Admission to Medical School...and a Scandal

I was quite sick (as always) during the premedical finals. Our work during the year did not matter at all. Everything depended on our finals. Everything. Fortunately, in spite of perennial sickness, I got reasonable grades in my finals. Chances were that I could probably get admission to a medical school with those grades. However, to my family, one problem remained: "Can we afford to send him to medical school?" Not only were there fees and other expenses, but it would also ensure five to six years of no earnings. They wondered, "What do we need more, food or education? Even with a degree in medicine, what is he going to earn? If he learns typing and gets a good job like his uncle, he can start feeding the family within a year. And if he studies engineering or gets a BA in physics or mathematics or economics, he can start teaching in two to three years."

They were not so wrong—the fact remained that I was not very good in biology or chemistry, which were necessary for success in the "medical line," and I had obtained distinctions in physics and mathematics, so it made more sense to go into a non-medical field. The family-dictated compromise was that I would apply to only one medical school. If I was admitted, fine; otherwise we would consider other options. I had no role in this decision; rather, my uncle Khushiram supported the medical route and my father went along with it. My grandmother weighed in as well. Even if they had asked me, I probably would not have contributed much to the discussion. I was an overprotected child who had made no decisions up until then and was essentially not even permitted to make decisions. Looking back, I know that applying to just one medical school was almost a sure prescription for failure. Maybe that was the underlying intent of the family. However, because they understood that there was the possibility of acceptance, they made sure I applied to the new medical school in town, Maulana Azad Medical College, which did not have a dormitory, so I could commute and save some money. Admission to that medical school was harder for the same reason—lots of poor people who could not afford to stay in the dormitory were applying—but it was the decision of the family. Because I did not belong to Scheduled Caste or Backward Class, I did not fit into that quota either (affirmative action).

⚜

In order to apply to medical school, I needed to obtain a certificate of residency in Delhi from the court of law. That was when I came face-to-face with Indian bureaucracy and corruption. The day after getting the application, I collected the needed proofs: the property tax receipt in my father's name; my high school diploma, which had my and my father's names; a ration card with both our names; and so on. Then I took the bus back to the court. I was directed from one office to another until I reached the proper place. It was a huge majestic courtroom, built in the tradition of British colonists. Regular court proceedings were going on at one end, and a clerk was sitting at the other end with a desk, a chair, and a typewriter. I was directed to the clerk and gave him the application and the documents. After barely looking at the documents, he asked for six and a half rupees.

"But the fee for the certification is only one-half rupee," I objected.

"Six rupees for my labor, my tea, my coffee." What he meant was a bribe. I understood and realized that I had no choice. But six rupees (about $1.20) was a large sum for that menial job. "Move on, kid, I have a lot of work to do. If you do not have the money, come back tomorrow."

"But, sir, how can I give you money for your tea right here? In front of the judge, the policemen? It is illegal; I will be arrested. I can give it to you if you come outside."

He gave me a funny look. "Don't be silly. Do you think all that dough is for me? The judge gets a rupee for signing the paper. The police, the higher-ups all get a cut. I get only one rupee from this. Now be a nice kid and hurry up."

I gave him the money. He picked up a form from one of the piles of papers on his desk, typed my name and the date, signed it, stamped it, and gave it to me. He barely looked at the documents I had brought with me.

༺⁂༻

I applied for the medical college and was invited for an interview. The interview process was a farce: eight or ten professors sitting around sipping tea and asking questions. "Where do you live? How many brothers and sisters do you have? Which bus will you take to come to the college? Okay, you can go."

Even though these questions were absurdly easy, I still failed. I was never good at orals and interviews. But this interview was just a front—the real goal of the process was to promote the personal cause of those professors. Nepotism was rampant. Probably there was no monetary bribe involved, but favors were definitely being doled out to politicians by admitting their children to the school without regard for their scholastic abilities.

We knew this but accepted their decision because my family did not know any politicians in high places, and we were generally a timid people. However, somebody else (a judge) made a stink and called the newspapers and the education minister; his deserving son had also been rejected on the basis of the interview. The judge had probably forgotten to call in for favors, thinking his son had good grades and would get admitted without that approach. Three days later, it became national news that the admission process to government-sponsored medical schools was rigged—was not done according to the grades, rules, and regulations of the college admission process—and that students from high society who knew somebody got in through the back door because of the interview process. The scandal mushroomed over the next two days. The admission list was quickly revised, and presto, I was admitted along with the son of the judge, who had secured the exact same scores in the national premedical exam as I had. It was front-page news, with my name in it! Interestingly, the judge's son later turned down the medical school because he got admitted into a better and more expensive one. Call it a stroke of divine luck that the judge had made all that fuss, indirectly, for me.

There was one more hurdle. During the physical examination, I got rejected once again. The doctor wrote that with my polio I could not face the rigors of medical life, what with night calls, and hours and hours of standing in the operating room, and working in the emergency room, running around, and so on. That could also have been a ploy to keep me out because they had found somebody else who "deserved" to fill that seat.

However, I had another stroke of luck. A few years previously when I had my ankle surgery and was laid up in the hospital with that huge hard plaster cast on my right leg, I had written an article about hospitals and doctors and blood tests and all the gore and "cruelty" going on there. It was a lighthearted article, making fun of the health-care system, written in a childish manner. I also wrote about the nurses and doctors flirting with one another, and so on. A nurse found the article lying on my end table and showed it to my orthopedist, who laughed hard and made a big deal of his fascination with it. He asked me what my future goals were. When

I told him I was taking biology in high school, he wished me luck and asked me to look for him if he could help me in achieving my goal. (This was strangely fortunate, because doctors did not befriend patients in those days; they were supposed to keep their distance and a stiff upper lip.) He wanted to keep the article to show it to his colleagues, and I was glad to part with it.

Now I needed his help. I took a bus and went to see him, told him my dilemma, and asked him if he thought I could physically fulfill my obligations as a physician. He felt it as a personal affront to him that his surgery was being questioned. Having read about the scandal and probably feeling some professional jealousy, he wrote a very strong letter arguing that my polio was no handicap at all, and hinting that they wanted me out because of the indignity of the exposure of their fraud. He also made a telephone call. His letter and telephone call worked like magic, and my rejection was overturned.

So that is how, in the end, my writing of humorous fiction may have helped me get admitted to medical school.

9
"Mr. Poet"

Maulana Azad Medical College was founded by the government of India in 1958 under the aegis of Delhi University. It was named after Maulana Abul Kalam Azad, a Muslim, who was then education minister of India. During the first year of its inception, the college admitted about sixty students. Ours was the second year; my class had seventy-two students, including seventeen women. So when we started, the school was in its infancy, with about 130 students and relatively a small number of teachers, for nonclinical subjects only. Clinical courses started after the second year of schooling. The college was attached to Irwin Hospital, the largest government hospital in Delhi, which had no dearth of clinical materials or specialties.

MAMC, as it was called, was started in a cluster of buildings—the old prison during the British *Raj* (Empire)—and some of the buildings were actually attached to the hospital. The anatomy auditorium was converted from an old ward of the hospital, and physiology lectures were held in old office buildings. Some of the dorms were originally prison barracks. New buildings were being erected fast, and the college later became a sprawling conglomerate of lecture halls, laboratories, offices, dormitories, and dining halls.

⁓⁓⁓

After my initial jubilation about getting admitted to MAMC came the hard part. The first few days of medical school were critically important.

It was mandatory to wear a white coat to school, or you were not allowed in. So we each bought two white coats, because one had to be washed almost every day. And all the teachers called us "doctor" right from day one, which alternately boosted us up or taunted us, depending on the tone of voice used. Within moments of entering the gates, we were all seated on benches in a big, long hall with eight-by-three-foot metal tables lined up near the never-ending walls. Every table had four stools on each side and held a cadaver covered by a tarp. Though we couldn't see the cadavers, we could feel their presence because of the heavy, intoxicating smell of formaldehyde in the room, familiar from our premed dissections of frogs and dogs. I was scared. And shaking, looking at this macabre scene. We all were. I looked around; every student looked pale and had dry lips. The anatomy professor was giving directions and introductions to medical school.

Then came the real test: the attendants came and lifted off the tarps. The dead people were lying there, some with their eyes open. One of the male cadavers had his penis erect, which became an unfortunate joke throughout the student body for months to

72

follow. Suddenly I felt a heavy weight drop into my lap. The young woman next to me had fainted and had rolled onto my lap. I was dumbfounded. I had never touched a woman, never even shaken hands with one, outside of my immediate family. I started shaking and sweating even more. Fortunately, a teacher saw the scene, ran to our bench, picked up the student's head, and brought her back to life. Now it was her turn to shake and sweat; she was so embarrassed that she could not look into my eyes for a long time, even though we were dissection partners for the next whole trimester.

Touching a dead human body for the first time was a harrowing experience. The skin was dry, shriveled, and rough. We had bought instruments for dissection: a scalpel with certain kinds of blades, a couple of forceps, a marker, and a book that gave step-by-step instructions on how to do the dissection. Devi and I were partners and were assigned the right upper extremity (arm and hand) for our first trimester. It took us several days and not-so-subtle rebukes from the teachers before we learned how to hold the scalpel right. Devi was better at dissecting than I. And even when I was the one to find a certain muscle or a nerve, she got the credit for it; she was a woman, a pretty woman.

Lunch was supposed to follow the morning dissection, but we had another thing coming. The "ragging" (hazing) was relentless and went on for days. Seniors (senior only by a year) teased you, nagged you, asked you to polish their shoes with your spit, asked you to take off your pants and run in your underwear to the next female student you saw and say "Good morning, madam." The women students all knew what the prank meant and looked around for the pranksters, who were hiding by then. They were more interested in the bullies and the jocks than in the little creature standing in front of them, saying "Good morning, madam." If you had a mustache, the seniors would give you a blade to shave off the right half, and so on. I was very meek and obedient and no fun, so I was spared from most of the bad ragging the big or resistive kids got. We heard some horror stories, though. One student jumped out of a second-story window while running away from seniors. He was hurt badly and hospitalized for a long time.

⁂

The afternoon was devoted to physiology. It was hot and tiring, and we all had our minds on a siesta. The teacher started by asking us to stand up one by one, introduce ourselves, and talk about where we lived, what our parents did, what we did for fun, how much time we devoted to our hobbies, and so on. It was a difficult task for me. I was good at theory, not at oral presentation, and there was nothing noteworthy about me. What could I tell him? My inferiority complex was taking over; I was having a panic attack.

When I got up, I mumbled my name. The teacher would not give up. He asked me to repeat my name, and to repeat almost all the answers. He started asking me all kinds of questions. The more I slouched, the more he persisted. He was enjoying my pain, and the whole class was having fun along with him.

"Yes, I am from a public school."

"These are my grades."

"I come by bus number twenty-one."

"I don't know what my goals are."

"For fun I write."

"I write Hindi poetry."

That was it: the poetry. They all laughed. Almost all of the seventy-two students had a nickname; that day mine became *Kaviji* (Mr. Poet). I did not like that name and forgot about it in later years. But the name stayed with me throughout the five years of school . . . and beyond. When I founded my college alumni association more than twenty years later, many students whom I hadn't seen for years met me and called me Mr. Poet. I recently was at a party in India where an old professor whom I had not seen for forty years approached me and said, "Hello, Mr. Writer." I almost fainted; I didn't know that professors, who pretended to be so aloof then, remembered their students' nicknames after all this time. I did not remember his name.

※

That first day—and the first week, and the whole five years—were tiring and miserable for me. I admit that whatever I am today is probably the result of those five years; nonetheless, they were miserable.

10

"We Have All Our Hopes Resting on You, Jagga"

Medical school in India consists of five years of studying and six months of mandatory internship before you get the degree of MBBS, Bachelor of Medicine and Bachelor of Surgery. The first two years are called the First Professional. The Second Professional ends after the fourth year, and after the fifth year you go for the Final Professional exam. You have to attend 75 percent of the classes to be allowed even to take the exam. If you don't pass the First Professional, you can retake the test after the summer, and if you fail again you are permitted to repeat the test in another year. If, however, you fail the exam a third time, you are expelled from the school; three years wasted. The First Professional has only two main subjects, anatomy and physiology. I was reasonably competent in physiology. Anatomy was another story.

Anatomy of the human body is the precursor to surgery. For most of the first two years we dissected the cadaver we were presented with on the first day, section by section, day after day. I was not good in anatomy. Once or twice a week there was an exam (called a stage) and our grades from those exams were considered for the final tally. The instructors gave marks after each stage. You had to get ten out of twenty to pass. I usually scraped by with a ten, while the other students on my bench got fourteen or higher. My perpetual fear of contending with verbal exchanges haunted me once again, as I always fumbled with my answers when the teacher came to our bench and asked questions while other students joked, smiled, and even flirted. That behavior was unimaginable for me—I was too meek, small, and sweaty. Almost every week the teacher would shake his head and say, "Dr. Jagdish, you are coming back after the summer vacation," meaning I was sure to fail the First Professional exam. This was not totally inconceivable to me, as only about half the students passed the First Professional the first time.

After school I had to take the bus home, which was the usual ordeal. Same scene day after day: I arrive home tired and scared that I am definitely failing my second year. My uncle Khushiram, sitting on the cot, greets me with a big smile. "Here comes our doctor son. The brightest kid in town. We have all our hopes resting on you, Jagga. It is very tough to support your medical school. I am sure you are going to get a gold medal and make us proud of our sacrifices." He would also hint that if I failed, I would have to leave the school because we could not afford to pay the extra examination fees the second time, and I would definitely lose my scholarship.

The next day I go on the same bus to the same college, sit on the same bench, take another stage, and hear another snotty comment from a different teacher.

My fellow alumni tell me that their best years of life were in medical school; they had fun. My years in medical school were the worst of my life. There was always a threat that I would lose my scholarship or be withdrawn from the school for a job, or I would be humiliated by a teacher worse today than yesterday.

In the end I was one of the few students who passed every professional exam the first time. I never got a gold medal, but at least my scholarship remained intact. In hindsight, I believe my uncle Khushiram was aware that very few students passed the exams the first time, that I was not the brightest kid in town, and that a gold medal did not mean that much. He was just putting a scare in my head, just as the professors were playing mind games with students like me. A few years ago, I gave a party for my professor of anatomy, and he was talking in flowery terms about me and my achievements. I asked him why the teachers treated us like crap in those days. "That is the system there, son. That is the British system there, not like here in America, the liberal country. That is how we were taught and that is how we teach."

When the results of the First Professional exam were published in the newspaper, my uncle Khushiram showed the paper to whoever would see. He stood in the street and distributed cookies, he was so happy. What a flattering day, with so many people congratulating me! I was going to become a doctor sooner or later. He never mentioned the gold medal after that.

༺❀༻

School was less stressful after the first two years. At least they could not expel you from school if you failed an exam; you got as many tries as necessary to pass. And nobody was really going to stop my studies if I failed an exam once or twice, even though the pressure from my uncle Khushiram continued. Yet my anxieties, fears, and feelings of inferiority never abated during my whole medical-school experience. It has been almost fifty years since then, but I still get anxiety whenever I think of those times.

Regular attendance in school was important. Studying was important. But the most important thing in medical school was your professor's whim. Teachers made your life easy or a living hell. I saw students fail because the professor did not like their attitude in class. Or because the student had made a joke about the professor's necktie, and he heard it. Or the professor just got up on the wrong side of the bed on the day of the oral exams. In some subjects, like anatomy, 60 percent of the students failed, while in others, like surgery, the failure rate was only 15 percent. Same students! Similar subjects! One female student who did not respond to a professor's romantic overtures was failed for several years until she got herself transferred to another school.

My knack for writing helped me survive the theory exams. We had to write essays, and the longer the essay, the better it looked. I would stretch the subject like a rubber band. For example, for a question on maladies of the middle finger I would elaborate to include the other fingers and the hand, and the disorder that can happen whether it occurred on the middle finger of the right or the left hand. I would brighten the essay with colorful pictures scattered all over the several pages—pictures of blood vessels, bones, muscles, and joints of a finger, and how they looked when swollen or deformed. Colored pencils were my best friends. (By the way, the middle finger is just fictitious; I have never seen such a silly question. Index finger or thumb, perhaps.) The professor had less than a minute to devote to that essay and would spend it turning the pages and admiring the pictures. And he gave me good grades. Usually there were six or seven essays to write in three hours' time.

Oral exams were a different story. Writing couldn't help me there, and I was still really awful at these. There were at least two professors during the oral and the practical exam; one was our own and the other was from another college, "the external examiner." My trump card was not how I responded to their questions, but what they had in front of them, perhaps my grades from the theory exam they had graded last night or the day before when traveling by train to Delhi. I vividly remember the two professors conferring with each other after one of my anatomy orals, and discussing the discrepancy between my performance in theory and in practical and oral. The outsider was highly impressed with my theory exam, and though reluctantly, the "internal professor" had to agree with him.

꧁✿꧂

Just as in high school, I was shy and poor. I did not go on any picnics or outings, and did not attend any dances or dinners. I was asocial and lonely. But I was thinking and writing. That was my enjoyment. I did have two or three friends, all geeks like me. We would hang around together and share our sad stories of sadism by our professors and the conditions at our homes. We would bring in lunch from home. (We did not have money to splurge in the college cafeteria.) Lunch was always the same: two *rotis* (pita bread) wrapped around cooked, spiced vegetables or potato. With our meager allowance, we would eat bananas or ice cream after our lunch. Sometimes we cut classes and went to a movie; there were two movie theaters around the corner from the school. After school we would study in the library until it closed, which was around seven or eight in the evening. Conditions in our homes were not conducive to studying, buses were easier to get after the rush hour, and the library had some books that we could not afford to buy.

I wrote profuse notes during the lectures. I couldn't afford as many books as some other students did, so the class notes came in handy. A number of other students would "borrow" my notes, and I became very protective of my notes before the exams, as I was afraid they would walk.

11

The Taxi Drivers' Union

We were still teenagers when we started medical school, and over-protected and pampered until we were at least married and had a couple of children, and even then most of us lived with our parents. So we were extremely susceptible to the bullies of the class—or jokesters, pranksters, or jocks, depending on how you looked at them. Or how they looked at you. There were five of them in our class, nicknamed the Taxi Drivers' Union. They were the by-product of the school's ritual of "ragging"—when they were being hazed by the upperclassmen, they banded together and started throwing their collective weight around.

In the first week or so of school, a fellow student was being harassed by them and he said, "Oh my God, they behave like taxi drivers. They should join the Taxi Drivers' Union." The title stuck. Others called them Truck Drivers' Union, some TDU. At our college reunions several decades later, if we say we are from the class of 1964, some younger doctor will say, "Oh, the class of TDU."

The leader was from a rich and famous family and had a car. (Only one other kid out of a class of seventy-two had one.) He was jovial, always smiling, the smartest of the TDU—and in fact one of the most intelligent in the entire class. He was also somewhat overweight. He was funny and made jokes about everyone, including teachers. And nobody made fun of teachers in medical school. His friendly ways and charismatic personality bailed him and his friends out of trouble numerous times. He was a ray of light, and he made light of everything. He was also an actor and participated in the stage productions of the school. Many of the dramas and songs were parodies of our professors. They were written by him and everyone knew it. He acted them out onstage, and the professors laughed their asses off. He was surprisingly humble and quite friendly to me.

The number-two guy was my friend from high school. He was an athlete and a bodybuilder, and my protector. He won several awards in sports during high school and beyond. People were afraid to confront him. Since we were friendly, I occasionally used his services. When a student intimidated me or did not return my books and notes, I would ask him for help, and he threatened the student, or beat him up, and got me the appropriate results. Thus he kept his bully status in the class and I was free to roam around without fear of other students, who were all bigger than I was. Sometimes I would give him my pocket allowance for his favors; sometimes he asked me in a friendly manner to fork it over.

The other three were always seen with them. They played hooky from school, went to movies, menaced other students, and became a nuisance to the teachers. As mentioned earlier, if you did not attend 75 percent of the classes, you could not even take the professional exam—yet this bunch missed many classes.

Sometimes one who attended class would answer for the rest during roll call. In some classes, through requests or threats, they got other students to answer for them. I was one of their stooges and would help them through some of the classes. Since I was generally a nerd, the teachers did not suspect me of participating in this scam. I would also lend them my notes and help them in other ways, like rigging their experiments in class or letting them copy from me during exams. In turn they assured my well-being. In my own quiet way I somewhat identified with them, although I would never admit it openly.

Once they drove to Simla, a vacation resort, most likely looking for girls. Overnight somebody stole the hubcaps of their leader's car. How could anyone dare? In response, the next night they went around and stole the hubcaps of all the cars parked on the nearby streets. They came back to Delhi with a trunk full of hubcaps and made a show of it for other students to see.

Their sexual escapades, their hazing of junior students, their juvenile behavior comprised much of the school gossip. The teachers who tried to stop their immature jokes were tormented in other ways. They once hot-wired a teacher's motor scooter and went for a ride. The principal called them to his office and admonished them. He tried to break them to find out who actually was the culprit, but each claimed responsibility for the action. Knowing that a maximum of two students could have ridden on the scooter, he could not have expelled all five from the school, or it would have been a smear on the school's and his own reputation. Rather, he admonished the teacher to be more careful about locking his scooter in the future. That is how they worked and controlled the system.

The girls in our class loved them, and there were stories of one or the other going around with them. We also heard that they were warned many times for having brought outside girls to the dorms.

Years later, I found out that TDU was also known in other medical schools around town, and the coed medical students from all over were anxious to see who these students were.

The student who named them TDU was a friend of mine. He was also a neighbor and well known in the neighborhood for his eccentric ways. While most of us called ourselves medical students, he called himself a doctor and even put up a sign outside his house proclaiming himself as such. Many people would go to him for advice and he would freely give it. He was not the only medical student "practicing" medicine on ignorant country folks and charging fees. There were no laws or regulations about practicing medicine, and there was no threat of malpractice. (Even now malpractice is not a menace in India.) When he was still just a student, I saw him give injections to patients.

❦

After graduation, my friend who named the TDU joined the Indian Army. Once he retired from the service, he started a private practice in Delhi, mixing medicine with yoga and meditation, and became quite popular. When his children moved to the United States, he retired and followed them. He found out he could not practice medicine here without a license, so he started looking around for something to keep himself busy. He eventually found a job teaching basic sciences to nursing and physician-assistant students. He always was the teaching type.

Another friend of mine joined the Indian Army and did postgraduate work in pediatrics. After retiring from the service, he became a consultant and worked in administration. One classmate became an ophthalmologist and opened a charity eye hospital in Delhi. Another opened a general charity hospital there. I lost contact with these classmates and seldom saw them when I visited India. As for those who came to America, I might have stayed aloof from them too, except that I formed a college alumni association and have kept in touch with them. Fortunately, my wife is far more social than I and can carry the small talk for both of us at reunions.

The leader of the TDU eventually settled in England, married an Englishwoman, had a great family, and won numerous awards there, including the Queen's Award. His personality never changed.

The number-two guy, who had been my friend in high school, came to the United States, worked hard, made his money, and went back to India. He helped a number of people there, financially and professionally. Once I visited him at his home in India: a huge farmhouse with several servants and bodyguards and guard dogs, where he lived a lonely, isolated life. He studied Indian scriptures in depth and enjoyed critiquing them.

A third member of the TDU came to the United States, became a surgeon, also raised a fine family, and is now retired and a golf junkie.

Tragically, the other two TDU members had a terrible end as young men. One had a heart attack after giving a passionate, heart-wrenching religious speech in England, and the body of the second one was discovered on a golf course in India.

The star of our class, the perpetual gold medalist, joined the U.S. Army, later became a professor, and was shot to death at a young age by his own son.

12

The Romantic Writer

After my humiliating experience in the first week of medical school, and after having been dubbed "Mr. Poet," I was encouraged by my classmates to run for the office of joint editor of the student body executive council. (The editor position was always held by a senior.) Though I had no idea what I was doing or why, and there was no way I was going to win, I ran anyway. My opponent was a formidable candidate and the election was hotly contested. I won, I will never know how

The executive council had formal meetings. I did not speak even once, and nobody cared to include me in any deliberations. When the school magazine was published, the editor had all the articles by him and his friends; I was not mentioned anywhere. Feeling insulted, I got the idea of a weekly wall magazine. It consisted of a glass-enclosed bulletin board, and students and teachers were asked to contribute articles. Very few people contributed, but everybody read it several times a day while passing by. I started writing new articles, new poems, even a who's who, and a "Did you know that . . ." gossip column. Even though I wrote most of the pieces anonymously, everybody knew who was writing them.

My poems ran the gamut: they were romantic or humorous or sad or sarcastic. The romantic ones were all directed toward the same girl, on whom I had a crush from afar for all five years of medical school. She was short, jovial, sociable, popular, and always singing to herself. She also had an invisible sign on her forehead: "Do not touch." Probably every male student in our class had his eye on her. My former female classmates tell me now that they used to bet with one another about who the subject of my poetry was. For five years I could not tell this person that I had feelings for her. That was not the thing to do in those days, at least not for me!

When my classmates asked for volunteers for a dramatic stage production, I raised my hand and did a pretty good job. (I sometimes wonder if the person sitting next to me raised my hand.) Teachers and students put on a funfair carnival. I went in a costume and was a main attraction. I also participated in a caricature skit. I went to the stage and recited a romantic poem, again directed toward this "unknown" entity. Maybe I was not as shy and squeamish as I think I was. I did all that but, as always, never gave myself any credit for it. And, I believe, others didn't give me any credit either. I since learned that if you don't feel good about yourself, others won't either. Then again, writing a poem and reciting it onstage, sweating all over, is not the same as taking an oral exam or being interviewed.

✦

During my internship, I wrote a story about an emergency-room physician that was accepted in a respected national monthly Hindi

89

magazine, *Sarita,* maybe equivalent to the *Reader's Digest* here. They published the story with my picture and paid me thirty-five rupees (then about seven dollars). I was ecstatic.

A year or so later I applied for a medical job with Employees State Insurance (ESI) Corporation, my second job after the internship. It paid more than the job I had, 650 rupees per month compared to 550, and there were hundreds of applications for three openings. I went for the interview but had no letter from a cabinet minister, no connections, and no medals or grades to boast about. There was not a chance of my getting this job, especially because I panicked during the interviews. The three stately professors who were interviewing looked bored as they asked the usual questions and dismissed me. Then one of them called me back and asked me to sit down.

"I have seen you somewhere."

(No, you could not have seen me. And no, I do not know any major politician. And I have no idea why you are suddenly being nice to me.)

Then he posed a question. "Did you write a story or something and get your picture in the newspaper?"

Now it was my turn to liven up. "Yes, sir, you may have read my story in *Sarita* last year." The other two professors woke up too and asked me to tell them the story.

A tired emergency-room physician, Dr. Nag, has been going from one bed to another for the past seven hours without lunch, only many cups of tea. He has done two lumbar punctures, certified two deaths (including that of a child), started numerous IVs, sutured patients, and read X-rays; he is now examining a bloodied patient. There was a street fight between neighbors over a woman, and the man before him was repeatedly clubbed. Nag asks the nurse to bring an IV, call the X-ray department, and bring in the family to give history. Suddenly, Satish the constable, who is always posted outside the emergency room, appears and wants to have a statement from the patient. The patient is dying, but the constable insists on getting the written version of the incident from the patient. Nag asks him to leave or he will call hospital security. After the constable leaves, Nag muses loudly that the corrupt policemen want their bribes from the offending party, and without regard for the condition of the patient, they want their case strengthened for a better bribe. These are the leeches of society, he says.

Later in the evening, after having been relieved by the other doctor, Nag is changing his white coat to his regular suit when he gets a call from his friend at the engineering college about the new movie playing in the theater across the street from the hospital. "But the hall is booked for the next six weeks," says his friend; "there is no chance of getting tickets even on the black market."

"Hold on," Nag says, and hangs up the phone. He runs out to Satish the constable and asks him if he knows somebody in that theater who can get two tickets for tomorrow's matinee. Within ten minutes he has two good tickets in his hand, and Satish has not even accepted any money from the doctor for those tickets. Nag calls his friend with the good news and goes home.

That night he dreams of the leeches of society, and in the line are the corrupt constable Satish and the corrupt doctor Nag.

The interview lasted for a whole extra five minutes, and I got the job.

❦

Since then, my writing has been sporadic and bumpy. I did not write for years. I did not think I could write in English, and a few attempts I made did not succeed. I did get published here and there: letters to the editor, jokes, commentaries, some actual articles too. When I started publishing a regular newsletter of several pages for my college alumni association, my writing took off once again. It was like déjà vu. I was writing for the same people for whom I had created the weekly wall magazine. My spirits came back. The association became successful, and credit was given to the fun and interesting read of our magazine, which was almost wholly written, edited, and published by me.

I started writing newsletters for my medical association, my hospital, and the psychiatric society. My "Ruminations," a satire on anything and everything, became a regular column in the newsletter of the New Jersey Psychiatric Association. Other state psychiatric associations started republishing the column. In addition to the psychiatrists, their office staff and their husbands and wives called me with compliments. The column was a tongue-in-cheek look at psychiatry, doctors, politicians, Indians, lawyers, short people, bald people, *me*. And a writer was reborn.

PART THREE

Doctor and Immigrant

13

The Doctor...and
Two #2 Pencils

The six months' mandatory internship at Irwin Hospital was a grueling job. All of us had to do our rotation in medicine, surgery, and obstetrics/gynecology in the familiar hospital where we had been going for our clinical education for years. I worked hard, day and night, with very little sleep and no breaks. The pay, 150 rupees (about thirty dollars) per month, was about the same as my scholarship during school. Finally, after six months of servitude, I was proclaimed a doctor. No major family celebration followed this event.

My family had made it clear that I needed to find a job immediately after my internship. While my former classmates were looking into residency programs and graduate courses, I started looking for a job. In India we did not need residency to practice medicine; residency was only necessary to become a specialist. The rich kids and the ones with connections were starting their own private practices. My best friend, Nagi, joined the Indian Army; his family also told him money was their immediate need.

It was hard to get into graduate programs, and it was harder still to find a job without personally knowing somebody higher up who was somebody. For weeks I was going from pillar to post, walking in the hot sun, taking buses, filling out application after application. No luck.

During my travels, I often visited my school and once ran into a professor of medicine, Dr. Hari Vaishnava. "Hey, Dang, what are you doing these days? Why don't you join my department for postgraduate studies?" I wondered why he was offering me admission while other more qualified students were dying to get in. He must have liked me. Or maybe I had not been as bad in school as I thought. Maybe he knew about all those anonymous poems and articles.

I explained to him as politely as I could that I had to decline his offer because my and my family's priority was for me to find a job. "Oh, what kind of job are you looking for?" I told him any job would do, but I would prefer to work for the Municipal Corporation of Delhi. "Why don't you go see Dr. Rao, the health commissioner, and tell him I sent you?" I told him that I had seen Dr. Rao the week before and he said there were no openings. Dr. Vaishnava picked up the phone, dialed a number, and said, "Hey, Rao, I am sending a student to you for a job; he is a good boy." And he hung up.

I swear that's all he said. I remember every second of the incident as if it happened yesterday, even though it was more than forty years ago. I lay awake all night thinking that Dr. Vaishnava had faked it all; he was known for his flamboyant behavior. How could he just say a sentence like that and hang up, and expect me to think anything of it? He didn't give Dr. Rao my name or tell him anything about me. Was he just talking into a dead phone line?

The next morning at ten I returned to the health offices of the Municipal Corporation of Delhi, just as the offices opened. I was told that Dr. Rao was at a meeting and would come back after lunch. I went and ate lunch and hung around until he showed up. When he saw me sitting on the bench outside his office, he barked, "Why are you still here? I told you there are no openings!"

"Sir, Dr. Vaishnava sent me."

His voice softened immediately. "Oh, so you know Vaish. Come in." Inside his office he unashamedly told me he had three job openings; I could take my pick. I chose a job at the tuberculosis hospital in Kingsway Camp Colony because it was on the direct bus route from my house, even though it was far. I was with him for less than five minutes, after which he scribbled a note on a scrap of paper, instructing me to go to the hospital the next day and give it to the superintendent there. I had a job!

⚜

Simply put, it was a half-time job with full-time salary. There were a thousand or so patients, across many units, all in some stage of tuberculosis. About twenty doctors collected in the large conference room at eight every morning to discuss chest X-rays, patients, and any major events of the past twenty-four hours— who had died, who had vomited blood, who had been given sedation, who had fought with another patient. Our superintendent was a well-known tuberculosis specialist, and he did most of the talking. He knew all the patients; they stayed there until their death, and he had been there forever. Most of the patients were on a combination of two or three tuberculosis medications available at that time. By noon we were tired, had tea or coffee, and dispersed to go home around one in the afternoon. Only one physician who was on call that day stayed behind. I stayed about once every twenty days. There was a nice clean room with a bed and a few magazines. I was assigned to visit one unit when on call, examine the chest of every patient in that unit, and write a short note on each of their charts.

About three calls came during the night, mostly for severe emergencies or death certifications. The telephone in the room never worked, so an attendant came in with a slip of paper, and you either wrote an answer on the slip or accompanied the attendant to the unit. Sometimes young nurses would stop by to flirt, to have tea, or to offer "entertainment." Either I was stupid or maybe I had some strong principles (superego? inhibitions? fear?), so I never responded to those overtures. There were stories of other doctors having fun. I stayed dumb (or principled) forever, even after I came to the United States.

❧

My afternoons were more or less free, so I would end up going to the medical school and hanging out with whoever was available. I made two friends, and we three would go to Chandni Chowk, a busy area of Delhi full of markets and restaurants, to eat lunch. The other two were graduate students and made very little money, and I had a lucrative job now, so I usually ended up paying for lunch. I was generally happy, now that I had completed my medical education. I had no major ambitions, no goals. As always, I felt that whatever will be, will be. I saw a lot of movies during the four months of my first job, usually with those two graduate students.

It was during one of those visits to the dorms that these friends brought applications for the ECFMG (Educational Commission for Foreign Medical Graduates), an exam to become certified in the United States, and we sat down together and filled them out. We weren't seriously applying; rather, it was just something to do. We had very little idea what it meant to pass the ECFMG or where it might lead us. We only thought that at least we would get to take a day off for the examination and get two #2 yellow pencils from "those Yankees." In the space for application fee, we wrote "The Indian Government does not allow foreign exchange." This was only partly true. If we had really been serious about going to the United States, we would have applied for the foreign exchange of thirty dollars, and after a lot of hassles could have gotten the money; none of us was willing or able to spend 150 rupees for this purpose.

The registration papers came back from the United States with the date and place for the examination. I made some excuse at work and took a day off. The three of us took buses and went to

Ashoka Bhavan Auditorium for the test. The test was essentially two hours of multiple-choice questions, which was entirely a new experience for us; until then we had only done essay, oral, or practical exams. And there was an additional test of spoken English. I passed. I also got my two precious #2 yellow pencils.

14

Eight Dollars and
Two Tins of Loose Tea

By the time I had my first job, my father had started a small clothing store in Delhi, and the family had moved back to Delhi, to a small apartment. Two of my father's younger sisters, my aunts Shashi and Kanta, were married at that point. My youngest uncle, Puran, was married as well, working as an engineer and living in a separate apartment. His wife, Kamlesh, worked too. I was still living at my uncle Khushiram's place for the most part, in the original small house in Rajinder Nagar. Eventually, when I quit my first job and began working for Employees' State Insurance (ESI) Corporation, it was located near where my parents lived, so I moved in with them. I was helping them financially and was probably paying all the household expenses. I kept a small amount from my monthly pay and gave all the rest to my father. I walked to the ESI clinic and worked from two in the afternoon to eight in the evening.

At my father's one-bedroom apartment there were seven of us: my parents and their five children, with a water pump all to ourselves. Meanwhile, my younger brother Harish was going to a prestigious school of architecture. There was a big sign outside the house with my name and degree, though I don't believe anyone ever knocked at the door to see the doctor. There were also the beginnings of talk of "looking for a girl" for me to marry.

꧁꧂

At the ESI clinic there were limited supplies of medicines, and treatments were rudimentary, but most of the patients got better anyway. Once or twice a month we were on call and slept in the clinic. We did house calls for emergencies, accompanied by an aide. We got paid thirty rupees for that service, so I readily volunteered for that when others refused. I was happy; I was carefree. Life was good.

Around six in the afternoon we took a break. We gathered together in a large room, had tea and snacks, and chatted. One day Dr. Sacha provided the food and tea. He usually came in a necktie (while nobody else did). He was from a rich family and had a girlfriend, another of our colleagues in the clinic. He was treating us to the food and tea as a celebration because he was going to America. Everybody was congratulating him and kissing the piece of paper that he circulated. It was the notification letter that he had passed the ECFMG. I looked at it, then took aside our medical director, Dr. K. K. Sharma, and told him that I had received a similar paper in the mail the day before. Dr. Sharma was quite fond of me and did not much like Dr. Sacha. At first he did not believe me and asked me to bring that letter. I took off, trekked home, and brought the letter to the clinic. Dr. Sharma looked at it, gasped, collected everybody together, and started the celebration again. This time I was treating them to snacks and tea. He announced that he would make sure I got to the United States before Dr. Sacha.

Going abroad was a prestigious thing; this I knew. Did I really want to go to America? I had taken the exam almost as a lark, with no serious plans, and my life in India was running smoothly now. Was I startled that this exam could determine my future? Was I nervous about the prospect of my life turning upside down, or downside up? Was I making any decisions? Who was making decisions for me? I was in a daze, going through the motions. Sometimes I think I have been in a daze much of my life.

⁕

The next few weeks were full of activity.

I told Dr. Sharma right off the bat that my family could not afford to let go of my salary and send me to an unknown land. After the clinic that night he asked me to ride with him on his motorcycle. He took me to my house to try to convince my father that it was an ideal scenario and he had to let me go. When he begrudgingly agreed, we all went to my uncle Khushiram and talked to him. But my uncle had other thoughts. He had spoken with a World Health Organization visiting physician from England and learned of the possibility of a job for me there, doing research into the renal system. He thought it would be a financial boon for the family.

I wrote a letter to the superintendent of the only hospital in the United States that had advertised in the local medical directory. The letter was a simple sentence. "Dear Sir: I have passed the ECFMG and am looking for a job." International mail was slow, but three weeks later I received a thick envelope. It was a very nice appointment letter from the hospital, a brochure of the hospital, and papers for a J-1 visa. They also wanted to know my measurements, so they could have my white uniforms ready.

I was going to start as an intern at Bergen Pines County Hospital in Paramus, New Jersey, and would be given free uniforms, free room at the residence, and a salary of $131 every two weeks. I must start by April 15, which was only about eight weeks away. At the same time a letter came from England about the research assistant position there in renal diseases. The professor said I could stay with him until I found an apartment, and the salary was about eighty pounds a month, less than the salary as an intern in the United States, but it was well known that the cost of living was lower in England than in the United States. It was a difficult choice and we did not know what to do. I insisted I wanted to go to America, though I couldn't explain why because I didn't know why. In hindsight, I believe I was trying to assert my independence; the job in England was procured by my uncle.

❦

I had no idea what I was doing. I didn't even know where America was. I did not know its capital. I didn't know that you needed a passport and a visa to go to a foreign country. I went to the office of United States Information Service; they were of little help, probably because I did not ask the right questions. Dr. Sharma took on the responsibility of sending me to America. He was respected and resourceful. There were so many hurdles in getting the passport and permission from the Indian Government to leave my current job. But he persisted, and with him, his motorcycle, and the hot sun, I went from office, to office, to another office.

We started with the Employees' State Insurance head office. The boss asked him in; everybody knew Dr. Sharma, and everybody loved this humble soul. "This is Dr. Jagdish Dang, sir. He wants to go to America and needs a no-objection certificate from you." (If you worked for the government, you needed a no-objection certificate to leave your job and leave the country, and it was very hard to get that certificate if your boss refused to release you from the job.)

"I would love to help Dr. Dang, but you know, Sharmaji, there is a total ban on giving no-objection certificates these days."

"You are the one who implemented that ban, sir, and you can make an exception, for me."

They discussed me for the next ten minutes, and the boss said at last that he would look into it. A week later Dr. Sharma brought the certificate and gave it to me. It could easily have been construed that I bribed Dr. Sharma, but everybody in the department knew that he was an honest, genuine article, and they all would go out of their way to help him. There *are* angels in this world; he was my angel. He also found a deputy commissioner to approve my application for a passport. Unfortunately, Dr. Sharma died not too long after I came to the United States.

⚜

My uncle Khushiram was trying to procure loans for my trip. Three thousand rupees ($600) one way to New York was a lot of money. Later I learned that Bergen Pines would have sent me the ticket if I had asked. And then there were the ready-made shirt (thirty rupees) and an overcoat ("it is very cold in America"), fancy Binaca toothpaste instead of the usual Colgate toothpaste, and two tins of loose tea ("they drink coffee there; tea is not available in America").

A friend asked if I had seen the Taj Mahal. ("They all talk about the Taj Mahal in America.") No, I had not. It was only a little more than a hundred miles away, so two friends—the graduate students—and I took the train and went to see the monument. I was too timid to go alone one hundred miles but bold enough to travel eight thousand miles! Nobody in my family or in the neighborhood had ever gone to a foreign country, let alone America, which was considered the bottom of the world ("down under"). And I, a scrawny ninety-nine-pound doctor, was embarking on this journey.

I was given eight dollars; that was the maximum foreign exchange you could take out of the country legally. You could buy some dollars on the black market, but I was told we could not afford any more than eight dollars, so it would have to suffice. We had no idea how far this money would go, or how far the hospital was from the airport in America. We did not know when I was going to get my first paycheck or how I would survive till then. Everybody in the household was excited and apprehensive.

15

Halfway Around the World
on an Empty Stomach

My whole extended family, as well as some chosen community members, came to Delhi Airport to see me off. At least a hundred people were there, and not a dry eye in sight.

My father, a strict vegetarian and a man of principles, took me to one side and gave me his parting advice. "You are going to the country of opportunities and vices. There will be all kinds of distractions: women, alcohol, smoking, gambling. Do anything within limits, but do not eat beef. You know eating beef is strictly prohibited in our religion." (Little did he know that it would not be women, alcohol, smoking, or gambling, but that on my third day in America I would accidentally eat beef.)

Always practical and prudent, my uncle Khushiram gave slightly different parting advice. He reminded me that the family was going into a big hole sending me to America. I must keep that in mind and send money back home, not spend it all on myself, because the debts had to be paid. "Remember all the sacrifices the family has made in making you a doctor and sending you all the way to America. We will expect a money order as soon as you get your first check." He also admonished me to be careful about American women, who would try to snatch me and my money away from my "real" family.

All the uncles, aunts, and even children had advice for me, mainly to stay away from American women. They were bad; they had a special lure. I was an innocent and would be such an easy target. The good-byes took forever. Then I walked into the secure area and looked back. Everyone was crying, this time loudly. I felt so alone. Only once or twice in my life had I traveled even a few hours away from home, and now I was going to "the other end of the world," alone. Interestingly, I was not really sad; I was mostly feeling the hidden excitement of an adventure. I had always been an overprotected child, and at age twenty-six, I was still a child in India, a short skinny thing with a limp.

No one in my family had remembered to give me any snacks for the trip.

❧

I spent the next day and a half in a trance: Lufthansa airplane, changing planes in Frankfurt, only half understanding what was being said by the pilot on the intercom and by the hostesses in person. At Frankfurt Airport I was so afraid of missing the connecting flight that I would not even go to the bathroom for all those hours. And every few minutes I checked the inside pocket of my jacket to make sure that I had those eight dollars intact. Looking around, I saw that I was probably the only person wearing an overcoat, an oddball in every sense.

On the airplane to New York, nothing they brought to me in the food tray was familiar—nothing. I had never seen containers; I did not even know how to open them, and I was too embarrassed to ask. Nothing looked palatable. Even the water looked and tasted different. I had not had rolls before, or plain bread, or juice in a container, or juice without a container for that matter. I had never seen *that* food. I did not know what foods might contain eggs; I was allergic to eggs. So I kept drinking water and sending the food tray back. My travel sickness was acting up too and I was getting nauseous. My memory is foggy, but I recall that I did not eat or drink anything until I heard a passenger ask for Coca-Cola. That sounded familiar and I too asked the hostess if I could have Coca-Cola. She was delighted to oblige; I guess she was afraid I might die or something, because I had had no food of any kind in me for a long time. I had several glasses of Coke after that until I reached New York.

With eight dollars in my pocket and a suitcase in tow, I was standing bewildered at Kennedy Airport when an air hostess caught my sleeve and asked my name. When I told her, she said something that sounded like they were paging my name on the intercom. "Paging" and "intercom" were both new words for me, and I looked at her questioningly. She politely took me by the arm and led me out the door to a man standing on the walkway in front of the building with his hands in his pockets.

Back in India, my uncle Khushiram, always so practical, had decided to save money by not sending a telegram to the hospital to announce my arrival and instead expected that the airline would do that on our behalf. The airline had sent what was called a telex, which fortunately reached the hospital the day of my arrival, but so late that the hospital could not arrange for a taxi and instead sent a Filipino resident to pick me up. (What if the telex had not reached there?)

He asked me to follow him to his car. I had never picked up a heavy suitcase and was struggling with mine, especially because its handle had broken by now. Under my breath I cursed the workmanship that allowed the handle of a new suitcase to break within a day and a half. I was surprised to see no servants or porters to help with the luggage, a familiar scene at railway stations and airports back home. I dragged myself and the suitcase to the parking lot and entered the Filipino resident's car.

I had never seen a toll and couldn't believe that you paid to travel on the road in America! A whole quarter to cross the bridge! I patted my jacket pocket to make sure my eight dollars were safe there. I also did not see roads paved with gold, or dollar bills hanging from the trees, as I had been made to believe. (Years later when I mentioned this phrase to a veteran Armenian American, he said he was actually looking for the gold-paved roads when he came here. Maybe I was too!)

The resident and I made some conversation, but it was hard with his accent and mine. And I was tired, lonely, anxious, sad, sleepy, and hungry all at once. The excitement under the surface was waning. By the time we reached the hospital, it was evening. I was given keys to the dorm room and told to report for work at six in the morning. And, by the way, I was on call the next night. Also, I was not to be late or I could be fired.

Welcome to America.

16

America—Land of Smiles and Strawberry Ice Cream

Strange as this may sound, I loved it right away. Not too many people from India really love the United States; some don't even pretend to do so. And no Indian immigrant I know loved this country so quickly. They may have loved things about it, but to really love this country is uncommon. The reasons I did were not the usual ones cited. It was not the American girls. It wasn't the beer, or the food, or the dollars. In fact I did not indulge in any of that. What really mattered to me was the smiles and the people. The people actually smiled! They laughed! They were friendly, accepting, welcoming, warm, and flexible. They were good people and they quickly won me over. I was ready to embrace (well, metaphorically speaking) this new world and these new people.

Of course, some aspects of American friendliness were jarring at first. When I arrived at the hospital, an elderly woman telephone operator came out of the booth and extended her hand to welcome me. I instinctively withdrew. I had never shaken hands with a woman before, and clearly this was just the kind of trap my family had warned me about at the airport. Later I became friends with Rose, and we would often talk and laugh about our first meeting.

In America I felt free, and the freedom felt so good. In my home, and my country, there was an atmosphere of suffocation— deceit, jealousy, envy, sarcasm, all the time. My mother and grand-mother never got along with each other. Usually mothers-in-law and daughters-in-law in India did not get along. And they dragged their husbands and children and grandchildren into the fray. There was too much so-called love, affection, and consideration for each other, but to me it was all a facade. There were the inhibitions, the criticisms, the humiliations. There was no peace in my house or in most other houses I knew, or in my mind. Family bickering and arguments, yelling and screaming were a daily routine. Maybe poverty brought that. Maybe that was the by-product of the joint family system, with several generations living under one roof. Contrary to popular belief, there was more of the rat race and love for money among Indians than among Americans, at least among the Indians I knew. There was constant tension.

During my professional and personal dealings in America, I have come across countless families, including a lot of dysfunctional ones. They have different problems here, a different set of social dilemmas—but I was fighting my own conflicts, and America gave me freedom from them. I was free. Just free. I was busy and lonely and sad . . . but free to be all that, happy and miserable at the same time, without having to explain to anybody.

I was also taken aback, pleasantly, by the work ethic of Americans. Everybody worked hard. Everybody took his or her job seriously. Everybody did his or her own menial chores; there were no servants to cook or to clean. Once I saw the superintendent of my hospital in the car, and I followed him out of curiosity. After stopping at the dry cleaner's to drop off his laundry, he picked up food to take home from a restaurant. That was a big revelation for me; in America status did not matter. It was the land of opportunities *and* the land of responsibilities. Dignity of labor was a new concept for me.

ᘓᗷᕽᘔ

Bergen Pines Hospital was smaller than it is now; it has changed its name and ownership too. In the 1980s all the hospitals in New Jersey were in expansion mode, with new buildings added, total renovations, and fancy equipment. Two decades later, with the advent of new technology, HMOs, shorter hospital stays, and same-day procedures, many of those expansions became superfluous, and many of those same hospitals had to reduce the number of beds, close wings or entire hospitals, or reinvent themselves. Many started offering specialized services; others touted having started specialized services without really having done it. Hospitals became pure business entities. Marketing and lobbying became an inherent part of hospital business.

In 1966 the Pines was a county hospital mostly catering to chronic illnesses. Like most American state and county hospitals,

115

it had started as a tuberculosis sanitarium, in an isolated area at the junction of three towns so that no town needed to be associated with tuberculosis. Later, urban sprawl took place around it, tuberculosis was almost eradicated, and it started wings for psychiatric patients, alcohol addiction, and other chronic illnesses. It had several small old buildings and a couple of new ones, many of which were connected to one another by underground tunnels. Its superintendent, Dr. Rufus Little, was an old-time tuberculosis specialist who still conducted one lecture a week on diseases of the chest and showed X-rays. The hospital did have rudimentary acute medical and surgical services, and it borrowed surgical residents from a hospital in New York. It had its own interns, and I was one of them. I believe if it had offered a residency in psychiatry then as it does now, I would have stayed there after my internship.

The dorm at the Pines had long corridors with small suites of rooms on both sides: two bedrooms and a bathroom, for two residents or interns, or one family. The intern with whom I shared my bathroom was Dr. Ma, from Taiwan. There were about eight single residents and interns and four families on our floor. We had a lounge with a television (black and white in those days, with two or three channels). There was a stove and a refrigerator, which was stocked with milk for coffee. The housekeeper did our beds and brought milk for the refrigerator. We would drink up the milk and it was always running out, so she started bringing more and more milk until the hospital took notice and we got a memo. However, we—especially I—kept drinking milk, and she kept bringing more. I believe I was drinking an average of a gallon a day. It was free. While other residents and interns cooked food, like chicken and rice and hamburgers, I would sit there and eat cashew nuts and potato chips and drink three or four glasses of milk every evening. After work I was tired and hungry and ate raw calories. I did not like any of the foods I cooked or they cooked on that shared stove. My difficulty in adapting to unfamiliar food was my biggest problem.

On my third day at Bergen Pines, I had been assisting in surgery from seven in the morning to three in the afternoon, holding the retractor (a surgical instrument that holds the edges of a wound open). Like everyone else on the team, I was starving when I came out of the operating room. Soggy hamburgers were waiting outside and all of us were gobbling them. I did not know what I was eating, but I knew I did not like it. In India I had seldom had any meat, maybe goat curry once in three or four weeks. This time it tasted different, so I asked what I was eating. I was told it was beef—and immediately thought of my father's advice at Delhi Airport. Yes, I felt guilty, for a while only.

I did not like the lunch food in cafeteria of the hospital, even though it was subsidized. Instead I ate in what they called the Pinette, where I had mostly ice cream and orange juice. At breakfast I ate cereal with a lot of milk. I also consumed gallons of Coke every week. When I was a child in India, my grandmother had prayed to God to give me some weight, even in the wrong places. Now I was eating junk and gaining pounds. Within six months or so I gained twenty pounds, forty or so by the end of the first year.

I had gone from 99 pounds, five feet three inches to almost 140 pounds, five feet three inches. The pallor had gone from my face, it looked fuller and had a glow, and my skin became quite fair. People made all kinds of guesses about my nationality, but none thought I was an Indian; many thought I was white or East Asian. But I was always hungry and nauseous. I needed real food, like homemade food, but unfortunately I would not get that during the first year.

I went to see one of our attending doctors for my continuous nausea. She took tests and an upper GI series but found nothing wrong. After taking my detailed history she concluded that my food habits were bad. She also told me that ice cream in America contained eggs, and since I was allergic to eggs and my main symptom of an egg allergy was nausea, it was no wonder that I was nauseous from eating all that ice cream. It did not stop my ice cream consumption, but I ate less of it after that revelation.

Work was busy, long hours. There were no unions for the residents and interns in those days. We were on call ten nights a month and every other weekend. Even the "free" weekend started around two in the afternoon on Saturdays. My friend, another Indian intern, and I would take the hospital shuttle to the Grand Union and lug bags of groceries back to the room. While he brought back real food to cook, I brought nuts and potato chips and bottles of Coke (no cans back then). We were very fond of "curd" in India and made several inquiries about curd to no avail. The friendly salesman even called his head office in Michigan to ask if there was something called curd, but the answer was no. We had never heard the word "yogurt." If I had discovered yogurt early on, I wouldn't have been starving and gaining weight at the same time; I could have easily eaten yogurt (curd) and rice with a lot of salt and pepper added, at least a few days a week.

∘⦿⦾∘

I am often asked about discrimination. Was there discrimination? Surely there was. However, it did not bother me during my first few years in this country. I rationalized it. Was I accepted here? Most definitely. Was I treated badly? Definitely not. I had seen more discrimination in India, between North Indians and South Indians, between high caste and low caste, between rich and poor, between dark-skinned and light-skinned, and in many other instances. I just could not get over the smiles, affection, and accepting attitude of Americans. I felt as if I were in heaven, and I still feel that way. Many Americans tell me that when they visit India, they feel the same way about Indians.

Did my accent give me much grief? Not really. I caught on to the accent of the American Northeast fairly quickly. To this day there are some words I cannot pronounce properly and have to repeat (thyroid, thermometer), but for the most part I adapted. Some words were simply different. We called a flashlight a torch in India. Every time I asked for a torch, I was the laughingstock of nurses. It took me a while to respond to "Thank you" with "You're welcome," since back in India we answered "Thank you" with "Thank you."

On many of my free Sundays I went to New York. In the beginning another Indian intern went with me, but soon he stopped going, thinking it was a waste of precious money; he was not as fascinated by America as I was. I wandered around 42nd Street, saw the magicians, and ate junk, even lost money in three-card monte. Later in the day I ended up at Radio City Music Hall to see a movie (Doris Day) and the Rockettes. Sometimes I would see a dirty movie. What was a dirty movie in those days would be rated PG-13 today. I also bought a nice-looking wristwatch from one of the stores on 42nd Street for three dollars. It stopped working after three days.

One Sunday morning, early on, I was not fully awake when I heard a song sung by the famous Indian singer Kundan Lal Sehgal. I thought I was hallucinating: I must be missing India so much that I made up this song in my mind! Almost in a trance, I got up and started walking in my pajamas toward the sound. The voice was coming from a door about four down the hall from mine. Most people were still sleeping. I timidly knocked at the door. Dr. Arif, a Pakistani, opened the door. That was my first introduction to a tape recorder, and to this day I have never lost my love for them. I love music and believe that music is the soul of life. I have adopted many traits of America, but I cannot let go of my Indian music and Indian songs.

I was also fascinated by cameras. In India a cousin of mine who lived with us for a while had a camera. I was going to high school and he was working and attending night college. He would show off with his camera, rightfully so, and I would fantasize about owning a camera someday. When I discovered that an Instamatic camera here cost only about twenty dollars, and a five-inch reel-to-reel tape recorder cost about sixty dollars, I bought both as soon as I could save up the money. I was recording tapes from wherever I could get any Indian songs and taking pictures everywhere. Some weekends I would travel by three buses to go to Elizabeth, New Jersey, where a friend from my school lived with his wife. He owned a tape recorder too. We would stay up all night recording songs from one tape recorder to the other.

⚬❧⚬

I wrote letters home nearly every day. My father was proficient in Urdu, an offshoot of various Arabic languages, which I did not read or write. For him to reply to my letters in Hindi was a hardship, but he still answered each one. Later my brothers Harish and Girish took over this task and replied to my letters almost daily. They all waited eagerly for my daily writings and the mailman became their best friend; mail was delivered three times a day in Delhi. This was when and how I became close to my father and my brothers, through the written word. Otherwise we did not know each other well, since I had not spent much time living with them.

When I wrote home that I had bought a tape recorder and described its beauty to my family, my uncle Khushiram wrote in no uncertain terms that I was wasting money on such vanities and had forgotten my duties as a son. He reminded me of the loan they had taken to send me to the United States. The funny thing was that by this time I had already paid the loan back, and then some. Incidentally, the Indian rupee was devalued soon after I came here, and a dollar became equal to seven and a half rupees instead of five rupees. Thus, in terms of my paying back my loan, even though I had borrowed $600 (3,000 rupees), I needed to return only $400. And I was sending home more than $100 a month out of my salary of $131 every two weeks. But I understood my uncle's reservations. I resented but greatly respected his opinions. By this time my uncle Khushiram had built his own house in Delhi, and my father and his family had moved to my uncle Khushiram's old house in Rajinder Nagar. It is hard to explain, but somehow "my family" had suddenly transformed in my mind from my uncle's to my father's, mostly because of the letter exchanges!

I wrote home about all the beauties of America. In one of my first letters I wrote how the water here came in two faucets instead of one, and you could have hot water, cold water, or in between, anytime you wanted. I even made a drawing of that. I wrote about the shaving cream here, which lathered with no brush needed. I did not have to take a bath with a bucket and mug, but instead I took showers with water aplenty and used as much water just to bring it to the desired temperature as we used there for a full bath. There was central heating and air conditioning, and a telephone in every room. I wrote about how people smiled and smiled, even with strangers. About the tall people, the smart people, the happy people. Their phrases, their accents, their relationships, their value systems. The marvels of supermarkets and department stores. There were tunnels under the buildings, so I did not have to walk in the snow to go to the hospital. I devoted several letters to the beauties of snow. And the greenery in summer. And the autumn leaves. The Christmas decorations and Christmas caroling. The cleanliness of the roads, the houses, the hospital. Big buildings, big cars, big men. Radio City Music Hall and the Empire State Building. The subway system and the bridges of New York City. I wrote and wrote and wrote. We in India saw America as only the lights and bars and skyscrapers, and gunslinging, as portrayed by Hollywood. I told them that an average suburban house here had more greenery around it than our whole block back home.

Peanuts and cashew nuts are practically the same price, I wrote. So are apples and bananas. While I couldn't afford apples or cashew nuts in India, here I ate them all the time. Many kinds of juice are available, and we even get free orange juice—it's always there in the refrigerator. (I had already described the wonder of the refrigerator in a previous letter.) Even pineapple juice is not expensive: fifteen cents for a tall glass in our Pinette! A bowl of ice cream for a quarter. (I wanted to write that the counter girls took pity on us poor interns and gave us two scoops of ice cream for the price of one, but I refrained; they might take it in the wrong sense.) I have found something new here, strawberries. They are even better than pineapple. And strawberry ice cream—just out of this world. You don't have to stand in long lines to get milk, and you don't need a ration card. Just go to the supermarket and buy milk. Whenever you want and as much as you want. A land of plenty, indeed.

On the road, a pedestrian has the right of way, not the

motorist. When you are crossing the street, cars stop for you! Traffic stops both ways if the yellow school bus is stopped for children getting into or out of the bus. Children are not half hanging out of the bus. Similarly, doors must close on the subway car before it starts. The platform is level with the train door and you don't have to leap into the train. The bus stops at any point if you wave, and a hundred people are not pushing and tugging to get onto the bus; in fact, the bus driver will not leave unless everybody is in and the door has closed. Children leave their bicycles in the driveway overnight and nobody steals them. People don't generally lock the doors of their houses. (That was forty years ago.)

I wrote everything, and they wrote me back about the things at home.

I sent home a lot of pictures. Taking pictures and mailing them to India was very expensive, but I did it anyway. I wrote to my grandmother how my cheeks were not sunken anymore and they even looked pink. She couldn't read, but everybody else read the letters to her, several times a day. And I ran to my mailbox in the hospital every day expecting a letter.

❦

Hospital duty was rough but enjoyable. I did not mind all that work. There was one intern on each floor, one junior resident covering several floors, and a senior resident on call for the whole hospital. We were reasonably busy, and when I was not I would go to the very comfortable interns' call room, turn on the table lamp, and write a letter home. Somehow I always found interesting topics to write about. Sometimes we got an extra call and were very happy; it meant an extra ten dollars in the paycheck. During free time on night call we sat around the nurses' station and made small talk with sleepy nurses and attendants, and drank coffee. They were curious to know about our culture and we were trying to learn theirs. Sometimes I would play chess with Rose, the telephone operator whose hand I had been afraid to shake when I first arrived at Bergen Pines. They say chess was invented in India, and in fact most everybody back home knew how to play chess (except me). Rose taught me how to play chess, at least the basic moves.

One night I was sleeping in the intern room with the lights out. I was wearing my regular intern shirt and pants. Suddenly I woke up and felt somebody lying with me. It was a female aide. She had only her bra and underwear on; the rest of her clothes were on the chair, and she had her long, white-painted nails all over me. I went into a panic attack. At the age of twenty-six I had never even taken a woman out on a date, or given one a quick hug to say hello or good-bye, or held one's hand. (I was just barely learning to *shake* hands with American women!) And here was an almost-naked woman lying wrapped around me. "Hey, wh-what are you doing here?" I stammered in alarm.

"I thought we would have some fun tonight."

"But I want to sleep. Please, put your clothes on and leave; somebody might see us."

"Nobody will see us. Besides, the way you were looking at me earlier, I thought you wanted to do this." She was probably right; I might have looked at her "that way." Marie was a pretty woman.

I had noticed earlier that she had long, light-brown hair, blue eyes, just a little lipstick, and no other makeup—a short, slim, Italian beauty in her attendant's white blouse and short skirt. I had always liked short women. We might have flirted with each other, but that didn't mean any such thing, in my dictionary. In India we used to flirt with nurses, and it meant nothing else.

"But wait—you told me you have two children."

So what? I am fully divorced, and I'm not asking you to marry me. Come on—let's have a good time, that's all." By this time she had directed my hand to her bra, and her hands were groping me everywhere.

I was sweaty and frightened to death. Again I asked her to please leave. She got up, put on her clothes without turning the light on or saying a word, and walked out.

For the rest of the night I lay there quite upset, working out the meaning of the whole exchange between us. I concluded that I was naive and stupid, and I had to learn to shed some of my cultural values and adopt some of the American ones. In addition I needed to read about them, and learn about them through television and movies if I was going to spend the rest of my life here.

In our future dealings Marie never indicated that she even remembered that night, and I avoided her for several days.

⚜

The difference between the two cultures manifested itself in other ways. Bergen Pines had a shuttle bus that took us to Oradell, from where we got a bus for New York. The shuttle took this two-mile

126

trip once every hour, so sometimes there was a long wait at the bus stop. One evening while I was waiting there to return to the hospital, an older man started a conversation with me; he too was waiting for the hospital shuttle. A short, chubby white man, he was a janitor there, and he knew I worked there as an intern. He was dressed better than I, with a hat and a suit. It was chilly and we were standing in front of a bar. I had seen the neon lights of the bar many times but had never gone in. I could not even imagine going into a bar; to me it was almost a sin. During my five years of medical school in India, I had probably drunk a little beer two or three times only, sneakingly. This person openly invited me: "Let's go have a beer at Hagler's; we still have a half-hour wait for the bus."

My freezing moments started again, panic setting in. To drink a beer? In a *bar*? With a stranger? With a *janitor*? (Back home we did not even sit with a janitor, or touch him. If by accident we touched him, we washed ourselves). All kinds of questions ran through my head: Suppose I get sick or drunk? Suppose I am allergic to beer? Maybe beer in America is sold in large bottles or huge pitchers? Suppose I have to share the same glass with him? How much will it cost?

But I accepted his invitation. We had a beer each, and a very pleasant conversation. I found out that bars were not as bad a place as they were portrayed in Indian movies. That beer was cheaper than Coke in America. That janitors were as human as anyone else. That I did not get drunk from one beer. I tried to pay for my share, but the man would not hear of it. I saw him a couple of times after that, and we exchanged pleasantries. Then I left Bergen Pines.

I often think of that incident more than forty years ago, especially when I am near Oradell. One day I was going to North Bergen County to do a home visit for a competency evaluation. Instead of taking the Garden State Parkway, I took Route 4 and then Kinderkamack Road. I went into Hagler's and had lunch and a beer, for old times' sake.

PART FOUR

Psychiatrist

17

Psychiatry? Why Psychiatry?

When I came to the United States, what struck me most was that doctors did not use a stethoscope much, didn't even see the patient at times. They just looked at the lab reports, EKG, the kinds of fluids being given in the IV, then wrote some orders and walked away.... This practice of medicine with no human touch was unacceptable to me.... Then I got to my psychiatry rotation.... Here, doctors actually sat down with patients, talked to them, got to know them, analyzed them, and so on.... I was hooked.

The above paragraph is from my "Ruminations" column in the newsletter of the New Jersey Psychiatric Association. That is the official line I give for why I chose psychiatry. Actually there were many reasons for me to go into psychiatry, some conscious, others I still don't know. Let me explore here some of the other reasons for my decision.

In the mid-1960s doctors could choose their specialty; except for some highly coveted surgical superspecialties, competition was minimal. I applied to four residency programs, three in the New Jersey/New York area and one in Massachusetts. I got calls for interviews from all of them: two in psychiatry, one in internal medicine, and one in orthopedics. Obviously I was already leaning toward psychiatry.

During my three-month rotation in psychiatry at Bergen Pines, Dr. Raul Mujica and other psychiatrists were very helpful to me. They would calmly interview patients in my presence and later let me ask questions. Then they would explain the pathology and treatment. The locked doors and screaming patients did not scare me.

Once I was interviewing a young patient, and he lunged at me. He was a medical student who had been taking speed, trying to keep awake at night to fulfill his study requirements at school, and it had made him psychotic. The whole department ran to help me and support me. I probably asked him a sensitive question in an immature way that might have escalated his violent reaction, but nobody blamed me for the incident. I did not get hurt, although I was no match for his size. Interestingly, that is the closest I have come to being assaulted in forty years of psychiatric practice. Contrary to popular opinion, I believe psychiatrists face less danger from patients in general than do most other doctors. Maybe it is because we are more aware of this danger and more careful, or because we know how to talk to patients in a way that calms them down. I believe that most times when patients are violent, they are hurting physically or mentally, and a word or a small deed by the health-care worker just triggers it.

When I left India, it was pretty much certain that I would return home as a cardiologist in five years or so; that was the "in" thing then. After my rotation in psychiatry, cardiology did not appeal to me. Only psychiatry appealed to me.

I had no help in deciding my specialty. For the first time at age twenty-seven, I was left to my own devices, having been treated like a child all those years in India. Other residents and attending physicians were not giving objective advice. Maybe I was not willing to take any objective advice. Back home everybody was always advising everybody else, more or less telling you what to do, but here you were on your own, responsible for your own actions, the land of opportunity and *the land of responsibility*. Welcome to America.

I thought I did not want to go into a surgical specialty, never sure whether I could do neat, expert work with my hands. Did those "stages" in anatomy class have anything to do with that fear? I often joked that I was afraid of cutting myself shaving in the morning, so how was I going to do surgery?

I also needed money, and a residency in psychiatry paid about $4,000 per year, versus $3,000 per year for other residencies. At that time it did not occur to me that this was being done to attract residents to psychiatry because they were not going there otherwise: psychiatrists had the lowest income among all the doctors. Even if I had known the reason, I would not have been deterred, because in my mind I was going back to India in five years or so and therefore needed that extra dough in the immediate future. I did not even know how useful psychiatry would be for me when I returned there.

I was tired of working all the time and felt that I could not take five or more years of the same. A resident in medicine or orthopedics was on call ten to fifteen nights a month, whereas one in psychiatry was assigned only three or four. (Maybe I was basically a lazy person.) Also, I was tired of fast food. There were no Indian restaurants in the United States back then, and I had been hungry for an Indian meal for almost a year. I wanted to have time in the evening to cook my kind of food and eat it. A residency in psychiatry meant almost every evening free, and both psychiatric residencies I had applied for gave subsidized (almost free) housing with a kitchen, right on the hospital grounds. I could be saving money and eating real cooked, spicy food at the same time! Also, if I got an apartment on the hospital grounds, I would not have to go through the hassles of renting an apartment, learning to drive, and buying a car in a hurry. I was always trying to simplify my life.

It is also possible that I chose psychiatry to analyze the inner workings of my psyche, my family, and societies at large.

⚜

On the four-day Thanksgiving Day weekend in 1966, about seven months after coming to America, I boarded a Greyhound bus to Boston. I had talked to the state hospital and told them that I would be coming for an interview that weekend. I reached Boston Wednesday evening, wondering if getting a taxi would be a problem in case nobody came to pick me up. Light snow was falling. As I stood absorbed in my thoughts, a tall, distinguished-looking man came to greet me with open arms. "Dr. Dang? I am Dr. McLaughlin."

134

Dr. William McLaughlin? The superintendent of the hospital? In person? Coming to receive me, a lowly intern? I felt honored and overwhelmed. He took me to his car and started driving
toward the hospital.

Dr. McLaughlin was a soft-spoken, humble, and gracious
man. While driving, he gave me a running commentary about
Boston, the Charles River, Cambridge, Harvard, MIT, suburbia,
weather in the Boston area, the hospital, duties as a resident, and
so on. I was accompanied to an apartment in the nurses' residence
and given all the necessary telephone numbers. Dr. McLaughlin
invited me to his home for Thanksgiving dinner the next day,
which I respectfully declined. The refrigerator in the apartment
was stocked with enough food for a couple of days. He came back
on Thanksgiving morning with two other people, and they took
me around to show me the hospital—its maze of buildings,
grounds, and departments.

Metropolitan State Hospital in Waltham, Massachusetts, was
a cluster of buildings on many acres of land. The buildings were
old, the lawns well manicured. There were acute patients and
chronic patients, open wards and locked units, separate floors for
geriatric patients and for those with medical infirmities. One large
building was a nurses' residence and another was for employees.
The administrators had their houses on the grounds, a little set
apart from the main hospital. I was shown the employee cafeteria,
where I could get meals at subsidized prices, and the hospital
garage, where they would help me with any car problems.

Friday we repeated the same exercise. Nobody interviewed

anybody. I wanted to know about all kinds of mundane details that would potentially affect the next five years of my life. How many patients would be assigned to me? How many calls would I make per month? How much of the time I would be on call? What kind of training would I get? What kind of apartment would I have, and would it contain a refrigerator? Would I be able to cook there? Was there a bus to the supermarket? All my questions were answered in detail during the walks from one building to another, opening various doors with keys and numbers.

Friday afternoon Dr. McLaughlin took me back to the Greyhound bus stop, and I had made up my mind; I was going to Metropolitan State Hospital for my residency in psychiatry.

I did go to a couple of other residency interviews, but half-heartedly.

⁂

By mid-April 1967 I was packing. Two friends offered to drive me to Massachusetts, and I took them up on their offer. Stopping at Howard Johnson's on the highways every hour, feeding them, and paying for gas for the whole trip was expensive but fun.

I was happy. I have basically been a happy person since I left India. It probably has nothing to do with India, or America. Just me. And my attitude. I was reborn when I left my homeland, harboring a different attitude this time around.

18

The Residency:
Learning Hands–On

The residency was a joke in some respects. As a senior resident remarked, we were really the cheap labor, doing the grunt work that the real attending physicians, the American doctors, did not want to do.

A number of patients were assigned to us. We worked them up—taking their history, examining them to determine their physical and mental status, preparing a diagnosis and a plan of treatment—and presented this information to the medical director, Dr. Edward Merrick, the next day. He briefly reviewed and discussed each case, then moved on. It was learning on the job. There was some supervision, some didactic lectures, but mostly treating patients by trial and error, and learning psychiatry. There were very few medications; the emphasis was still on psychotherapy. One elderly psychiatrist was still doing insulin therapy. Electric shock treatment (ECT) therapy was common, and an occasional patient was referred for lobotomy for intractable schizophrenia.

That was the time of LSD, marijuana, the sexual revolution, the Beatles, Maharishi Mahesh Yogi, and open rebellion.

We were supposed to read works on psychoanalysis by Freud and Jung and harbor liberal views of human behavior. *I'm OK— You're OK* by Thomas Harris and *Human Sexual Response* by Masters and Johnson were required reading. Many psychiatrists were involved in their own kind of sex therapy with their patients, or at least there were rumors. Some of our supervisors had long hair and wore hippie clothes and beads. I suspect they did LSD also. Candlelight vigils and demonstrations against the Vietnam War were common. I myself attended a couple of the demonstrations and candlelight vigils. Many young kids would run away, wander cross-country, and get involved in drugs and sex (nobody knew about AIDS yet). They would roam from one city to another, one state to another, wash dishes at a Howard Johnson's or clean cars, and spend their nights in the woods, in abandoned houses, or in their broken-down cars.

Many years later, when I was practicing in New Jersey, a man in a business suit and with a briefcase in his hand came to see me in my office. He asked me if I remembered him. No, I didn't. He told me he was a hippie who had run away to a commune in Colorado in 1968. I had briefly treated him in Massachusetts for psychosis from LSD. After about five years living as a vagabond and fathering two children in those mountains, he returned home, went to college, and now was a vice president at a major bank in New York. When he read my name in the telephone directory by chance, he had an impulse to come and see me. It was a friendly visit; he just wanted to see the surprise on my face. I never saw him again.

Men wore their hair either shoulder length or as a crew cut; I chose the crew cut. (It is hard to believe, but I too had hair at one time.) I bought a cheap guitar and smoked cigars. I hated the taste and smell of cigars but smoked them anyway to look more distinguished, "like a psychiatrist." Our psychologist, Dr. Saul Berman, taught me how to clip a cigar and light it the right way. Smoking in the hospital was not banned. There were cigarette vending machines all over the hospital, thirty cents for a pack, any brand. Dr. Merrick probably smoked more than a pack in the six hours he was in the hospital. Marijuana was common too, but I never smoked it, was never even tempted—I was too fearful and legal-minded. I often said that I would be the first person to smoke pot the day it became legal. Me, always trying to be politically correct.

We treated schizophrenia with psychotherapy, primitive medications, and ECT. Everybody was on Thorazine, Mellaril, Haldol, Elavil, Tofranil, and Valium in various combinations. We saw patients with types of paranoid delusions we seldom see now: Russian spies were after them. Doctors were planted in the hospital by the FBI. The girl next door was the Virgin Mary, and they were Jesus Christ. The red punch was made with blood, and the stirrer was really the Devil in there. They heard voices of their ancestors and saw imaginary snakes on the walls. Fighting among patients was not uncommon because one thought the other was talking about him to the imaginary voices. I knew about a patient of a colleague who killed herself by jumping from the fourth-floor window. I kept thinking about her for a long time; she was a polio survivor and used to limp. Once I had to make a home visit to certify the death of a teenager who had committed suicide at her house by slashing her wrist and throat, and whose body lay in a pool of blood.

Many of the severe symptoms were treated successfully later with the advent of antipsychotic and antidepressant medications. The drug manufacturers realized the potential of making money by treating mental illnesses and fervently went into research. A hospital that had ten thousand patients then has five hundred now, thanks to the newer medications. Metropolitan State Hospital closed many years ago, and there is now a luxury condo complex on those beautiful grounds.

19

The Odd Couple

The old two-story building where I lived was called the nurses' residence. I had two large corner rooms separated by a bathroom and a hallway. There was no kitchen, but the apartment was furnished and had an old refrigerator. I got free housekeeping and laundry. Rent: four dollars a week. Very comfortable. I loved it! I bought a double hot plate for thirty-five dollars and was in business to cook and eat. Although I still sometimes craved Indian food, I had learned to eat hamburgers and french fries by this time. And any spicy food was good enough for me, with a little Indian mixed in. There were no shops with Indian spices, but allspice and barbecue spices from the supermarket were fine.

Minnie, the housekeeper, was very nice. She was always smiling and advising me and going out of her way to help. Since there was no kitchen, the dishes had to be washed in the bathtub, which she did. (I usually washed them again after she had gone.) She would clean the refrigerator and the hot plate. Officially the housekeepers were supposed to do only the medical laundry (white coats and pants) for free, but they did everything—even the dry cleaning, of which I did not have much. Minnie told me about her children, who were my age and lived in New York, and about her alcoholic husband. She also told me gossip about other doctors in the building, and cautioned me about the nurses and nursing students there. She was glad that unlike some other doctors, I was being "a good boy." She would bring me extra blankets and sheets and cleaning detergents, and spices. I know for sure that she was not doing that for other doctors.

I bought a television, black and white, fifteen inches wide, with a stand. When work was finished about four thirty, I walked to my apartment and started cooking, while learning about American culture by watching such accurately revealing classics as *Leave It to Beaver, F Troop, Hogan's Heroes,* and *Perry Mason.* Usually I ate dinner alone. I would watch television until the nightly National Anthem and go to bed way after midnight. I also read a lot. I especially enjoyed books about American history, social norms here, race relations in America, and legal and ethical problems in medical practice. Despite always having loved to read, I was still a slow reader, but I voraciously devoured every word. I even read novels as if they were scientific books, trying to cram it in all. I sometimes underlined words or phrases in the novels and then tried to use them in everyday conversations.

∽♥∾

Right above my apartment lived Angus, another first-year resident, from New Zealand. We became close friends. Angus was tall, handsome, and white, while I was short and Indian. But we were always together, like an odd couple. There were other Indian residents who did not seem very comfortable with our friendship. Maybe other white residents felt the same way about Angus and me. But we didn't care and were always horsing around together. We would race to the apartment for lunch, cook hamburgers and french fries, and eat together. He was a miser and did not want to spend money in the diner. But he was fair in his dealings. He calculated his share in some weird way and would leave on the table a quarter for each hamburger that he ate and a dime for the fries. I am sure he gypped me on that. But I didn't care—it was the thought that counted!

Within days of meeting me, Angus said I had to change my name. "Who wants to remember Jagdish? It has to be anglicized. What did your mother call you?"

"Over there everybody called me Jagga."

"Very good, I will call you Jack. Close enough to Jagga." The name stuck forever. Except for my Indian friends, everybody called me Jack from then on. I like Jack more than any other name I have been called.

Jack Dang sounds Chinese. A Chinese nurse had the hots for me. I looked Chinese and had a Chinese name, so I must be Chinese. I was not giving her any attention and of course was not talking to her in Chinese. She felt offended and cried to my supervisor for insulting her. "He doesn't have to go out with me if he doesn't want to, but he doesn't have to ignore me either." It was very hard for me to convince her that I was not in fact Chinese.

The name Jack Dang has given me some other minor problems too. Recently when I wanted to open a bank account in the name of Jagdish "Jack" Dang, my friendly banker refused to do that. New bank rules since 9/11: every account has to be exactly in the same name as on the driver's license. Some of my Indian friends snigger at that name.

Angus was not a reader, so I would sometimes do his homework for him. In return, he taught me not to put my elbows on the dining table, not to fold my hands in front of my chest when standing, the significance of Christmas carols, and to keep smiling and joking even in the face of adversity.

There were tennis courts on the hospital grounds. Some evenings the two of us played tennis and drank beer. Yes, I could play tennis, in spite of poliomyelitis. He bought the cheapest beer (I did not buy beer) and charged me a quarter at the end of the evening for each beer I drank. Our tennis playing was a facade, an excuse to drink beer. Some hospital workers would gather around and watch us make fools of ourselves. We also went shopping together, looking for the cheapest sweaters, tires, chicken legs, colas, and hamburger patties.

❧

After I moved to Massachusetts, I realized that I needed a car urgently. It was embarrassing to go by the hospital bus, meant for hospital workers who commuted to Waverley Square, and lugging groceries to my apartment was worse. And I could not ask people for a ride all the time. I was told I needed to learn to drive and get a driver's license before I bought a car.

The driving instructor came and asked me to sit in the driver's seat. He gave me the key and said, "Start the car, doc." I looked at him. Sadly, I had never sat in a driver's seat and did not know how to start the ignition. He had never seen a grown man behave this way; he did not know that until about two years before I had never even sat in a car. He had to start teaching me the basics, explaining each part and each step. I believe his services at that time were $9.50 an hour. After about eight lessons I had had enough and went for the driving test. I failed. Then I went to my room and cried.

About a week before that I had bought a brand-new, sporty Plymouth Barracuda for $1,750, on installments. Angus had convinced me that I was going to get the license, so why not have a car ready? Shopping for cars was his hobby anyway. (He was fond of big cars and had sent a couple of huge used cars to New Zealand; he said it was a big money-making business.) So we went around to various dealers and ended up buying that car—which was now sitting on the hospital grounds, and I had no license to drive it. By the way, he also told me that when I drove that car, women would stop me on the road and want a ride from me. No such thing happened. Women know whom to stop and hitch a ride with.

A few more driving lessons and I went for the test again. The examiner asked me to drive the car. After a few hundred feet he asked me to stop.

"You pass. . . . I have seen you drive around on the hospital grounds with your friend; you are okay." Had somebody talked to him? Dr. McLaughlin? Angus? My instructor? I never knew.

Angus and I made a few trips to New York. I would drive and he insisted on paying for half of all expenses: tolls, gas, and fast food. Sometimes we slept in the car on Broadway. It was his hobby to go to the Bowery and look at and talk to the homeless, the beggars, and the winos. I was scared to death for him and me, but he would take movies of people scrounging around in the garbage cans for food, and homeless people lying around like bags of potatoes on the sewers and in the alleys. He would carefully select a man or a woman near a bar, give him a quarter and then take pictures of him or her running to the bar for a drink. I also made trips with Angus to Montreal and Maine. After the riots of 1967, when we heard that Newark, New Jersey, was burning, we drove there just to see that. Talk about vicarious interests!

⁂

Angus also taught me the basics of baseball. Comparing it to cricket, which is played in India and in Europe and New Zealand, he showed me the differences and similarities. We watched baseball on television and drank beer. Naturally I became a Red Sox fan and hated our archrivals, the Yankees. Once I was eating lunch in a small diner near the hospital when suddenly there was a lot of excitement and commotion. Red Sox hero Carl Yastrzemski had walked into the diner at that moment. The manager was excited and overwhelmed, and announced that all the patrons at that time would eat lunch for free and whatever they had paid would be refunded. I just had a glimpse of Yastrzemski, and he walked out. Maybe he stopped there to use the restroom.

Years later, after I moved to New Jersey and my children and grandchildren became hard-core Yankees fans, I found myself overtly rooting for the Yankees, but hoping that the Red Sox didn't lose.

20

Introduction to Dating, Hippie Style

Each evening Angus would go out with a different young woman. It was the hippie era, and he fit right in: counterculture, open minds, open drugs, and free love. Once we were driving in my new Barracuda up and down Highway 128, and he waved to a woman in the car in the next lane. She slowed down, I slowed down, and we parked at the shoulder. He jumped out of the car, went to her and talked for less than five minutes, waved me off, and went with her in her car. The next day he told me they went to her house, and when they were making out, her husband walked in, so Angus jumped out the window half-dressed. Every morning he treated me to another of his escapades from the evening before. He was careful to choose dates he wouldn't have to spend money on.

❧

During my residency I dated a couple of women, briefly. They dumped me. Or maybe I dumped them, because right from the beginning I had decided that I was going to go to India at the first chance I got, and get married there. That may have been the ulterior motive behind my fleeting experiences with dating. After every date Angus would ask me if I went all the way, and when I shook my head he would shake his head vigorously; I was a lost cause.

One of my dates asked me if I would join her friends for a party after dinner. I accepted the invitation. We had dinner and went to a movie, and then she took me to the "party" around midnight. It was in a small third-floor apartment in Cambridge. The living room was dark and dingy. Cindy introduced me to the host, Michael. He was a happy man who welcomed me wholeheartedly. "So this is your doctor friend. Look, guys, this is Doctor Jack, Cindy's friend." Three or four people out of about eight in the room waved briefly; the others were too stoned to observe. I was told the party had not started yet; they expected some thirty more persons to show up later. We were welcome to do whatever we wanted to do, in whichever room we wanted to use. Pot and booze (and probably other stuff) were plentiful. Most of the people lying around were half-naked, half-stoned hippies, and the music was loud. The scene was familiar; I had seen it in movies. I was choking with the smell of whatever it was. After ten minutes I told Cindy I wanted to leave. She waved good-bye; she had already found other friends and had forgotten about me.

One evening Angus and a few of his girlfriends were in my room until late. We were drinking beer and talking and watching television. He left for his room with one of the girlfriends. The others left too, all except Katrina, who started flirting with me. She was quite drunk by then and slowly started undressing herself. By the time she was done, she passed out naked on my bed, her legs slightly apart. I was also somewhat drunk. I kept drinking and kept looking at her. What kind of society was I trapped in? I could not even *think* of having sex with my friend's girlfriend. I fell asleep in the same huge bed, without changing into my pajamas. Next morning when I woke up she was gone, and I had a headache.

During the first meeting in the hospital that morning, Angus and I were sitting at a distance, across from each other. He winked at me and inquired by raising his eyebrows and smiling slightly, and when I shook my head he heaved such a loud sigh that all the people in the room turned their heads toward him. He had set up Katrina and me, and I was obviously a lost cause in matters of sex! But I was a very happy person, I thought.

⌘

Eileen was a nursing student—slim, short, young, and attractive, with freckles and long, brown hair. We went on many dates: movies, dinners, drinks, even drive-in movies, and foreign (sexy) films. We did some necking, and that's all. She wouldn't let me go any further. I didn't really try that hard.

One day I heard that she was seen having sex with a nursing attendant. That evening when we were eating out, I confronted her with the rumor.

"So?" she asked.

"So? He is older than your father."

"So?"

"He has five children; he says he is happily married."

"So?"

She made it very clear that evening that what she did was her business, and that I was being intrusive in her affairs. "Who are you, asking me these questions? You are almost my father's age too. I can sleep with whoever I want to. If you're jealous, we don't have to see each other anymore." I tried to tell her that my being jealous had nothing to do with it, that there were some norms of society. Then I realized that she was being adamant and I didn't really know the norms of this society that well.

The next day the usually affable attendant took me to a corner and told me in stern words to stay out of the business of "his girl" or I would pay a heavy price. "You made her cry last night. She called me late at night and was sobbing and I had to take her to the park and console her. We had sex in the park to calm her down. I told her you were not a good person and never to see you again." That was the end of my dating experience in America.

⚜

Years later, after he moved to New Mexico, Angus and I lost touch with each other. I kept hearing about his escapades and girlfriends. I went to see him once, driving from Colorado in my rented car. He was glad to see me but we had nothing in common anymore, and I did not come back happy after meeting with him. He had a jovial facade and was a miser as always, treating me to pizza and cheap beer. Several years later Poonam and I heard from a mutual friend that he died a tragic death. He was found dead in his room by his then girlfriend with massive doses of some experimental drugs in him. It could not be established whether it was a suicide, accident, or homicide. He was rumored to have made many enemies in high places, including the sheriff and the commissioner of mental health, by having affairs openly with their wives; he was a show-off.

Angus meant so much to me during my first couple of years in Massachusetts. Always a clown, he taught me a different kind of lifestyle. In hindsight I wonder if he had more difficulty adjusting to America than I did.

PART FIVE

Husband

21

My Yellow Jacket and the Girl from Aligarh

During my residency I was sending money home and saving the remainder for a trip to India. My three brothers there were getting their education; eventually one became an architect and two became doctors. The house was getting a facelift. My family was living comfortably and was happy with my performance. We were still exchanging letters fairly frequently. That was the only practical means of communication, since telephone calls had heavy static, were very expensive, and were sometimes unavailable.

I applied for a credit card but was turned down because I had bad credit. I was not good about sending in the monthly payments for my car loan—I was always forgetting it and paying the late fee. I got so tired of it one day that I sent them the entire balance along with all the monthly stubs. I was able to do so because in addition to helping my family, I was saving quite a bit. It was a great pastime of mine to look at my bankbook every week and smile. One day I wrote home that by November 1968, I would have enough savings to come home and get married. Within weeks I received a letter that I was informally engaged to a girl my age who had an MA in economics, came from a very nice family, and so on. They had enclosed a picture of her. She looked fine and I accepted the engagement. I did not have the courage to tell anybody here, especially Angus; I would be branded even more stupid than I looked.

This is how it happened. I was the hero of the family, was supporting them from here, and had even "escaped the clutches" of the American women. I was a doctor, had a car (they had received several color pictures of my car), and I looked handsome enough in the pictures. My mother's brother Krishanlal knew somebody, a distant cousin, who had a beautiful marriageable daughter who had completed her MA degree, and her family was looking for a suitable match for her. He visited them, showed them the album of color photos from America (in India a color photo was a rarity at that time), and an *informal* arrangement was made. After all, I was coming to India soon. We were a match made in heaven! Oh, by the way, she might be an inch or so taller than I. "That's okay; in America they don't mind that." (In India it is considered something of a mismatch.) I was actually going to marry this woman without having ever laid eyes on her. I wrote her a letter, she wrote me a couple. Both sides were starting preparations for a wedding. A doctor returned from America marrying an Indian bride and taking her back with him was a rare event at that time, though it is very common now.

Twelve hundred dollars would take me to India and back. Also, I spent a lot of time and money buying gifts for everybody— a tiring process, but very exciting. I knew the biggest hit would be the tape recorder, with everybody speaking into the microphone and marveling at the playback. Neighbors would collect in the house, wanting to see the "American toy that records your voice."

⁂

With all the stops on the way, my trip there took over thirty-six hours and was very tiring. Many people came to the airport to receive me, including a number of the family members of my future in-laws. I don't think Raj, my wife-to-be, was there. I was busy meeting with my immediate family and the kids—brothers, sister, nephews, nieces—and was jumping around with them even before we entered the taxis. A little later in the day a message came from my future in-laws that the engagement was off. They had noticed that I was limping, a fact that my uncle and others in the family had "forgotten" to tell them. The immediate excitement was dampened quickly. I was a sport and told everybody not to worry—to enjoy and let me enjoy my visit to India.

I have never been a very religious person, even though I spend about five minutes or so every morning sitting down and thinking of Hindu gods and scriptures, a sort of meditation. I always did that in India and then here. But I do not have any special affiliation to Hinduism and do not follow too many rituals. I consider myself a spiritual person. Maybe it is a cop-out. I have read about religions and gone to Sikh, Muslim, Christian, Jewish, and other religious ceremonies. In my childhood I accompanied my grandmother to Sikh temples as often as to Hindu temples. Still, she never could impart much religiosity to me. Later in life I started thinking that religions were a main reason for world tensions. I am especially incensed that most of the religions I know treat half of their constituents, women, as inferior to the other half.

During my childhood I often walked over to a temple near my house (then it seemed very far), and spent hours wandering there. Birla Mandir is a huge temple with lawns and buildings. It gave me peace of mind. It was almost a ritual to visit the temple before my final exams. Now, to reduce the grief of my family, I proposed that we all visit Birla Mandir. It was a big hit. We spent the afternoon going to the temple by taxis, eating, drinking sodas, taking pictures with my new camera, laughing, joking. For the moment the family relaxed—the rich uncle from America was there, and we were all going to have fun with him for the next several weeks.

Then the sense of reality set in quickly, and everybody was scared and worried. I was there only for a month or so, and it was not going to be easy to find a match for me in that time. I was going to go back into the clutches of the American women, and once that happened, nobody was ever going to see me back in India again. Most of the relatives knew about the broken engagement and were no longer eager to come up with offers for a boy whose engagement had been broken. Broken engagements were another of the infinite number of taboos in India.

Many families wanted to send their daughters to a foreign country; it would increase their financial worth and their social standing. Many girls secretly vied for such a rare chance. But there were also rumors that boys came from America, got married to Indian girls, and then didn't end up taking them there. Or when they did take them there, they quickly divorced them. Sometimes they were already married in America or had steady girlfriends. There probably was a person who did do each of those things, and the story took on a life of its own. Thus there were families who were not ready to take those chances and send their daughters with strangers to unknown lands like America.

Whenever I told Americans about matchmaking in India through newspaper ads, they made fun of it. But that was a fact of life over there. It is interesting that a similar custom is so popular here now: dating and matchmaking through the Internet.

After a few days so my family could recover from their disappointment, we started advertising in the newspaper. The response was lukewarm. Nobody was in a rush as we were. A few responses came by mail (we didn't have a telephone yet). The same ritual was repeated each time. We got dressed up and went "to see the girl." About five members from our family met about the same number from hers, including "the girl and the boy," either in the girl's house or in a restaurant, or rarely in our house, for an hour or so. If the families liked each other, and the boy and the girl gave a tentative yes, the investigations started; family members found contacts who knew the other family. What were the girl's or boy's "actual" education, manners, behavior, character, liaisons? What was the family's reputation in the community?

As I said, the response was not so great. Either we did not send a response back or they would keep quiet. After the earlier incident, I made sure they all knew about my limp, and that did not go well with my family. Why did I have to be so blunt about the truth, they wondered? Family members asked me why I was so picky. The truth is that I had very few requirements, almost none. I just wanted a woman, reasonable in looks and education, who was willing to go to America with me and spend the rest of her life there.

Precious time was being wasted. I would spend time sightseeing at various places in Delhi. I took all my brothers, sister, and cousins to Agra to see the Taj Mahal, and we had fun. My family made sure that I attended every party, every wedding, to show me off. In their minds, I was the most eligible bachelor. But apparently, to the rest of the community, I had lost that clout with the broken engagement, which was no formal engagement, really.

꩜

One evening I went to the wedding of a distant cousin and was having a good time horsing around. I had the movie camera, almost unknown in India then, and was joking and singing and even ribbing people here and there. I was wearing a yellow jacket that I had purchased here for four dollars on clearance. The four-dollar jacket stood out and was a big hit; it looked so American. I was quite aware of the fact that all eyes were on me. "See that guy with that huge camera; he is here from America." A cousin of my father had known that I was going to attend the wedding and brought all her family to see me. She had a niece by marriage, named Indira, whom she wanted to marry to somebody from a foreign country. My father's cousin knew about my limp and my broken engagement and my car and my profession.

Wherever I went, she followed me. She wanted her family to carefully see how I walked, talked, and behaved. She also started conversations about my lifestyle in America. Her family was very impressed with me. I could almost hear them thinking, "He speaks Punjabi. He makes jokes. He smiles a cute, shy smile. He is so humble. So simple. He is still an Indian at heart, eats a banana instead of an apple, drinks tea instead of coffee, and remembers his religion, his culture, his family." They did not know that I had been craving the Indian tea that I did not know how to make in America, and yearning for their small ripe bananas.

Two days later we learned from a messenger that Indira's family wanted me to see her. When I heard the message, I gave a flat no. Indira was too young—only nineteen while I was twenty-eight. Not educated enough. Still in school for a master's degree, which even if completed would have been considered only equivalent to a BA in America. I gave several other reasons too, but those were flimsy at best and my family was very upset. "You have to see every prospective girl. Who knows where the heavens have made your match? Also, your father's cousin will feel offended. And what do you have to lose in going and seeing her?"

I was sitting around the house all day at that point, basically doing nothing. Finally I said, "Okay, I will go."

♣

Meanwhile, in Aligarh, about a hundred miles from Delhi, Indira was fervently studying for her final exams for her MA when late at night her uncle arrived by train and told her to close the books and get ready for a trip to Delhi the next morning; a boy was coming to see her for marriage. No details given.

Marriage was the furthest thing from her mind. She started crying.

Her uncle was not deterred. "We are all going tomorrow, first thing in the morning."

Her mother took her aside and told her to stop crying. "He is a good boy. We saw him at the wedding last week. He is a doctor from America. If he likes you, you will get married this week and go with him."

"What about my studies?"

"This is it, *bete* (honey)."

22

A Spectacular Wedding
on Four Days' Notice

As usual, both families made elaborate arrangements for me to go see this girl from Aligarh. The meeting was going to take place in Delhi, in the house of her uncle. There were about eight of us and eight of them, in a small room in a small house. We crowded around a long dining table, with Indira at one end and me at the other. She was a good-looking nineteen-year-old, with long, black hair braided down to her hips. She wore a *kameez* and *salwar* (long tunic over loose-fitting pants); girls from Punjab did not wear saris until they were of marriageable age, and she was a year or two younger than that. Norms had changed since my mother's time, and girls were no longer getting married at fourteen or fifteen.

Both families were excited—they because they were getting a rare chance to send their daughter to America, and we because a family with good reputation in the community was ready to consider this union. Me? I was oddly indifferent. I think sometimes I get excited at mundane happenings and am blah when I should normally be excited. I also surmise at times that all my successes have been a matter of chance rather than my doing, and so have my failures.

Most of Indira's family were sitting around me and mine around her. Her younger sister Shashi sat next to her protectively. There was small talk. And a lot of snacks on the table—sweet and salty, fruits and nuts. And tea and coffee (for the American). I remember my uncle Puran asking her what school she went to, and I asked her younger brother, Virender, what school he went to. I was feeling totally relaxed and making jokes, while she was feeling extremely tense and claustrophobic. That was the way most matches were made.

I stole frequent glances at Indira, but she kept looking at the floor, as she was supposed to. She told me later that once she tried to look at me and saw me staring at her, and almost died with embarrassment. I was enjoying all kinds of snacks and answering her family's questions, mostly about my hospital, my work, my car, my camera. In contrast, she wasn't eating anything and was mumbling answers to questions from my family. This was how she was expected to behave, although somebody from my family later suggested that maybe she had a speech problem, and it should be explored further. Little did they know that she would turn out to be the most talkative and most sociable person.

An hour or so later we were on our way home. When we were walking out, I looked back and saw her standing on her toes, staring at my back. I felt relieved that she was looking at how I walked; somebody must have told her about my limp. To this day she denies that she was looking at us going away or that she was particularly concerned about the limp. She says she was just numb and confused and robotic.

My family was totally impressed with the reception, the girl, and her family. They were ready to say yes. I was the sole holdout. My reasons were the same as before: her age, education, and immaturity. My family was in a hurry; nothing else was in sight, and my time to go back to America was approaching fast.

Her family was also all uppity about this match. Even though nobody really cared about Indira's opinion or asked her for it, when her mother asked her in confidence, she nodded yes. She later told me she was fascinated with the whole idea of getting married and going to a foreign country, not knowing much about the country, or about me. Never having been close to a man, other than her immediate family, she felt almost high with the thought of marriage. She said she even dreamed of me a few times. She was sorry, though, that she would have to leave her studies unfinished.

The hopes of Indira and her family were fading fast when they did not hear from us. They knew I would be going back soon. They sent a couple of messages, and our answer was always that we were thinking about it. I sent a letter to my hospital and extended my vacation with a leave of absence for an extra month. We did see a few other girls during that time, but nothing materialized.

In the Hindu religion there is a month called *Pausa* (part of December and January) when it is considered inauspicious to make major decisions or actions, or hold major events like weddings. We had fallen into that month. Our family could easily have kept quiet, and her family would still have hope that maybe we were waiting for the month to end before answering their inquiries. But my uncle Puran was asking me almost every day why I was being stubborn about this girl. "She is the prettiest girl we've seen. She's a little young, but so what? She could always mature with you, and go to school in America." I thought and thought and thought, and one day I said yes. After having been in the United States for more than two and a half years as a medical doctor, I agreed to marry a girl whom I had barely seen from a distance. That's me, a psychiatrist from India.

My people started dancing, her people were celebrating, and Indira was trying to grasp how much her life was about to change.

Then I sent them a message: "Not so fast." They got scared. Now what was the problem? Did I want a large dowry? What else could it be? I invited them to come and have a meeting with me. Her uncles came, without her, of course. I put a few conditions before them. One, no dowry; she was not going to wear those saris for too long anyway, so why waste them? Two, it had to be a simple wedding. Three, she must go with me within a week. For that she needed a passport, which sometimes took months. They were overjoyed to hear the conditions. Yes, they knew somebody in some ministry who would get the passport within days. They loved the idea of no dowry, but they could not agree to a simple wedding. They could not send her to America quietly because the community would start rumors. A quick wedding and sending your daughter to a foreign country without fanfare seemed fishy. Also, they had to show off their American son-in-law. I gave them three days for the wedding or there was no engagement. They finagled one extra day out of me.

They had brought some sweets and a ceremonial gold coin. My parents and uncles hugged them, and Indira and I were officially engaged.

Her uncles took the train to Aligarh that night to tell Indira and her parents that she was engaged to be married in four days, and to go to America in ten days. They told her to set aside her studies; the family had to get ready to go to Delhi in the morning for four grueling days of preparations for a huge wedding. She burst out crying, and her heart was beating fast. She did not know whether she was sad or happy, or what. She has very little memory of the next four hectic, confusing days.

❦

Wedding invitations were printed, hand-delivered to local people, and mailed to outsiders. For the locals, emissaries were carefully selected and dispatched so as not to offend particularly sensitive relatives, lest they not come. I had to go personally to a few relatives to break the news, especially the ones who had tried to match me with girls they knew. They would be offended if they heard it from other sources. On the other hand, if I went personally, and told them the news in my diplomatic, jovial way, they might not be thrilled, but they would have to be civil with me and at least show some delight on the surface. Relationships are everything in India, and the appearance of affection is very important.

Because the inauspicious month had just ended, there were

so many weddings planned in Delhi that it would be difficult to find the necessary tents, bands, horse, buses, and caterers, especially on such short notice. My mother's brothers came in handy; they had connections and the arrangements were quickly secured. My in-laws were also in Delhi, running frantically, as their arrangements were at least ten times more elaborate and expensive than ours. As in many other cultures, in India a daughter's wedding is considered the most expensive and most stressful event in a father's life, and probably the most momentous too.

My wife tells me that when she went shopping with her aunts for her bridal clothing, jewelry, and make-up paraphernalia, she was always looking around to see if she would get a glimpse of me doing my shopping in the stores. She was excited by the thought, even though she knew that if I saw her there she would probably run away and hide. She had never done any major shopping before and had never been the focus of attention. She has a lot of stories of financial and interpersonal family problems in her childhood, not unlike mine. During the preparation frenzy, her uncle asked me casually if I would like to take her out for a few hours. I declined the offer. I had my reasons. I was going to get married to her in two days anyway; suppose I didn't like her or she didn't like me; would I stop the process halfway? Even though they had asked me to go out with her, the family elders would have taken umbrage at it. They would have sent her younger brother with us. Or maybe her cousin would be watching us from a distant table in the same restaurant.

❧

The day of the wedding arrived. Relatives coming from long distances were already there. Even my aunt Kanta, only a few years older than I, arrived from Bombay with her small children in tow, after a thirty-six-hour journey by train. This is a curious phenomenon in India. For any affair, all you have to do is give a couple of days' notice and everybody gets there. No RSVP, just come and be happy. It's as if they all have nothing else to do and are sitting idly waiting for the invitation. They would probably be confused if you gave a month's notice. Surprisingly, it is still true today; Americanization has not changed this custom.

I was relaxed and calm, probably the only one in the household who was. Everyone else was running around making sure of something or other . . . or just running around to run around.

The *baraat* (marriage procession) started from our house around seven in the evening. I was all decked out, with a nice suit, a crown on my head, and garlands and flowers all around my body. I rode on a horse, also decorated, which followed a twenty-piece band with lights and fireworks on the streets. A couple of hundred people followed behind the horse, dancing and singing. The procession continued for a few blocks to several waiting buses. We boarded the buses, drove toward the bride's uncle's house, and reconnected with the horse and its owner a few blocks away from his house. Then the procession started all over again with increased vigor and display.

As we arrived at the bride's uncle's house (the same small house where I had first met her), there were large tents in the street, brightly lit and decorated. There were large tables and chairs, to accommodate all of the five hundred or so guests from both families. Various rituals were performed. The guests were fed hearty meals. My wife's cousins, friends, and others from their side surrounded me. They were teasing me, ribbing me, making fun of the "handsome American guy" who had come to "steal" their sister. Later Indira was escorted from inside the house and asked to sit at the same table across from me. She was clad in a beautiful red sari with heavy embroidery and tons of jewelry, and full makeup, a first for her. She kept looking at the ground, as is customary for an Indian bride. My cousins (I had no friends left in India at that time) joined the fun-poking carnival.

After dinner the guests were given gifts, and they boarded the buses back to our house, or to their own homes. My immediate family stayed behind, as the real wedding ceremony was to start around one in the morning, an auspicious time chosen by the astrologer/Hindu priest. There were a lot of hymns and holy fire, with the bride and groom going around the fire, making vows, and a whole lot of hoopla.

Sometime during the wedding ceremony, the priest proclaimed that Indira was now an integral part of the Dang family and had to renounce her previous ties; her first name would have to change too. He looked in the astrology and astronomy books (though I am skeptical as to whether he understood those complicated charts) and said her new name would start with the letter

P. All my aunts and uncles started giving suggestions of names starting with P and looked toward me. I liked one name, Poonam, already thinking I could anglicize it in America to Pam. So, then and there, Indira was renamed Poonam, and that name has stuck with her to this day. All our Indian friends and family call her Poonam, and Americans call her Pam or even Pamela. Almost nobody knows that the name on her passport is still Indira. Only her father still calls her Indira. (This name changing thing does not happen anymore.)

It was probably four in the morning when the Hindu priest finally pronounced us man and wife. Indira and I got into a special car (*doli*) decorated with flowers. At the time of departure her family and friends cried their hearts out; as they say, a part of their family was leaving them forever. She was becoming a part of another family. I believe it is a good Hindu tradition, a sort of closure to the weeks and months of celebrations and hoopla. In her case the merriment and excitement had been rather short, but she was literally going halfway around the world, and her family didn't know whether they would ever see her again, or what kind of life awaited her there.

We reached home at dawn. There were more rituals there at my home, a visit to the temple, and breakfast with the bride. Finally, people who had arrived from long distances started leaving. By the afternoon we were all immediate family members, talking and laughing and joking, and discussing the good and bad of the preceding day.

I don't remember too much about our first night together as

man and wife, but Poonam insists that we did go to bed for about three hours after coming home. This nineteen-year-old girl who had never even shaken hands with a man had her innocence taken away in those three hours. Lucky that her aunt had talked to her about the birds and the bees the day before, or I would have objected since she wouldn't have known what it was all about. She was thinking, "Is this how Americans do it?" She didn't know that for me, too, it was a maiden experience, pardon the pun. But since I was twenty-eight, a doctor, and from America—the land of beautiful, sexy girls—there was no need for my uncle to explain *those rituals* to me.

Two days after the wedding there was reception given by our family. Again, hundreds of people came for dinner under a large tent right in our street. A few people from Poonam's family were also invited. Her aunt asked her if "everything" was okay. My wife smiled, looked down toward the floor, and nodded. Incidentally, it was the same aunt who was wheeling and dealing and sending messages back and forth, bent upon getting us together in the first place.

Thank you, Aunt Pushpa. One more person deserves the credit for this fortuitous matchmaking forty years ago: my uncle Puran kept pressuring me.

23

Pinball in London,
Blizzard in Boston

The week after the wedding was very hectic, again. Indira, aka
Poonam, had to obtain a passport. She also needed a physical
exam; X-rays; vaccinations for smallpox, typhoid, and cholera; a
visa application; interviews at the American Embassy; reservations
for the trip; and an airplane ticket. In between, we had to visit our
relatives from both families for dinners and felicitations. I also
stole moments when we would visit fancy restaurants for tea and
snacks, or go see a movie. She was exhilarated but nervous. She
had never been part of the glamour scene or the center of attraction before, especially in the company of a strange man from
America, now her husband. She had a new name and a new identity; she would soon have a new country. It was all mind-boggling
and overwhelming. How could a normal person handle that?

Two days after the wedding, on our way home from the
embassy, I decided we should see a movie. I stopped the taxi near
the Rivoli Theatre and bought tickets for the balcony, the most
expensive seats in the house. It was a sort of a private booth with

two very comfortable cushioned seats. Poonam started feeling uncomfortable and looked pale. When I asked her why, first she wouldn't say, but then she admitted, "I was just thinking: suppose my grandfather saw me sitting in these plush private sofas watching a movie with a man? I would get severely punished." She still did not grasp the fact that she was a married woman, not an over-protected child anymore.

Less than two weeks after the engagement, we left Delhi. At the airport, the scene from when I left for America three years earlier was repeated. My family and my new in-laws' family were all there in full force. There was a lot of crying and hugging, advice and admonitions, congratulations and prayers. During the flight, Poonam had the same reaction that I had had three years before. Strange people, peculiar language (we in India learned written English, not spoken English), odd-looking food, although this time I was there to explain all that new stuff to her. After she cried a little bit, we started talking, really *talking* for the first time, about ourselves, our childhoods, our dreams, our future life together. She did not eat much and soon fell asleep with her head on my shoulder. I felt good. She, however, was still somewhat numb; my reassurances were not working. We had an overnight layover in London. The airport bus took us to the hotel, to be awoken in the morning for the second leg of the trip.

࿐

London evening in late January can be gloomy. It was dark, and the fog and mist made it quite spooky. After settling in the hotel,

I thought we should go to the hotel restaurant downstairs and eat dinner, as we had the dinner vouchers given to us by the airline. Poonam refused. Nauseous from the smells and the sights, she asked me to go alone; she wanted to take a nap. I told her I would be back in a half hour or so and left. I ate at the restaurant and soon got caught up playing pinball machines. I wasn't tired, and besides, why should I go upstairs and disturb her sleep?

Upstairs was a nineteen-year-old young lady who had been extremely sheltered until a couple of weeks ago. Now she was in a strange land with a stranger from another world who spoke her language but did nothing else that she had been accustomed to for all her short life. She waited, and waited, standing in front of the hotel window on that dark, misty London evening. When I did not come back for an hour or so, she started getting nervous and scared. "Who is this man? Where is he? Is he meeting someone in London? Is he gone? I don't even have my passport. I have no money. I don't understand the accent of the people here. I don't know his address in America, or even in India. I don't know how to use the telephone. . . ."

When I opened the door, I saw her standing, staring, and quietly crying.

"What happened?" I asked.

"Where did you go? What did you do? Why did you leave me?" She ran toward me, laid her head on my chest, and started sobbing. "Don't ever leave me alone again. Don't ever leave me alone again."

I told her that I had started playing pinball machines after supper. Without hesitation she smiled. She wanted to know what those machines were, and suddenly she was hungry. "Will the second dinner voucher still be good?" she asked.

So we went down to the restaurant, where I bought her some food and showed her the pinball machines. She ate very little and played a game. When we returned to the room, she burst out sobbing again, saying over and over again, "Don't ever leave me again," until she finally fell asleep. I wondered whether she had gone downstairs to make sure there was something called a pinball machine, and I wasn't lying and really meeting someone else. What did she dream of that night? I'll never know.

But I do know that the next morning she was cheerful again. I learned then one of Poonam's remarkable traits: she does not keep grudges. And any disagreements we have had in the almost forty years since then, she has taught me not to rehash those the next morning.

⚜

We suffered through another tiring flight and were finally in Boston. And welcomed with a blizzard and nobody at the airport to receive us. I told her I didn't make friends easily, and we had no family there. In fact, Boston had so few Indians that if we saw one Indian a week, it would be a lot. What a contrast: the warm, lively, almost frenetic airport in Delhi versus the cold, lonely, impersonal airport in Boston. Poonam could not imagine that no one had come to meet us after we had flown all the way from India. We took a taxi to the hospital in that blizzard. She had never seen snow before, so she was fascinated and happy, but sad and lonely at the same time.

I came back from India with many questions and uncertainties of my own. For one thing, I had been in a minor car accident just before I left for India, and I had left my car in a repair shop. I wasn't sure whether it would still be there when I returned. And while I was certain I still had my residency, there was that little bit of nagging doubt in the back of my mind. After all, I had extended my vacation twice, broken all the rules of a residency; maybe there was no job. And if there was no job, there was no apartment. All these thoughts were bugging me throughout the journey home, and I had given Poonam a hint about this. But she didn't care, she said, as long as I was with her. Now I was wondering, what if? This blizzard made matters worse. Where would we go, and how? Neither of us was wearing a heavy coat or boots appropriate for the snow we encountered.

It was around four in the afternoon when we arrived at the apartment. It was New England, and it was getting dark. Well, my key to the apartment worked, and my things inside were as I had left them. At least I had not been evicted. And the warmth of the apartment made us feel good. I started orienting her to the refrigerator, the television, the central heat and hot showers, the black rotary telephone, the furnishings, and the clothes. She was amazed; everything was like a dream for her.

When we got out of the taxi and I was paying the driver in that snow, somebody had seen us from his window. This somebody called the hospital operator and told her that I was with a woman clad in a colorful sari. The operator called everybody and his brother. They put two and two together.

The doorbell rang. A dozen roses were delivered, courtesy of Dr. Ehrenberg. "Welcome, Mrs. Dang," it said. I told her that Dr. Ruth Ehrenberg was our very motherly assistant superintendent, and the roses meant that I still had my job. Poonam did not really understand the significance of the roses, but she knew it was something nice and was in high spirits.

A little later our housekeeper, Minnie, brought us some chicken and rolls and boiled potatoes, and greeted Poonam with her signature American smile. Poonam was a vegetarian in India, and like me when I first arrived, had never seen rolls or boiled potatoes. I started telling her about the foods here, the variety of foods and how to eat what. I showed her that milk and butter were available in abundance, and fruits and vegetables, and she would not have any difficulty as a vegetarian. Unlike me, she was a quick learner. Very soon she started liking the foods here, even preparing foods the American way, and she was eating meat.

❧

"So you did what you should not have done, you bloody fool." It was Angus, always a clown. He came over the next day after work; it was dark. He asked Poonam to stand up, turn around, put her hands on her hips, lift her chin, and so on. He finally nodded approvingly, and asked her to sit down. "Yes, she is okay," he said, then added to her, "You have to take off the sari." Poonam looked at me with horror. Even though I had told her a bit about Angus, she did not like his remarks. "We will have to go shopping soon and get her some dresses." I had not prepared her for that. Believe me, at that time Poonam was not ready to even think of wearing skirts; she could have killed him. Indian women did not show their legs in public, and a sari was a sari. Even a long skirt would not have been acceptable to her yet. Some aspects of the new life would take longer for her to adjust to than others. I needed time to get her accustomed to them.

Then, in a very serious tone, Angus said, "Now that you have brought the Indian broad, what are we going to do with the one you left here?" He did not get that even a joke like that could be devastating. Thankfully, Poonam did not fully understand his accent and kept smiling. Still, soon after he left, she told me she did not like Angus. I could stay friends with him, but I should not expect any special courtesies from her.

That was when Angus and I began slowly drifting apart. Sometimes I felt guilty about this, but Poonam had plenty of culture shock to deal with already without the extremes of his attitude and temperament.

24

Making Snowballs in a Sari

I brought back my car from the garage, and every time the weather was conducive, we would take a ride. Poonam had never seen anything like a supermarket or a department store. And she had never gone anywhere in "her own car." She loved bringing bags of groceries home and trying to cook new foods. (Servants and cooks were the norm in India, not here.) Wandering in the supermarket became our favorite pastime. Seeing twenty-nine types of toothpastes and seventeen kinds of breads was for her like being an Alice in Wonderland, as it had been for me almost three years earlier. I believe that is a common experience of immigrants to this country. My residency in psychiatry gave us enough money and free time that we could do all that. We were like teenagers finding each other and exploring this world. She *was* a teenager, and she made me one by bringing my youth back. We were having our honeymoon in the supermarkets and Laundromats, and enjoying it, discovering the New World anew. We have been having a perpetual honeymoon for the nearly forty years since.

On one of Poonam's first days here, I was working in the hospital when Dr. Ehrenberg called and pleaded with me to go home right away; I must bring Poonam inside or she would get pneumonia or frostbite. Somebody had seen her playing in the snow and making snowballs (she was wearing a short-sleeved shirt, a sari, and open sandals), and had called Dr. Ehrenberg. That same evening we went to a department store, and Poonam bought her first pair of pants, boots, coat, and gloves. We often talk about that incident and laugh. There were many such happenings that made our memories. What a difference between the two cultures and two countries! Neither is better or worse; they are just different. You can frown upon the differences or embrace them. Poonam and I have attempted to do the latter at every step of our lives, and we are happier for it.

Because there were so few Indians around, every time we came upon each other in the stores or in the streets, we stopped and talked, told each other stories, exchanged telephone numbers. Everyone was hungry to find some semblance of the past. We started making friends, and visiting them, or inviting them to our place. Poonam was good at making friends among the Indians; she still was shy among Americans and did not relate much to them yet. We found Parwanis, Rathis, Kamals, Sherings, and Sharmas, and were meeting with one another often.

On free weekends we visited New York City and stayed with the Goyal family. They were very hospitable. We learned a lot from them—they taught us what to do and what not to do. New York was not as cold as Boston, and we could walk around 42nd Street and Times Square. We went atop the Empire State Building, traveled the subways, visited the Statue of Liberty, and took a

Circle Line cruise around the island of Manhattan. We never forgot to take pictures and send them home.

In the spring we decided to go to Cape Cod. I knew nothing about Cape Cod; I had just heard from people that it was a great vacation spot. We drove all the way to the tip, to Provincetown, and walked around the beach a little. We were the only people on the beach, walking around at dusk. It was getting chilly, so we decided to spend the night in a motel. But there was a problem: I had never checked into a motel or hotel on my own before. (The airline had reserved the room in London for us.) I did not know how much it cost or any other protocol. Poonam, of course, did not know either. We laughed about the whole thing, giggled for a long time trying to think of a scheme to check into a motel without getting embarrassed. (We still giggle about that evening whenever we think of it.)

We decided that I would go first and weigh the odds, come out, and if all went well, take Poonam in. As you can imagine, it was a smooth transaction. The man at the front desk told me it was off season, so the rate of one room for two people would be twelve dollars a night; next week it would be twenty-four dollars, as high season started then. I gave him the money, came out, and parked the car, and we went in to spend the night there. It's funny how you remember those small incidents. Ordinary people doing mundane activities are sometimes what make for great memories.

⚜

At the hospital I thought I was an important person. Apparently the administrators thought so too; they gave us a slightly bigger apartment, with a real kitchen and stove and a sink and two large bedrooms. Rent: six dollars a week. The apartment was in another building, attached to the hospital, so now I did not need to go outside to get there. It was easier to take night calls.

For many months when I got a call from the emergency room at night, Poonam went with me. The first time she went, the nurse greeted her warmly, and then said casually, "You know, Mrs. Dang, before you came I was number one for Dr. Dang." We all laughed. After the work was done and we were walking home, Poonam asked, "Was she your girlfriend? She is pretty but she is so much older . . . and fat." I had the time of my life trying to explain to her the American ways—they were different from Indian ways, and that was how all Americans talked. People flirted much more casually and differently, but it didn't mean anything.

Another difference in the culture came as a shock to her. During the summer when our housekeeper Minnie was away, a young girl came to deliver linens and help Poonam do little chores. During casual conversation she happened to mention that she was the daughter of our superintendent, was a student in school, and this was her summer job as a housekeeper. Poonam stood stunned for a minute. How could the daughter of "a man of status" do such menial work? It took her a while to learn the work ethic of her adopted country: dignity of labor, no false pretenses.

She also learned that we didn't eat home-cooked food all the time, that women drove as much as men and even drove buses. We were going to the Laundromat, and bowling, and playing mini golf. Somewhat reluctantly, she even cut her hair short and got her nails done. She was watching television and learning American slang. She made friends with an American couple, Don and Doris, and was learning the customs here.

How Poonam changed so quickly is hard to understand. Three or four years after her coming here, we lived in New Jersey and my uncle Puran was visiting us; he was relatively new to the United States. We were hanging out in the front yard when our friends Irwin and Barbara stopped by. Poonam ran to meet them and greeted them both with hugs and kisses. My uncle looked on with horror. He could never imagine a woman giving a man that kind of open welcome. Suddenly both Poonam and Irwin realized what damage had been done to the psyche of my uncle, and froze.

Most of our friends were Indian, and we had get-togethers almost every weekend. As was usual with Indian gatherings, and still is, the men go to one room and the women to another, usually the kitchen. The men drink (then it was scotch, now it is wine), talk politics, badmouth American traditions, share their bad experiences with trips back home to India, and watch sports on television in the background. Meanwhile, the women gossip and help one another with the cooking. They talk about their clothes, their shopping experiences, and the latest scholastic achievements of their children.

In those early days, friends became our extended families. We drove distances to visit one another, to eat together and talk:

about what sales were going on at Filene's Basement, what new foods we had found in the supermarkets, which bank had the higher interest rate, and what gas station gave a free plastic logo cup when you filled up there. We played cards and talked about our jobs. We complained about the hard work here but appreciated the paychecks. Most of the men were engineers and doctors, and the engineers were making more money because the doctors were still doing internships and residencies and had no quick way of getting a license here and practicing medicine. Our goal at that time was to stay here for a few years, save enough dollars, and go back to India. We bought appliances that could work on 110 as well as 220 volts, to use them when we returned "home." With time our goals kept changing, and most of us ended up staying here permanently.

PART SIX

Brother, Friend, and Father

25

A Licensing Catch-22: The J-1 Visa

I came to the United States on a J-1 visa. The rules were simple. You came here as a student, did your residency, got your education, and then went back to your country of origin after five years. Sometimes you could get an extension for a year. However, once they got here, most people did not go back. Who wanted to leave this wonderful country? This was the land of opportunity. This was *the land of milk and honey*. The roads might not have been paved with gold, but at least they were paved.

The problem with the J-1 visa was that you did not really get the education that you came here for. You were the worker bee; most of the learning you did was on the side, on your own. You could not apply for the specialty boards in psychiatry unless you had a license to practice in at least one state. But you could not get a license to practice medicine unless you passed the licensing exam, and you could not take the exam unless you had an immigration visa. Therefore, as a J-1 visa holder, you could go back to your country of origin in five or six years with no graduation certificate or board exam. And without the piece of paper, you were really going back with no graduate degree at all and no education to your claim.

All we J-1's would talk about was this very severe problem. What were we going to show them back home, after wasting five years of our lives? One way to get immigration papers was to marry an American citizen. Many of us J-1 men were going with women, partly for infatuation, partly for love, partly for sex, but in the back of our minds we did have an ulterior motive that it was the only way to stay here forever. Some of us were contacting immigration lawyers. It was pretty well known that an attorney who knew the ropes could apply to Congress for a waiver of your visa regulations. The bill would stay buried in congressional files, and as long as it was "in consideration," you could live here as a person with no status, so to speak. But the cost was steep. You paid the attorney $1,500 as a retainer, and if you were ever granted immigration, you promised to pay another $1,500. Marrying an American citizen would be cheaper.

As for women doctors, I knew only two J-1 visa holders. One did not have great reputation; she was smoking, drinking, and probably sleeping around. There were rumors that she had secretly married an American citizen purely for the purpose of her immigration. We lost track of her after a while. The other was considered a great catch among us Indians and Americans alike. She was also sort of a tease with a holier-than-thou attitude. She went back to India and had an arranged marriage with all the traditional fanfare.

Me? I did not like either of those two choices, getting an attorney or getting a wife for the sake of a visa. I never liked conflicts, and these choices were conflicting, uncertain, and stressful. I was almost sure my hospital would get me an extra year or so, and then I would leave, after saving money for a few years. Poonam would go back to Delhi to stay with my parents. I would go to England, finish my graduate studies in psychiatry, then head back to India about two years later to practice psychiatry in Delhi with a degree from England, which was as highly recognized in India as the one from here, maybe even more so.

As always, I made light of the situation, but it was serious and required some action. An eternal procrastinator, I did nothing about it and just waited. Like my father, and later my son, I lived day by day.

⚜

Enter Richard Nixon. Whether it was pressure from the American Medical Association, or there was shortage of doctors, or for some other political reason, in 1970 President Nixon signed an order stating that all J-1 doctors could apply for immigration. I was not even aware of this when our superintendent, Dr. McLaughlin, called me to his office and practically ordered me to apply for an immigration visa immediately. He had received a memo from the Commonwealth Commissioner of Mental Health that all of his doctors should apply as soon as possible, because they were not sure when the government might rescind this order.

I, who had been somewhat worried about this problem, did not jump up with a grin and shake his hand. I said quietly, "I will think about it." Now Dr. McLaughlin was pleading, "Please, this is very serious. Do not take too long. We need you here." He called Dr. Ehrenberg in, thinking she had more clout with me, and she talked to me too. Dr. Ehrenberg was single, but all of us treated her like a mother. She was from Britain, originally a German, but had been here for more than thirty years.

Despite my outward nonchalance, I was delighted. There couldn't be any better news than this. Poonam and I celebrated with many of our Indian friends. But our friends who had hired lawyers were upset when they learned that as long as their application for a waiver was in the hands of the legislature, they had no status and therefore could not apply for immigration. If they wanted their status changed back to J-1, they would need time and more money. If this ordinance was rescinded when their turn came, they would again be behind the eight ball.

(This was one instance when my procrastination was beneficial. There are times when procrastinators win!)

With the joy came stress. After getting the immigration visa, I would need to go for the licensing examination, and then the psychiatry boards. During this time I would also need to plan my practice. Doors were starting to open, the future was looking brighter, but the process for getting through those doors was long and daunting. I needed to study, become serious, and start dusting the books I had and buying new ones.

The immigration offices were crowded, with all kinds of people asking questions and applying for this visa or that. The officers there treated you like crap. They asked you questions—irrelevant, annoying questions. When I went to apply for the immigrant visa, the lady grimaced when she learned that I was a doctor. She asked me if I knew how to speak English. Then she started asking me questions that didn't make any sense, and she made a face after every answer I gave. I vividly remember her asking me whether I thought Canada was part of America, and then asking me to spell Massachusetts. She kept my passport and dismissed me abruptly, saying, "You will hear from us in due time."

The immigrant visa came in the mail within two days. I still don't know what the harassment was for.

⚜

Approximately five years after becoming immigrants, we got papers to apply for citizenship. This involved an interview, a few simple questions, and an oath of allegiance in a large group in an auditorium. I was excited about it, went for it right away, got it. Poonam wanted to wait. She felt ambivalent, just briefly, and went for it after about a year. Most of our family members who arrived in this country later became U.S. citizens in due course. Some really had difficulty renouncing their ties to the mother country and procrastinated for variable periods of time before going for it. In my practice and socially I have talked to so many immigrants, and each one has a unique story about getting citizenship; for many of them it's simply euphoria.

26

The New Arrivals

In the 1960s many Europeans had more or less open immigration to the United States, but other countries were severely restricted. Then the government changed the visa rules from Asia around 1970. People from India started trickling in, and just a few years later there was an avalanche of Indian technical people here. So many engineers came from Asian countries that there was a surplus, and articles regularly began to appear in the newspapers about skilled engineers digging trenches and working in hamburger joints.

My younger brother Harish had finished college as an architect and applied for his visa. He was approved soon after I sent sponsorship papers for him. This meant writing a letter with a promise to give him a place to stay and support him financially until he became independent. As evidence I had to send proof of my job and my savings. After arriving here in late 1969, he wandered around in Boston, sightseeing. At one point he applied for a job at a couple of architectural firms, and got an offer from one. He scratched his head and told the interviewer that he would give his answer the next day.

"Any special reason?"

"I want to confer with my brother before I accept this job."

"Is your brother an architect?" the interviewer asked.

"No."

"Then why?"

"I can't accept a job without asking my brother. He is older than me, you see."

"But you are an adult. Can't you make the decision yourself?"

Harish was confused. To an Indian, it would have been highly disrespectful to the older brother if he accepted a job or a school or a girlfriend without discussing it with the elders in the family. The next day, after discussing it with me and with Poonam, he took the job.

After Harish came my uncle Puran, a few years older than I. By then he was an engineer with a degree from the Indian Institute of Technology (IIT), a prestigious university in Kharagpur. Then came Harish's friends. It seemed like I was writing letters of support and sending sponsorship papers to India almost every month, along with a statement from my bank. Then there was the work involved with giving them rides for job interviews, and transporting them to and from their jobs once they got them. Poonam was busy making dinners, taking care of their laundry, and so on. And yet somehow it did not seem so stressful at the time. We also continued to throw parties for our friends and attend their parties and get-togethers.

⚜

In January 1970 Poonam gave birth to our son. She went to Waltham Hospital in the evening. I waited at the hospital until late and then returned to see her in the early morning. Finding no signs of the baby yet, I came to my hospital and started working. I was seeing a psychotherapy patient when the call came. The doctor told me the news. I thanked him and went back to the session, thinking I would go to the hospital afterward and see my son. The nosy telephone operator was listening in; she knew my wife had gone to the hospital the night before. She called Dr. Ehrenberg and gave her the news.

Dr. Ehrenberg, in turn, walked into my office, told me to leave immediately for the hospital, and said that she would see my patient. She was so considerate! No wonder I loved America and Americans.

As I was going into the maternity floor, the obstetrician met me in the corridor, congratulated me, and casually told me that he had given two units of blood to Poonam.

"But why?"

"Her hemoglobin was low after the delivery. It was ten."

I was stunned but did not let him see my emotions. I wanted to scream at him, "Ten grams is considered pretty good hemoglobin for Indian women, especially after delivering. In India, I would not have considered a blood transfusion even if it had been seven. There is a big difference in hemoglobin between Indians and Americans!" But I did not say anything, just thanked him, and kept walking. I do not like confrontation.

Three days later Poonam, Harish, and I brought the baby home and started looking into buying the crib and the bassinet, finding a diaper-cleaning service (no disposable diapers in those days), and other things required with a new baby. The next day when I came home for lunch, Poonam was crying. She thought that maybe she had hurt the baby while giving him a bath and his neck was broken. Not knowing any better myself, I called Mrs. Bess Asekoff, the wife of our medical director, who was very affectionate and understanding. She came immediately, saw the baby, and started laughing. She explained to us that all newborns have limp necks and wanted to know how come we did not know that. Hadn't we read any manuals on childbirth? And shouldn't I know it as a doctor? And didn't I know that Pam was having normal baby blues? And hadn't anybody given Pam any instructions on how to bathe the baby? The answer to all these questions was no. There were no parent classes in the hospital, and I had not yet learned about the baby blues. The nurses and doctors, everybody in the hospital thought we knew all these things, especially since I was a doctor. But we had come from India with no exposure, no experience, and no commonsense knowledge of the real world of babies. And certainly no parents with us to help us through these things. Now Mrs. Asekoff arranged for a nurse to come and teach us the basics of child care, and also brought me a book to read on the normal development of an infant.

⟳⟳⟳

As a standard practice, Waltham Hospital had sent information about the birth to a statistical bureau. The next day I got a call from a local newspaper reporter who wanted to know the name of the baby. She thought the hospital had inadvertently forgotten to write the name when it sent information about the birth. I explained to her that we had not yet named the baby. I had sent all the information to my parents in India—the place, the date and time of birth—and I was waiting for their suggestion by return mail. Then I told her that my parents would go to a Hindu priest, who would look into a confluence of stars in his book and would then come up with a proper suggestion for his name. "Hold it," she said. "I've never heard any such thing. Could I come and interview you and your wife in detail?"

The reporter and a photographer came to the house, we did a long interview, and there was an article in the newspaper, almost a whole page with a large photo of the three of us, entitled "Name That is Written in the Stars." She also was intrigued by some of the other cultural issues and wrote about them. People here had not yet seen many Indians and did not know much about the cultural differences. Once when we were driving from Boston to New York, we stopped in a small town in Connecticut to eat. Poonam was wearing a colorful sari, and people slowly started to gather around us and whisper to one another. They thought she was an Arabian princess. As foreign as the American culture was to us, we were every bit as foreign to them.

Finally we received the mail and the suggestion from back

home, and formally named our son Vivek. His name became a problem when all the Indians started calling him Vicki, which is a male nickname in India, but a female name here. When he started going to kindergarten, we were dismayed to think that he would be called Vicki all his life. So we hired a lawyer and officially changed his name to Victor, once again conforming as best we could to American society and culture.

⚜

The hospital administration was very kind to me. When they saw that we were four people living in a small apartment (including Victor and Harish), they moved us to a house just before my uncle Puran came. The house was also on the hospital property, but quite far from the main campus. It was an old, small Cape Cod, but it seemed very large to us then. Rent: six dollars a week. It was mostly furnished; we just needed to buy a few things here and there. Having a house was very handy, what with all the family coming here, and friends staying with us for the weekends. It was almost a party at our house every weekend, with several adults and a baby. We all did everything together as a family: ate and slept, played cards and chess, took care of the baby, went food shopping, took our clothes to the Laundromat, listened to music and watched television together. At that time I was the only one among our friends who had a house and a car, a wife and a baby. It was a happy life.

27

A Promotion and
a Visit to India

During the third year of my residency, I had a rotation in child psychiatry. I did not like seeing children with severe psychiatric and behavioral problems, with psychoses or autism or developmental disabilities. I could not engage myself in play therapy. Even during my regular adult rotation, I was more into geriatrics and old people. Geriatric psychiatry was almost unknown and certainly unpopular, but I would go to that unit and work there willingly. The hospital was happy with my interests because other residents did not like dealing with that population. Perhaps it was my Indian upbringing and the ingrained respect for the elderly, or maybe I was lazy and somehow found that working with the elderly was not as hard. In any case, many people consider me an excellent geriatric psychiatrist, and I have almost forty years of experience with that population. I even wrote a paper, "Group Therapy in Geriatric Population," in 1970, before group therapy was popular or geriatric psychiatry was known.

One of our visiting supervisors from Massachusetts General

Hospital was Dr. Jacob Christ. There was a well-known joke about him. Originally, when he joined the department of psychiatry at Mass General, he wrote a telegram saying "J. Christ" was arriving on a certain date. They thought it was from a former patient who had the delusion that he was Jesus Christ, and nobody went to receive him. Anyway, he took a liking to me and wanted me to do a fellowship at Mass General. "At Mass General? Who would take me at that high-class institution?" My superiors at the hospital thought it was a great opportunity for me and that I was a shoo-in, if Jacob Christ recommended me. Dr. McLaughlin said he was sad to let me go, but he did not want to be a roadblock in my progress.

The interview was scary: night calls every other night, twelve-hour shifts every day, half the money, and I would have to rent an apartment. Most importantly, I would be one of the very few foreign-looking residents there. As a matter of fact I saw only one other, a Filipino. And he talked down to me; I got the feeling that he did not want to see another Asian there to compete with him.

I turned down the position. I wanted to have a family life and some fun, and that would not be possible if I spent two years at Massachusetts General Hospital. Sometimes I wonder what would have become of me if I had taken that fellowship. By now I would probably have written hundreds of scholarly papers, maybe a book or two. I would be on a lecture circuit throughout the country, and beyond. I would still be burning the candle at both ends. Maybe I would be very happy; maybe I would be miserable. There are so many crossroads in life; we don't know what would happen if we take one path or the other.

⁂

Exactly three years after starting my residency at Metropolitan State Hospital, I was made a staff psychiatrist there, and my salary more than doubled. Victor was three months old. We had a second car. Poonam was driving. Harish came one day and showed us a brochure he had brought from Harvard University. Just for the heck of it, he was going to apply for a master's degree in architecture. We all encouraged it. He applied and was accepted. The university wanted proof that he could support himself and afford the fees. My bank book again came in handy. Harish quit his job and finished his master's in a year or so. They even gave him a scholarship during the year. Later on he found that the Harvard degree did not bring much money with it, and for the thirty years since then he has been working as a stockbroker and a financial consultant.

After a year or so of being a staff psychiatrist, I was becoming restless. It was time to move on. There were many problems. Even though I was going to get my immigration papers, I still had no license, and prospects for getting one were very bleak. Studying for the Federation Licensing Examination (FLEX exam) was like going for a whole medical school curriculum all over again. All the basic sciences and the clinical subjects had to be studied. One who had not even looked at a sore throat for five years could never hope to pass FLEX. People advised me to do a one-year residency in internal medicine, which I could easily get, before taking the exam. But that seemed out of the question at such a late stage.

Without a regular license I had to work in a hospital where they would let me work on a temporary year-to-year license. So I was committed to working in a state institution for the rest of my life; those were the only places I knew would get permission from the state for a temporary license. Could I ever get a regular license to practice medicine in the United States? I also wanted to get out of Massachusetts because there weren't enough opportunities for growth there, and I wanted to explore other worlds.

In late 1970 we decided to visit India. When I went to see Dr. McLaughlin about my three weeks' vacation, he and Dr. Ehrenberg told me it was the wrong time to leave. Union negotiations were imminent, and they needed me to be around during that time. They said I was going to be a buffer between the administration and the union, as the union leaders would probably listen to me. Somehow, they were of the opinion that my presence at the talks would help. They wanted me to postpone my vacation, and in return would give me an extra week of vacation (informally) if I went to India the following year. That was a bonanza for me since I was planning to take an extra week anyway, without pay, so I postponed my trip. I didn't end up doing anything at all during the negotiations; it all worked out without my involvement. I don't know anything I could have done anyway except just be there.

The airline business was changing in late 1971. Air India came out with a promotional round-trip fare of $450 from New York to Delhi, quite a departure from the usual $1,150. For the three of us that was a huge saving, and the extra week of vacation was a bonus.

At that time I had also started looking around for a new job. I had no idea what kinds of jobs were out there. I just knew that I needed to be approved for a temporary license and that the job should pay substantially more than the $12,500 I was currently making. I applied for literally any psychiatry job I saw advertised. And then we went to India.

❧

Going back home is a major project for us immigrants. We have to buy gifts for everyone, and do it very, very thoughtfully. At the same time we have to make sure that what we buy is liked there. What is cherished here is not necessarily liked there. First it was Gillette razor blades, and then it was German-made tape-recorders and Japanese transistor radios. And American clothes, and sneakers, and certain foods like pistachios and chocolate. On one visit I took a lot of potato peelers and they were a hot item there. Later it was perfumes, and cameras, and movie cameras. We could not take too many electronics because of both import customs regulations in India and the sheer expense. In recent times, most everything has become available in Indian cities, but the gifts continue.

During our 1971 visit, the family was full of joy and celebration, but there were already some culture clashes rearing their heads. The biggest objection for everybody there was that we would not let them smother Victor, who was less than two years old. We were actually very liberal according to American standards, but we put our foot down when it came to some things. For starters, we would not allow everybody and his brother to hug and kiss him ninety-five times a day. And, since Indians did not believe in diapers, they wanted him trained immediately. They did not like our restricted food habits. They wanted us to visit every relative and friend and have a home-cooked meal at their place. My family did not want us to visit Aligarh, where Poonam's family still lived, for more than a couple of days, but I disagreed. My family could not understand why we would want to stay in a little town when we could be in Delhi the entire time. And as far as they were concerned, Poonam no longer "belonged" to her former family, nor did Victor.

Aligarh was in fact a small, not-so-clean town at that time, with few sanitary facilities, and there was not much to do there. But I felt that Poonam's family had a right to have their daughter, grandson, and son-in-law visit them for a week or more. Poonam generally went along with whatever I said; I was on her side anyway. So one day we took a train and went to Aligarh. From the train station we took a man-driven bicycle rickshaw to their house. Luckily, Poonam remembered how to get to her house even though in all those years she had lived there she had never gone anywhere to or from her house alone. It was evening and getting dark. We got off the rickshaw and knocked at the door. When the landlord opened it, he could not believe his eyes. How could a son-in-law come without any celebration? He felt further insulted when I picked up my own suitcases and insisted on carrying them upstairs myself.

Very soon the whole neighborhood was there to welcome the "community son-in-law" and grandson. They forgot the daughter. And they all were talking about how humble their son-in-law was, because he did not want any fanfare and even picked up his own suitcase. Had they known about our visit in advance, the whole neighborhood would have been waiting to receive us at the train station with flower garlands and sweets. But I was being myself and was not trying to show off. Having been in America for five years, I had forgotten the concept of servants.

Our stay in Aligarh was somewhat rustic, but comfortable; they were still using a hand pump for their water supply. We saw a couple of movies and went to their only market a few times. There was not much to do there except rest and relax, so I spent my time reading novels. Friends and neighbors of my in-laws kept coming and visiting us, and for the first time I got acquainted with my in-laws and their wonderful affection. And we ate home-cooked meals three times a day.

I left India after four weeks, with Poonam and Victor remaining there for an extra month. I gave my parents strict instructions not to interfere in the diapering of Victor, and to let Poonam and Victor visit Aligarh again for at least another week. My parents did not like it but had no choice.

⚘

Back in the United States, I took a bus and started visiting places for job interviews. The Massachusetts state hospitals all had the same salary structure, so it was no use going to any other hospital there. New Hampshire had better salaries but not by much. Angus had moved to New Mexico and was making much more money, but his hospital had no openings. I went for interviews in Cleveland, Chicago, and Detroit. The bus trips were very tiring, and I did not have enough time and money to spend on motels, so I squeezed my trips together, catching up on sleep with naps during the bus trips. Nothing really worked. Nobody wanted me. And in some cases I did not want them. In addition, my travel sickness was acting up.

I had a strange experience in Chicago. I was being interviewed by the director of a mental-health clinic there. He said his clinic was in a ghetto and would be ideal for me because I could make good money and have a good life. He could arrange for many amenities, more than I had in Boston, and it would be a stepping stone for an eventual private practice. He offered me $17,000 a year, more than I had in mind. He said he was in desperate need of a psychiatrist and had grant monies that he had to use. He would give me an extra stipend of $250 a month, which would be enough for a rental apartment in a good location. He wanted me immediately and even had an apartment in mind. When I brought up the topic of a temporary license, he smiled ear to ear. He knew about it; we had discussed it on the phone. I quietly mentioned that even though I had the immigration papers, there was no chance of my passing the FLEX exam in the near future, having practiced nothing but psychiatry for five years.

What he told me next was shocking. "Dr. Dang, you go and appear in the exam; I will make sure you pass. I am here in downtown Chicago, and the AMA office is right here. I know everybody there. If I need you in my mental-health clinic, you will pass the FLEX—nobody can stop you. I know all about it. The politicians here do for me and my people what I want them to do."

To this day I don't know why I did not take his offer. Partly it was that I did not believe him: how could he ensure that I would pass the exam? Looking back, I believe that it was possible; anything is possible in politics, and in Chicago. The other reason for my rejecting his offer was that I was scared. I was intimidated. If he had this much power in Chicago, what could he do to me when I wanted to leave him in the future?

I left Chicago with a heavy heart.

28

A Painful Farewell
to Massachusetts

Since coming to the United States, I had enjoyed sending Christmas cards to everyone I knew, writing short, funny, personal notes under the printed part of the card. One of these was to Dr. Rufus Little, the superintendent of Bergen Pines Hospital in New Jersey. I did not really know whether he was still the superintendent, or even whether he was still alive. He was an older man who had suffered from a speech impediment after some sort of illness, nobody seemed to know what. (Most people surmised it was from old tuberculosis of the throat). He had a sharp eye and we were all scared of him during our internship. We thought he knew every move we made at the hospital and at the residence. He had his spies all over the hospital, so we thought. His executive secretary was Miss Lee, and we would go to her whenever we needed something. She was his biggest spy. We thought she even knew how much milk each of us was drinking in our residence. In fact, we did not have any reason to fear her; she was very nice to us interns.

That year, 1971, on Dr. Little's Christmas card I wrote simply, "Looking for a job. You got any?" I knew it was a shot in the dark as he could not help me. He probably would not even remember me from when I was an intern almost five years earlier.

He called. "Hello, Dr. Dang, I got your card. So, you are looking for a job. I have your file in front of me; I see that when you left here, you went to Metropolitan State Hospital in Waltham, Massachusetts. According to our files, you went there for your residency in psychiatry. Is that so?"

I was shocked. It was Dr. Little! Same speech impediment, which made him very hard to understand. He had looked up the telephone number of my hospital.

"That's right, Dr. Little. I finished my residency in psychiatry two years ago."

"Well, we need a psychiatrist. You were very good as our intern. We would like to have you back to work with us."

Of course he did not remember me; he made it up. On the other hand, maybe he did have spies and had a full file on me. "Sir, I don't have a license to practice. I wish I did."

"You can work with us on a temporary license as long as you want." Wow! He explained to me that the county hospitals in New Jersey could have doctors work with a temporary license, same as the state hospitals. Talk about luck!

He invited me to come visit him. I was not sure about anything; the whole conversation seemed surreal. Did I hear him correctly? Was he offering me a job? Did I want to go back to New

Jersey? Could they pay me even the same as I was getting in Massachusetts? Well, no harm in going to see him. But I was skeptical. I told him that my wife and son were arriving in New York from India next week and I was coming to pick them up; I could come and meet him then.

ᗡᕼᖇᕼᕤ

After picking up my family from Kennedy Airport, I drove them to New Jersey and on the way explained to Poonam about my trips, the job hunting, that I was having no luck so far, and how we were now going back to good old Bergen Pines for a job interview. Poonam and Victor stayed in the car while I went in.

I met with Dr. Little. He took me around, showed me the psychiatric floor where I had done my rotation as an intern, and said he needed a psychiatrist urgently and he was offering me a job. He said that the final decision rested with the medical director, Dr. George Simpson, who came to the hospital only on Fridays. He also said the job paid around $21,000 a year, much more than I was currently making. I would have accepted $18,000. I was shaking with joy. Could I be that lucky? I made an appointment to come back the following Friday and meet with Dr. Simpson.

We drove to Boston. I told my amazing story to my brother and my uncle, and their faces fell. They could not believe that I was going to leave the family just for a little more money. How could I leave them in the lurch? Where would they go? What would they do without my assistance? In reality they were both established, or nearly so, and in fact had no trouble finding their

212

own apartment before I left Massachusetts, but it seemed they had a lingering sense of insecurity about it.

The next Friday I met Dr. Simpson. He had shaggy hair, a careless demeanor, and a Scottish accent. He reminded me of a scattered, confused professor. He gave me very little time, took me to the same unit, and said, "We need somebody right away, and Rufus likes you. So the job is yours if you want it; we'll arrange for your temporary license. The salary will be about twenty-three thousand dollars a year." The money was increasing by the minute. After that visit, Dr. Little called almost weekly, raising the salary each time, and wanting to know the date I could join them.

⋘⋙

It was very difficult to leave Metropolitan State Hospital. When I went to Dr. McLaughlin with my conventional two weeks' notice, he almost had convulsions. First he was upset, then angry, and then he started pleading. Dr. Ehrenberg and Dr. Asekoff, even Mrs. Asekoff, were employed to entice us into staying. The nicest guy I ever knew, Dr. McLaughlin, got so angry that he threatened to ruin my career if I left them in a hurry, without giving him at least a year's notice. He could not change my salary, which was fixed by the state, but he would give me a couple of thousand dollars a year from the plumbing account! I myself was torn with the thought of leaving, but their pressure made my resolve less painful.

One day Dr. McLaughlin came to my house while I was working in the hospital. The house, of course, really belonged to the hospital. Poonam was playing with Victor in the backyard. He sat

213

on the steps and talked to her for a little while, then started pleading with her to convince me to stay. "Do you have any inconvenience here? Even though we are not supposed to let anybody else live here other than the immediate family, we ignore that your uncle and brother-in-law live here. We don't charge you for landscaping, snow removal, electricity, and other amenities." Poonam also had mixed feelings about the whole idea of leaving but said she would go along with my decision.

My family, my friends, and all the staff members at the hospital were against my decision. I knew if I didn't do it then, I would never leave there. It was almost double the salary, even though much of it would be used in renting and furnishing an apartment. And it would be hard work, but in a general hospital I might get some additional exposure to help me pass my licensure exam. In a total psychiatric environment I was out of touch with doctoring, exams, and licensure; it was like being in a cocoon. Starting a new life filled me with new excitement and new fear. Many times I have called myself weak or lazy. Maybe I am not that weak after all; I stuck to my decision of moving to New Jersey. So many dilemmas and no help from anybody.

I called Dr. Little and told him that in all sincerity I needed to give my hospital longer notice and could only join Bergen Pines in two months. This may sound unbelievable, but Dr. Little said that if I came immediately he would offer $28,000, in one month it would be $25,000, and if I did not join them in two months, the deal was off. I don't remember exactly what salary I got in the end, but I did give Dr. McLaughlin two months' notice, and neither he nor any other administrator showed up at my farewell party. And when my friends gave me a party, my family members made excuses not to come. It was a sad ending to a very happy life in Massachusetts for five years.

29

Our Special Friends, the Glassmans

Before I left Metropolitan State Hospital, Dr. Meyer Asekoff, our medical director, died. Poonam and I spent a few days in the Asekoffs' house sitting shiva, meeting their visitors, family, and friends, and consoling Mrs. Asekoff. A couple was visiting them from New Jersey. Mrs. Asekoff introduced us and told them that we were relocating to New Jersey. That was the beginning of our lifelong friendship with Irwin and Barbara Glassman.

They were bubbly and excited to learn that we were going to be their neighbors; Bergen Pines Hospital was only a few miles from their house. After that Poonam and Barbara were on the phone several times a week, and when we visited New Jersey in preparation for the move, the Glassmans took us around, showed us the neighborhood, and took us to visit various apartment complexes where we could rent an apartment.

That was my first real taste of corruption in America. The director of the mental-health clinic in Chicago had talked about rigging the system, but I did not have to experience it firsthand.

Even though corruption in India existed in everyday life and I had read reports of big-time corruption among politicians in America, I had not witnessed any such thing and had not even heard any stories from normal, everyday people. So it came as a shock. The garden apartment complex that we liked in Fair Lawn did not have any vacancies at the time we wanted to move. Barbara told us to stay in the car and went back to see the superintendent. She came back with the news that if we gave the super one month's rent in cash, under the table, an apartment could be available. I laughed my head off. So there were some "normal" people in America too. I obliged him with the money; we did not want to look around too much and we wanted to be near the Glassmans.

Between the visit and the move, Barbara looked around for furniture for us and saved us several trips. We were on the phone practically every day. A lot of anxiety associated with the move was alleviated. I asked around and found two able bodies who would fill a rented truck and drive to New Jersey, then go back to Boston by bus. The whole move was smooth and sad and expensive. Immediately after arriving in New Jersey, I started my new job and left Poonam to explore the area with Barbara, and to furnish and stock the apartment.

❧

The job was not hard, but it was time-consuming. I could not come home on a whim or for lunches as I had in Massachusetts. The administration was delighted to know that I liked working with the elderly—none of their other psychiatrists did—so I was

217

made the medical director of their geriatric floors in Building 12 soon after joining them. During the day I would go to the main building and sit in the library, trying to gauge the progress of other doctors. Nearly all of them were feverishly studying for their FLEX licensure examination. They had done a medical residency and were practicing, yet were still very nervous about the test. Many told me that I had no chance. I had already applied for the FLEX exam from Massachusetts and sent in fees, or I would probably have postponed it. I had made some friends who were doing fellowships in internal medicine; even they were scared of what was coming ahead.

Several states recognized the FLEX exam, but not all. For example, Pennsylvania had its own exam for licensure, and it was in the Northeast, so I applied there too, thinking that if I did not pass FLEX, maybe the Pennsylvania test was easier or they needed more doctors, and if I passed that, I would move there.

There were ten subjects to study, including basic sciences, and each one carried the same weight in scoring. Naturally I was a weakling in all of them except psychiatry, and even that I was not sure of anymore. I had no books on those subjects. I bought some, borrowed a few from the library, and started planning my studies.

Ever since high school, I had always had a method to my madness in terms of studying for any exams. I spent a lot of time in planning and organizing my studies, as opposed to actually studying. In India we did not have multiple-choice questions, so I would start guessing what the essay questions would be and write down how much time I was going to devote to studying that particular topic. Then I would compute the total time available for the rest of that book and that subject. I planned how I would formulate my answer: beginning, middle, and end. In medical school we had to draw figures. I had a system of how many figures I would draw, what color pencils I would use, and where in the answer I would place those pictures to be most striking to the teacher. I knew that he did not have time to read the whole essay, so I would imagine myself in his shoes and plan my answers so that the headings would show him how much I knew. Having been a monitor in class and also a tutor, I believe I had mastered that art. I also made it a point to answer all the questions even if I was not sure about the answer, hoping that the teacher might take pity on me and give a couple of points for my effort. I always got good grades in my theory papers because of these tactics. However, as mentioned earlier, I was quite poor in orals and in interviews.

FLEX was going to be a different experience: there would be no essays, only multiple-choice questions. My strategy shifted to planning by subject. I very quickly learned that if I read about diabetes in the medical textbook, it was eighty pages; it would take me three days to read it because I was working full-time. There would probably be five questions on diabetes. After reading those eighty pages I could probably answer three questions correctly, and the medical resident would answer four out of five. Net loss: one. The book on obstetrics and gynecology was about 160 pages. After spending six days reading it, I could probably answer forty out of ninety questions, and the schmuck who was ignoring this book because he was still busy reading about diabetes would give twenty-five correct answers. Gain of fifteen points, right off the bat. Also, if I just answered the diabetes questions at random, I might get one or two correct, and save time for reading other questions.

☙❧

Poonam was expecting again, my new job was taxing, and as usual I had the habit of falling asleep as soon as I opened the books to read. Poonam was extremely supportive, staying up with me and making tea and coffee for me so I could stay awake at night. But all the cards were stacked against me. It was really embarrassing when I overheard two so-called friends betting with each other ten to one that I would fail.

I sat for both the FLEX and the Pennsylvania licensure exams. They were extremely hard. I did not understand many questions, let alone hope to answer them correctly. All the pictures of X-rays and blood slides looked the same to me. The patient histories were intriguing but confusing.

I remember when the envelope came. I was at work and Poonam opened it. She called, crying and screaming. I had passed the FLEX exam. I did not believe her until that evening when I saw it with my own eyes. Even then I wondered if it was some sort of mistake. We were ecstatic. This permanent license to practice would open so many doors.

The letter was not a mistake, because a few days later another letter came from Pennsylvania; I had passed there too.

Nobody was happier for us than Barbara and Irwin Glassman. They reminded me of my uncle Khushiram in India, who used to stand in the street showing my grades to whoever cared to see. They were also sad to think that my license was good in several states, since I often talked about looking for opportunities for private practice in other states. We were seeing each other regularly, and they were getting accustomed to Indian food. Their oldest son, David, especially liked our food and the spices. We participated in the bar mitzvah of their twins.

I wrote an article entitled "How to Pass FLEX Even If You Are a Dumb Psychiatrist" and sent it to *Medical Economics*. They called and wanted to meet with me. I met with an editor at lunch in a restaurant near the hospital. He wanted to see evidence of all the things I had written, about the diabetes and gynecology books, about my being a psychiatrist, and wanted just to meet me to authenticate the article. A photographer was sent to take my picture with the books I read, especially the Rypins' books (the Cliffs Notes of medicine) that I had emphasized in my article. The article was published, albeit in a different format and with a different title, but it was published—my first publication in the United States. I was paid $250.

❧

Poonam and I had quite an exciting trip when I took her to the hospital for the birth of our daughter. We had a flat tire. Until then I had never had a flat tire and did not know what to do about it.

Also, it was a chilly autumn day and her contractions were increasing in frequency. We happened to be in front of a small neighborhood hospital, which is now a nursing home. I went in and brought out a blanket for her; I also called the police from there. A police cruiser stopped by. The cop started laughing. "It only happens in the movies—a flat on the way to the delivery room, and a doctor's wife! I will write about it in my diary." He called an ambulance and a road repair guy. But our adventures still weren't over: the ambulance took Poonam to the wrong hospital—Valley Hospital instead of Pascack Valley Hospital. In the end everything turned out fine: she made it to the right hospital and gave birth to a beautiful daughter. I had the tire fixed and was in the waiting room when Nita was born, while Barbara was taking care of Victor in our house.

⋆

I may mention here our first meeting with Irwin's parents and Barbara's father. It was 1972, and there were not too many Indians in New Jersey yet. It was the first time these three old-fashioned Jews had eaten dinner at the same table with such a different-looking family, let alone in the house of their children. They were uncomfortable, more with Barbara and Irwin than with us. Barbara and Irwin felt the tension in the room and were trying to act natural and jovial to ease it. Poonam and I tried to keep the conversation going, having been in awkward situations in the past, but the three older people were very quiet. We thought the evening was a disaster. Yet we were wrong. Those same three parents would become very fond of us as time passed, and we met each other frequently. They would often visit us. We later visited them in Florida. When they passed away, we attended their funerals.

30

Is Addiction to the Stock Market Genetic?

After the partition of India, my father became a stockbroker in partnership with one of his uncles and lost all his savings. That was the beginning of his financial downfall. Even after he left that business, he kept investing in stocks on the side and kept getting into debt. We were literally starving and he was being somewhat careless. One day my uncle Khushiram took his older brother (my father) by the hand, led him to their mother, and asked him to put his right hand on her head and swear never to indulge in stocks in his life. It is said that my father never lied in his life, so that was the end of his involvement in stocks.

Twenty years later, when I (my father's true son) was a first-year resident, Angus taught me the ABCs of the stock market. Both of us bought our first stock, in partnership with each other. I think we bought 100 shares of a clothing company called Askins at five dollars a share. As soon as we made fifty bucks of profit each, we sold it. That was how I got the habit, and have never stopped my interest in it. I do not really think I am addicted to it; I do not buy or sell stocks more often than any other doctor I know. I went through the October 1987 crash, suffered heavy losses in the dot-com bubble burst of 2000, and have also been burned many times in between. Some doctors have joked, "When Jack buys something, it is time to sell it." But I have heard some other people complain that everything they buy goes down and when they sell something it invariably goes up. I think by its very nature the stock market makes you think that way.

That does not mean that there is anything wrong with the market. After all, in the past I also made a lot of money in it. My children went to private schools and private colleges. They had the most fabulous weddings of their time, and I helped them in buying their cars and houses. I have a lot of life insurance, which my children and grandchildren will inherit. I have taken some spectacular vacations and saved a little in my retirement plans. All this did not come from my jobs and psychiatry practice. But, in sum, stocks have probably been a losing proposition for me.

If gambling is genetic, we are an example of such a family. Two of my brothers are heavily into the stock market, and as mentioned earlier, my brother Harish is a stockbroker. (These days they have a fancy name for it—a financial advisor.) I believe my grandfather was also into the market, and so is my son.

I never bought any real estate other than my house and office, and even in those I lost money while my friends were buying and selling real estate and doubling their profits within a year or two.

I was too involved with buying stocks; that is so much simpler than buying rental real estate and taking care of it. As always, I took the path of least resistance. Sure, some people did lose their shirts in real estate too, but more lost it in the stock market. Then again, the grass does look greener on the other side of the fence.

This is not just a phrase; it is real. When we lived in Fair Lawn, my next-door neighbor and I were talking over our fence on a nice sunny day. "Jack, Karen and I always appreciate how good your grass looks."

"That's funny, Barry. Pam and I think the other way around." We started laughing, and discussed the phrase in detail, and promised each other that one day we would have a neutral person look at our backyards and give us his opinion.

Poonam and I sometimes talk about all the good deals of real estate that we let go in the past. I believe everyone thinks that way about something or other. I made some good investments early in my career, such as buying stocks in my children's names of then AT&T and IBM. When I made big profits, I got into buying and selling. ("Gambling again, son?") They say the biggest mistakes are made when you make deals out of fear or greed, and the stock market involves both.

I have also lost major sums of money when I could least afford it because friends gave me bad advice. During the "gold rush" of the early 1970s, a friend was deep into the gold market and I invested money in his venture. Also, at that time I loaned another friend a large amount, and he bought Arthur Treacher's Fish and

Chips stores in California and went under. Later I gave money to another person for an oil-well investment.

I guess everybody has made some foolish decisions. Doctors are often considered bad businessmen; perhaps I am a typical doctor.

31

My Sister, Sarika

I have to cover this subject carefully. In our family we seldom talk about it.

Almost every society I know treats men and women differently, men a little better than women. This happens even with Americans, even in the twenty-first century. Conditions for women in India are deplorable. I believe the environment has changed somewhat, but it is still not good. Physical and emotional domestic abuse is not uncommon, not only from the husband but also from his family and extended family. The wife who was abused as a daughter-in-law goes on to do the same to her own daughter-in-law, and the cycle goes on. Granted, it is significantly better than the situation in many Middle Eastern or African countries.

In most of India, there is no celebration when a daughter is born. A daughter is called Laxmi, a goddess, maybe to buffer the grief, or to cover it up. When a son is born you rejoice in many ways. You write to people, call them, and go there personally to give the good news. You distribute sweets, and you may even hire a band to play in front of your house for the neighbors to join in the celebrations. At the time of a daughter's birth, you just inform a few people, and they say somberly, "You are blessed with Laxmi." Most of the so-called enlightened Indians or intellectual elite will be furious to read this, but even some of them have had a fetus aborted after finding out that it was female. Most educated, rich, upper-class Indians will probably not feel hurt by having one or even two daughters, but will try to go for an abortion if the third child is also a daughter. In some remote villages the statistics are overwhelming: the ratio of boys to girls born there is 80:20. Where does this huge number of girls disappear? It should not be hard to figure out. The daughter-in-law in a joint family gets maligned if she gives birth to daughters. She herself starts feeling guilty and inferior.

The dowry system is a big blotch on our culture, and in spite of denials and legal restrictions, it is not really getting better. An ordinary man is buried under a huge debt after marrying off one or two daughters, much more so if he happens to have a third or fourth to give away. A son, on the other hand, brings dowry and riches at his wedding. Also, the son is there (hopefully) to take care of the parents when they grow old; the daughter becomes the "property" of the other family. Bride burning, for reason of a low dowry, is much less common in modern India, but it is not unknown. In olden times the system of *suttee* dictated that, after the death of her husband, a widow sat live on the pyre when her husband was being cremated. Hindus by the hundreds stood around chanting mantras in honor of the *sacrifice* of the widow. Sometimes she was forcefully picked up and held there if she refused to do that. Thankfully it is not practiced anymore. However, in essence, a widow is dead for all practical purposes after her protector and provider has died.

⚜

I had a sister, named Sarika. She was born after four sons, and would have been a cause for celebration, especially because I had heard my mother wishing that her next child should be a daughter. In spite of that, my parents and grandparents were glum at her birth, and they received very few, muted congratulations.

There was a large time gap between each of my mother's children and the next. I was the oldest and my sister was twenty-one years younger than I. When I left India she was about five years old, young enough to be my daughter. I had very little memory of her, especially because I never really lived much with my parents. As mentioned earlier, my brothers Harish and Girish became close to me through the intellectual letters we exchanged almost daily after I came to America, but Sarika never wrote to me.

My parents, I believe, loved Sarika more than they loved their sons, but she was *just* a daughter. She was a pretty child. She was considered a bright kid in her class. But she also became moody and reclusive. The family blamed my parents for spoiling her rotten. Some accused my mother of putting extra pressure on Sarika by comparing her to her overachieving brothers.

Sarika became stubborn and angry. Before long she started deliberately breaking things in the house, showed paranoid traits toward our parents, was hallucinating and hearing voices, and had

230

suicidal ideas. At that time people in India used denial when it came to mental illness in a family member. Neighbors and extended family should not know this fact at any cost. Who would marry a mental patient? Who would marry her brothers or others in the family? Who would visit the family where a mental patient resided? This fact-hiding is still practiced in India, but I believe it is reduced.

I was getting reports of Sarika's behavior in the letters from my parents and brothers in indirect and hushed references. During my first trip back to India, I was a resident in psychiatry and saw paranoid schizophrenia in her. (In those days we in America did not have much concept of bipolar disorder.) She participated in my wedding somewhat reluctantly and angrily. It was hard for her to consider me as her brother because I was so much older than she and had abandoned her forever. My youngest brother, Sanjiv, who became a doctor in India, did one year of residency in psychiatry merely to understand her better; they were both living with my parents at that time. Later he switched his specialty to ear, nose, and throat.

Sarika's illness kept getting progressively worse. She was becoming violent to my parents and brothers, and was hurting herself. She had shock treatments. She had remissions and relapses. She steadfastly refused to take medications and was hospitalized several times. Most mental hospitals in India at that time were run by the government and had appalling conditions. On our trips, Poonam and I visited her in the hospital and cried all the way home. We were willing to foot the bills for a private hospital, but there was none in or around Delhi, the capital of India. My parents were getting old and could not, or did not really want to, take too much responsibility. During one trip we decided to admit Sarika to a private psychiatric hospital in Lucknow, and Poonam and I took her there against her wishes. I even gave her tranquilizer injections. We went by overnight train, a treacherous trip; there were very few flights then between Delhi and Lucknow. Later my parents brought her home because they said that even the private hospital did not treat her well since there was no oversight by the family. Also, she was refusing medications and treatment activities, and the doctors felt that she had received the maximum possible benefit from their treatment and was "cured."

Almost immediately after one hospitalization, Sarika took a heavy overdose of her tranquilizers as a suicide attempt and had to be admitted again to the government hospital, where she lived in horrible conditions. She stopped eating and drinking, and tragically succumbed to dehydration and infections. My parents were visiting us here in America when she died in India. She was cremated without them being there. My youngest brothers, Girish and Sanjiv, and the extended family, went through the torment of rituals: priests and prayers and cremation and condolences. A closure to a sad chapter of the family. But is there ever a closure? Just a denial.

⚜

I often think of Sarika, especially because every day I see patients with schizophrenia, bipolar disorder, or depression. They talk about hearing voices, threatening and accusatory voices. They have paranoia and grandiose delusions. They talk about being better than everybody else, having imaginary powers, or being watched and persecuted. They have suicidal thoughts and make suicide attempts. They stop eating or they eat excessively. They become violent with the family, and they break things. They accuse people who are near and dear to them. They stop taking medication (paranoia prevails), and suffer relapses.

During the earlier years of my residency, we did not have effective medications to treat psychosis and schizophrenia. The only choice during a relapse was hospitalization. The system was being abused; it was easier for the family and for the health-care workers to admit a patient to the hospital than to treat him or her on an outpatient basis. I remember one incident in particular. I was eating lunch at a diner near my state hospital when an attendant came in with a few papers about a patient they had just examined in the emergency room (they all knew where I was during the whole time). Having no other blank paper with me, I picked up a napkin, wrote the name of the patient, the date, and the word "Admit," and signed it. No questions asked, he was hospitalized.

With the advent of better medications around 1970, patients actually started getting better, with longer and sustained remissions. Hospitals started emptying themselves of psychiatric patients. Then the so-called mental-health reforms happened. The government spent dollars to start mental-health centers. Outpatient treatment in local mental-health centers rather than warehousing patients in remote state hospitals became the norm.

Hospitalization of a psychiatric patient became harder and harder all over the nation. A state hospital with ten thousand patients a couple of decades ago probably has six hundred now, and some of those may have been transferred from another hospital that was closed.

During the earlier period of the change, I predicted that politicians were making a big mistake in insisting on discharging patients from the big hospitals. One mental patient would harm a family member of a big politician, I said, and the laws would revert. I was wrong; the trend continued. Many patients were discharged to their homes or boarding homes. They kept attending out-patient services and got hospitalized briefly when they had a relapse. Some of them ended up being homeless, sleeping under the bridges. Many patients were sent to nursing homes, with only a few of them returned to the state and county hospitals.

My beef is that the pendulum has swung a little too far. Now you have to jump through hoops to involuntarily hospitalize even a legitimate, needy patient. While admitting a patient by an order on a napkin was an abuse of the system, now the judge may refuse to hospitalize a young psychotic man who held a knife to his mother's breast two hours ago but has calmed down because he received an injection in the emergency room. Or a suicidal patient may go into the hospital voluntarily but sign out the same day against medical advice, even though the crisis team has been told the patient has a history of several serious suicide attempts.

They get better and they get worse. They are sent to group homes, educational facilities, shared residences, and day programs. I wish we had the same facilities in India. Now there is some awareness of mental illness there, but denial remains prevalent. Stigma is still a major problem with psychiatric treatment even in America. It certainly was a factor in retarding timely, appropriate recognition and treatment of my sister's illness.

PART SEVEN

Advancing Professional

32

Admitting Privileges for the Less Privileged

Our new baby girl, Nita, was crying at night, and the tenant above us was giving us trouble. Every time we got up at night and moved around to change diapers or whatever, the guy upstairs got disturbed and started banging on the radiator and the pipes. We also knew that he was drinking most of the night and there was no reasoning with him. I thought I would probably stay right here in New Jersey, so I didn't mind putting down roots. It was time to look for a house.

The real-estate agent was greedy; she was showing us high-priced houses that were clearly out of our range, but we didn't know any better. Whenever I mentioned that I had no savings, she reassured me that getting a mortgage would be no problem. She was right. When we found a house that we liked in Fair Lawn, it was much more than we could afford, but when she took us to the bank, they welcomed us with open arms. "A doctor? No problem, you don't need to provide any down payment." (The power of an

MD after your name!) Barbara and Irwin went with us for the closing of the house, which in itself was quite a learning experience.

Shortly after that, Irwin's job transferred him to Colorado. We
were so sad to lose the Glassmans as neighbors. Largely through
the efforts of Barbara and Poonam, we have stayed in touch with
each other, seen each other at least once every two years, and participated in each other's good and bad times.

⚜

Now that I had passed the FLEX exam and finally had a full license
to practice psychiatry, I wanted to start a private practice before
too long. I did not want to work as the employee of some other
doctor or some hospital for the rest of my life. Practicing on my
own would be more lucrative once I got established, and I would
be more independent, though I would have to work harder.

To start a private practice, I needed to apply for admitting
privileges in the local hospitals. This would mean that I could
admit my own patients there if they needed hospitalization, and
also that the hospital and its doctors would sometimes call on me
as a consulting physician. Any hospital whose consulting staff
I joined in this way would also expect me to be on call for emergencies and to help staff its clinic. So, while still working at Bergen
Pines, I began to apply for admitting privileges at various hospitals.

However, big-name hospitals wouldn't even give me an application or did not respond when I sent one in. A foreign name, a
foreign face hurt their competition with other hospitals; nobody
was ready to embrace me. A Dr. Benjamin Bergman interviewed

me at one hospital and told me in no uncertain terms that I was not wanted or needed. I must have an established office within two miles, be board certified, and meet several other conditions. Many years later, when I was well known in the community and in the New Jersey Psychiatric Association, the same Dr. Bergman met me at a conference and invited me to join the same hospital. When I asked him if he remembered that I had applied in 1972 and been turned down, he unashamedly responded that conditions were different then, and that it "might have" happened. It was clear to me that he remembered that interview. An Indian was not welcome there at that time, but by 1982 he was. The chief of psychiatry at another local hospital would not even return my calls; again, I sounded foreign.

Am I sure that my Indian nationality was the problem, or is that just paranoia? I am sure. Actually, my experience was not half as bad as some other doctors'. I have heard and read, and seen firsthand, that it was happening all over. It was especially bad with surgical specialists. I know personally that some doctors had to fight their way through lawyers and courts to be considered "equal," only to be harassed later by the chief of the department forever and ever. Some were even referred to the Board of Medical Examiners for investigation of their licensure, on flimsy grounds. Conditions in the New Jersey/New York area had started to improve in the early 1970s, but it took much longer in some other states. I was always somewhat timid. I did not want to take any aggressive action and kept applying to hospitals, going for interviews, and waiting for their replies.

꧁꧂

I was finally able to get admitting privileges in two hospitals in Paterson: St. Joseph's and Barnert. Many conditions were imposed, like free clinic service and free on-call emergency service, and I was supposed to be 110 percent available if I wanted to continue those privileges.

The chief of psychiatry at St. Joseph's Hospital, Dr. Floyd Fortuin, was a very fine man: tall, slender, and distinguished-looking. The first time he met me, he asked me whether I had an office. I told him that my house was a mother-daughter house with a side entrance and would be an ideal location for a psychiatrist's first office. He suggested that I should look into his office on Park Avenue in Paterson. It was a house converted into offices, like so many others on that block. He had his office downstairs, and upstairs was available since his tenant had left some time ago. It was furnished and free until I started getting patients; then I could pay him whatever rent I felt was reasonable. He joked that he was old and feeling lonely there and that I would bring some life to the office. I enormously appreciated Dr. Fortuin's generosity and mentorship.

So that is how I started my private practice.

Dr. Fortuin also asked me to join him at Christian Sanitarium in Wyckoff, which is now Christian Health Care Center, a senior care center and full-fledged psychiatric hospital. He told me that he was bringing me in because he was very fond of me; otherwise they would not let me set foot in there. You had to be a Dutch

Christian to have privileges there, he said. Once we walked in, he introduced me proudly to everybody. They were all civil to me, but I could see that I was not welcome there. They loved Dr. Fortuin, so I was being tolerated; I did not apply there. Today you find hardly any Dutch Christian doctors there. What forty years have done to the practice of medicine in New Jersey!

❧

Now that I had an office and a brand-new private practice, I resigned from my full-time job at Bergen Pines Hospital after having been there about two years. It would have been wise, however, for me to keep at least a part-time job to pay the bills until my private practice took off. I had no patients for a while, and sitting idle was not helping my morale. I started getting restless and thought of going west for a job. Poonam and I decided to fly to Colorado with both children, spend a couple of days with the Glassmans, and rent a car; then I would go interviewing for jobs. An ambitious plan was made. Only problem: no cash.

I went to my bank and asked if I could get a loan. I truthfully told the manager that I was going west to look for a job and needed money for any emergencies. No problem, he said. He gave me a bank draft for $10,000 and asked me to sign a piece of paper. That's it. No collateral, nothing. Those were different times. And being a doctor did not hurt. After about four weeks when we returned, I went to the banker and told him that I did not need the money. "Thank you very much. How much do I owe you for the interest?"

"Nothing. You gave me the check back; here is your loan paper. We are even. I should probably charge you ten dollars for the processing fee, but what the heck, you are a good customer." As I said, those were different times.

During the trip I went to Wyoming for an interview. It was a summer day, and I was going to be interviewed for a state hospital job. We parked the car and were met by throngs of people in the local park. It seemed like the whole county had called a day of celebration; they were going to see an Indian doctor with a funny name, for the job in the state hospital. Many of them had not seen anybody looking like me before. They were grilling huge steaks, and we were treated royally. To us, they were foreign too—tall, scary guys with big hats and funny accents. When one of them took Victor away to show him the fish in the lake, Poonam started screaming to me in Hindi that our son was being kidnapped.

I was offered a job. I was going to be the only psychiatrist around, so a two-seater plane came with the job; I was told I would need the plane even to run out for milk or cigarettes. They would keep me on a pedestal, but it was scary. I wondered what they would do to me if the mayor's daughter under my care killed herself.

I turned down that job. As a matter of fact I turned down many jobs during the trip. It ended up being a vacation more than anything else. I was learning the capitalistic way of taking a vacation and calling it a business trip.

33

Diplomate Exams and a Suitcase Full of Muffins

Now that I was practicing and had a full license, I had to start thinking about taking the boards in psychiatry. We Indians love higher education and are always looking for ways to collect more diplomas and certificates. The shingles outside a doctor's office in India have at least five or six degrees listed after his name. Here, generally an MD will suffice. In 1966, when I was still in India and received my letter from Dr. Little of Bergen Pines offering me an internship, many thought it was a bogus letter. How could the superintendent of a hospital write only "Rufus Little, MD" and address the envelope to "Jagdish Dang, MD"? How could the employee and the employer have equal status? Status is a big thing for us. Interestingly, what made that letter look authentic was the thickness and the whiteness of the paper; most of us had not seen that kind of paper before.

Going for the boards and the graduate qualification document was very important for me, although most people at that time did not think it was necessary. I started looking for books and buying new ones to prepare for the boards. It looked like an uphill battle, almost an impossible task—but I decided that I had to do it. Conditions were tough. New practice, immediate and extended family expanding, and my poor knowledge base was obvious. Again, I started planning and organizing. How much time for what subject, and various priorities and concerns? Yes, Poonam was again making coffee at night, and I was falling asleep on the books. Working hard, I passed the written test. Orals were going to be the real test for me.

Orals consisted of seeing three patients and discussing them with the examiners: two psychiatric patients and one neurological. *Three* times facing the monsters (examiners, not the patients)! Studying for this did not really matter that much. It was your presentation that they were looking for. The orals in 1975 were scheduled to be held in St. Louis. I decided that we were going to make a vacation out of it. Also, I was afraid of my travel sickness. So my family of four flew to St. Louis two days before the exam and did sightseeing for a day. After I took the exam, we would all fly to Colorado and take off for two weeks of traveling all over the West.

When we asked Barbara and Irwin what we could bring from New Jersey, they thought it would be nice if we could bring some Thomas' English muffins, which they did not get in Colorado and had been craving. We did not have much luggage, so I packed a small suitcase with muffins for them. Problem: they would go stale in three days. So when we checked into the hotel in St. Louis, I asked the hotel desk clerk if they had a refrigerator where I could store some muffins. They were pleased to oblige. I brought down the suitcase. The desk clerk was baffled and called his manager, who wanted to see what we were storing. I opened the suitcase and showed them almost two dozen boxes of Thomas' English muffins. They grinned and let us store them there. I am sure the desk clerk told his wife that night that Indians were very fond of muffins; they traveled with a hundred muffins. By the way, I don't even like English muffins.

⚜

On the day of the oral exam, I was not the only nervous person. Everybody was on pins and needles. In between the sessions I saw an examinee, a psychiatrist, take a bottle out of his pocket and swallow what looked like at least ten tablets of Valium, five milligrams each, without water. And he did not even collapse.

The first patient they asked me to examine was a young woman with a personality disorder, my weak subject. The second was a woman with midlife depression, my favorite topic. Two different white men and women were always there, and one or two more came in and out of the room every few minutes during each session. They were smiling and smirking, trying to be helpful (or were they taunting?) and I was dying with each passing moment. My shirt was probably wet with sweat by the time it was all over. I was sure I had failed in examining the first patient and passed with the second. A few weeks later I got a letter stating that actually it was the other way around. Their comments were that I was acting like I knew all about the subject of depression in women in their forties and did not go through the mechanisms of examining the patient fully, as a student should. I should have asked her the date, the month, the year, to subtract 7 from 100, and so on. Why did I pass in examining the patient with personality disorder? I think they just took pity on the anxious diminutive man, or that I behaved like a student and asked her all the right questions, personality disorder being my weak topic.

When it was time for the neurology case, the patient could not be found. The two examiners conferred for a little while and apologized for the unavailability of a patient. Then one of them took off his shirt and tie and asked me to examine him, and both kept shooting questions while I conducted the exam. Answering questions on a normal patient can be very easy or very hard. They made it easy for me; after all, it was their fault that there was no real patient available. I passed that one.

If you failed two or more patients, you had to go back and do it all over, after a year. However, if you failed one, you would go back the following year and be examined on one patient only. Next year the oral exam was in Los Angeles, and I passed the one patient they gave me, and thus became a diplomate in psychiatry. The patient was an obese, mentally retarded, psychotic young man who was obviously hallucinating. He seldom made any eye contact and answered very few questions, mostly with grunts and babble. I applied my trickeries again. It was the time of *One Flew Over the Cuckoo's Nest*. In preparation for the board exam I had seen that movie three times and read all about it from psychiatric journals and newspapers. It was a hot topic those days, and I even remembered the names of the actors who played doctors in the movie. California had banned electric shock treatment (ECT) for a while. I read a lot about that too—good, bad, and ugly—and the legal aspects of ECT. Any question the examiners asked me, I brought them back to *Cuckoo's Nest* or the ban on ECT in California, where I was being examined. Yes, they did ask me many questions on these two subjects, and I was ready with the answers. They forgot the patient, and I obliged.

Even though the psychiatric boards were not a big deal in the 1970s, with recent pressures to perform and to compete, those who did not go for it regret it now. I would never have felt like a complete psychiatrist without the boards.

Once I volunteered to become an examiner for the American Board of Psychiatry and Neurology. I was turned down outright, no special reason given. It was almost unknown in the 1970s for a nonwhite to be given a position of importance in psychiatric circles in America.

In 1991 I passed the boards in geriatric psychiatry and then the recertification exam in 2001. I do not think I will go again in 2011. But who knows?

⚜

Meanwhile my practice was going okay. Not great, but not bad. I was running from one hospital to the other, and to clinics and my office. After a couple of break-ins, Dr. Fortuin moved his office. I rented a modest office in Wayne and obtained admitting privileges at the general hospital nearby. However, even though I admitted a number of patients to that hospital and my office was only a stone's throw away, I could not break through the so-called Italian Mafia there. All my efforts were useless; I got very few consultations from that hospital. (Admitting privileges are supposed to be a two-way street: the hospital and the doctor help *each other* find patients.) Renting an office near that hospital was a bad idea; it had no benefit but extra commuting.

Years later, an opportunity fell into my lap to change my office. New construction for a medical office building was being proposed in West Paterson. Because I was one of the first ones to consider it, and the builder wanted some names of doctors who were buying the condos at preconstruction prices so that he could attract other doctors, I got a good price. I got my mortgage at a good rate from the same bank that was building the condos and bought a small but very nice corner office. Going from a rent of $250 a month to a monthly mortgage of $1,350 was not an easy decision to make, but it was one of the best decisions of my life. Location, location, whatever, my income increased substantially.

Later, when I was fully established in West Paterson, the so-called Mafia was gone from the other hospital, and many Indian doctors worked there. I got several invitations to come back and do consultations, but I refused. I officially stayed on their staff as a consulting physician until recently, but never went back to do any work there; I just could not forgive them for the treatment I got in earlier years.

❧❀❧

I was happy with our house in Fair Lawn, but Poonam had other ideas. She wanted a bigger house, a new house, a colonial. She was actually going around with real-estate agents and looking. And we signed up for a house that she wanted, in a new development in Morris County. She actually wanted Bergen County, but that was beyond our reach; we were a one-income family, and that one was a psychiatrist, not a surgeon.

Building a house from ground up must be among the most stressful events in one's life. Our builder was bad; most builders are, in my opinion. When we applied for the mortgage, we gave almost all our savings in the down payment. Any upgrade to the house had to be paid up front, and we had no more money. The basic house plan was *very* basic. Upgrading needed to be done in the kitchen cabinets, bathrooms, electrical wiring and plumbing, doors, windows, everything. The paint in all the rooms was white; we had to pay extra for each room if we wanted color. Poonam went to the site almost every day and came home crying. Nothing was going right, and money was tight. I did not want to borrow but talked to some friends in case I needed some money in a hurry.

Our lawyer was not helpful. I know it is fashionable to make fun of lawyers, and I do it the most in my writings, but we actually felt that he was getting money from our builder for torturing us. We were forced to close on the new house in the midst of winter, in a snowstorm. Our Fair Lawn house had not sold yet, and we repeatedly lowered our selling price because we felt trapped and squeezed in our money situation.

Eventually we moved to the new house and sold the old one. All was well in the end. We started liking our new house, although after being there almost thirty years we still think that the builder was a crook. Like everybody else, we did a lot of upgrading; we are still doing it, throwing money into the bottomless pit. We also bought better cars and raised our standard of living to compete with the Joneses.

◦෴◦

In the meantime more family kept coming from India, to visit or to stay. Our frequent trips to Kennedy Airport in New York to receive them or see them off became routine. We would then take them around to see the tourist spots of New York, Philadelphia, Boston, Niagara Falls, and Washington, D.C. (I believe most immigrants do that.) They kept applying for immigration and arriving one by one by one, to live here or get a chance to bring other family members. We helped them get settled. Eventually they all became citizens once they became eligible five years after immigration.

Most of Poonam's family and mine are here now and well established in their own right, some on a much higher rung of the ladder than we are. Poonam's father visited us and later came back to settle here. My parents also visited us several times. I kept sending a little money here and there, and kept visiting them, taking gifts with me. My father continued his small cloth shop in Rajinder Nagar, which was more a place to spend time than to earn money, and later retired. My three brothers married in India, and we all went to their weddings. (Harish and Girish now live in the United States; Sanjiv lives in India.)

My uncle Khushiram used to call me the Columbus of our family who brought the family to the New World. Once, when we were visiting him in India, he started telling my children about my childhood, and my Columbus-like accomplishments. He must be exaggerating, right? Suddenly he took a neatly folded yellowed paper from the inner pocket of his jacket and showed it to us. It was a copy of my medical-school grades that he had kept close to his chest all the time for thirty years. He told my children that I was the only doctor in the family who passed every exam the first time. I don't remember sending him a copy of my certificate of psychiatric boards; if I had, he would probably have kept that too in his pocket!

34

Fellowship in the American Psychiatric Association

Always a joiner, I became a member of the APA in 1970, when I was still a resident. When I moved to New Jersey, I joined the state branch (the New Jersey Psychiatric Association) and also the North Jersey Psychiatric Society. I attended most of their meetings and was a vocal participant, but I was thoroughly ignored. You had to be white (and Jewish) to be anybody in those days. I was probably the only foreign-looking psychiatrist in those august bodies. But I kept pressing my cause, in a very small way. Even though we psychiatrists talk a lot about championing the cause of the poor and downtrodden, we are hypocrites when it comes to our own affairs. We are snobbish and elitist. That may be one reason why we get trounced by doctors, psychologists, social workers, the Church of Scientology, Medicare, and the government at large.

When I was active with the county medical society and the state medical society, I was made chairman of the mental-health committee of my county medical society. Another psychiatrist, a so-called friend, was always criticizing my actions. Maybe he felt slighted that he was not made the chairman; after all, I was a foreigner. He was a respected member of the profession and had a voice. One time he got up to the microphone and started talking about my actions in derogatory terms. Everything I did was wrong, so how did I dare to continue to be the chairman of the committee? I was furious but sat there listening to his diatribe. Like other foreign doctors, I was accustomed to frequent indirect insults, but this was extreme.

The next day I called a judge friend and invited him for lunch. I asked for his advice on whether there was a case for slander. He admonished me, "Jack, I am Jewish myself, and we Jews had to go through this kind of humiliation for decades. There is no recourse; I suggest you grin and bear it. They will recognize their prejudice in due time." He told me that if I went through the motions of making any charges against him, it would cost me thousands of dollars, no witness would come forward to defend me, and I would lose in the end. I would also be maligned by the psychiatric community. He was right.

Many years later, when I was flying in the high society of psychiatrists, the same psychiatrist introduced me to an audience, saying, "Jack here, my friend, brings luster to our profession." I can never forget those words.

ॐ

Fellowship in the APA was extremely difficult to get. While you could become a fellow in other specialties by passing the boards or being a member for four or more years, the APA had very stringent standards. You had to be a member for eight years, have passed the boards, and show *excellence* in at least five of nine categories. Some of the categories were doing community service; working in the mental-health field and medical society without compensation; active participation and holding office in local, state, or national psychiatric societies; publishing books and papers of distinction; and having clinical, administrative, and teaching qualifications. Talk about the superiority complex! In addition, you needed three fellows to write detailed recommendations about your professional and personal character.

I applied in 1993 but got no help from anybody, no call from an officer. A friend said in passing, "By the way, your application for fellowship was rejected." Rejected by whom? The New Jersey branch? The APA as a whole? No answer. We psychiatrists, the champions of communication, are mum on issues that matter.

More than not being able to get the fellowship, I was upset that I was ignored. Nobody called me to explain the application process, or even to tell me officially that I had been rejected, and why. I knew I was qualified. I had passed two boards. I had been a shining star when it came to community service. And I had excelled in working in the medical society and mental-health associations, and in teaching, and so on. Actually I was probably doing more uncompensated work for the society and the community than most of the fellows. What went wrong?

Many things were wrong in my application; just qualifications were not enough. I learned later that I did not inflate my qualifications as the APA expected. I did not know three fellows who would give me professional and personal references. I was also an Indian! When they called us FMG (Foreign Medical Graduate) or IMG (International Medical Graduate), they actually meant FLMG (Foreign-*Looking* Medical Graduate).

⚜

Always timid and politically correct, this time I became feisty and confrontational.

I wrote a long, angry editorial, and it somehow got published in the newsletter of the New Jersey Psychiatric Association. It was a scathing description of how we psychiatrists consider ourselves above everybody else. I described the fellowship committee as an old boys' club, and all those requirements for fellowship being redundant, elitist, and impossible for a normal human being to fulfill. Dr. Sigmund Freud, Dr. Marcus Welby, and Mother Teresa would not be deemed competent to join the elite fellowship of the APA. I also mentioned that the three fellows' letters were merely a facade to keep minorities out of the club. For example, I would never know three fellows intimately. Unless three Indians were somehow able to breach the fence, no Indian would ever become a fellow of the APA. I suggested changing the requirements to eight years as a member, board certification, and one fellow's recommendation, or excellence in two or three qualifications.

In the next issue of the newsletter, the chairman of the fellowship committee wrote a reply calling me all sorts of names (returning the favor) and telling me I was wrong. The editor was

257

chided for publishing my letter; how could he let me thrash all the big guns of psychiatry? He wrote a short note that the subject was closed . . . and quietly resigned.

The subject had not closed. *Psychiatric News*, the newspaper of the APA, picked up the story and wrote pros and cons of my editorial. People wrote letters to the editor, and the fellowship subject never died. At the next dinner meeting, several fellows came to me and said I was being inconsiderate to them; they were my friends, so why didn't I ask them to write a recommendation for me?

"What personal recommendation can you give me? Do you know if I am married or single? Do you know what hospital I work in or where my office is? Do you know about my community service?" I was told very calmly that there was a process and I had to follow the system. I was supposed to write letters, inflating my qualifications, and give them to three fellows who knew me well. They would then write a nice letter on my behalf. They did not have to know me personally; I had to tell them about myself. The chairman of the fellowship committee (who was present in that meeting) had many sympathizers, but I too had a few. I was asked to apply again. I refused.

When the subject of fellowship kept coming up again and again, I was finally asked by Dr. Levon Boyajian to please reapply and leave the matter of three fellows to him. I considered Dr. Boyajian my mentor and had a lot of respect for him. I believe some people in the know had commissioned him to approach me.

I told him I would seriously consider it. Not to be left behind, three or four other fellows called me too and asked me to give their names as references.

⚜

The next year, 1994, I became a fellow of the American Psychiatric Association. That same year I was appointed to the fellowship committee of the New Jersey Psychiatric Association. The chairman retired. Now I was in the seat to accept or reject applications for fellowship in the APA. Since becoming a fellow, I have promoted several excellent South Asians to become fellows. The district branch fellowship committee has a meeting once a year, and we consider all applications. Whenever a well-qualified South Asian's application is being discussed, every member quietly looks toward me. I nod my head almost imperceptibly, and the application passes without much discussion. The wounds have not fully healed.

Some people in the APA did not let the subject go. Under pressure from some big chiefs, the APA held a referendum to reduce requirements for fellowship to what I had proposed. It was defeated by a slim margin. However, the APA later changed the requirements. Those who fulfilled their previous requirements were called distinguished fellows, and others with minimal qualifications were given plain fellowship. Psychiatrists, the elitists! Two categories of fellowship!

Now I am a distinguished life fellow of the APA. This title and three dollars will get me a cup of coffee at Starbuck's. However, this whole episode does show that (a) discrimination is alive and well in America, but (b) only in America can a foreign little country doctor shake the foundations of a powerful organization like the APA with his pen and bring about a change in the system.

I proudly display my fellowship honor.

PART EIGHT

Community Leader and Social Critic

35

Cure for Shyness:
The Kiwanis Club of Montville

Contrary to popular belief, I am not a very social person. I lack the art of making small talk, although some people think I am the life of the party. I can be in front of hundreds of people, giving a lecture, and can mesmerize them with my anecdotes and jokes. And later, I do not feel comfortable in one-on-one conversation. I believe I have learned from the Montville Kiwanis Club the ability to conquer stage fright and act confidently in large groups.

Dr. Sunil Shah is a neighbor in Montville and also a colleague at a hospital. A gentle soul, Dr. Shah is one of the best human beings I have met in my life. He is strict in his principles, frugal in nature, a religious Hindu, a vegetarian, a philanthropist, helpful to everyone. He is an ear, nose, and throat surgeon. He has opened a charitable clinic in his village in India. He told me one day in 1978 that he belonged to a local service club and would like me to come to attend a meeting as his guest. I had never heard of the Kiwanis Club before. He explained to me that it was a community service club just like a Rotary Club or Lions Club. I still did not understand it, because in my mind you joined these clubs by giving large donations as they did in India; there, only the elite could join them, like joining a country club here. But I accepted his invitation to attend the meeting—and I was hooked right away.

A bunch of people sat around, eating and drinking, and talking about helping people in the community. This was an entirely new concept for me. And they were all jokesters. I felt comfortable, as if I belonged there; one more jokester couldn't hurt. Joe, Tony, and John—and Fred, Tom, and Jordan—it seemed like I had come home. Almost everybody who was anybody in Montville was a member. (Well, all the men, anyway. Several years later they started having women members too.) They were having fun while helping the community. You did not have to pay enormous dues, and you did not have to know somebody in high places to join. I joined and I never looked back. My sense of humor and self-deprecatory jokes were helpful.

A few years later I became the treasurer, then the secretary, then the vice president, and ultimately the president. We did a lot of social and volunteer work. I learned the concept of community service, involvement in social affairs, and the idea of giving back something to the society that had given me so much. And having my picture in the local newspapers and published interviews, and my name in the news about the community work, did not hurt. I also helped write the newsletter for the club.

The notion of community service was not taught in India in my day. Here, everybody understands the concept. In my town you cannot graduate from high school unless you do a certain number of hours of community service. Back home, if some rich person was distributing blankets to the poor, it was thought he must be running in the next election and was doing the good deed to assure votes for himself.

As an offshoot to the Kiwanis Club, I joined the Montville Fourth of July Committee and Montville Board of Health, and I became an officer in those organizations. I organized the Fourth of July parade and sold glow sticks during the fireworks. I did so much work that I, an Indian, was given the coveted award of citizen of the year in the conservative Morris County town of Montville in 1991. It was probably the finest day of my life. Joe O'Dowd introduced me: "Here is one immigrant who is giving back to this country more than this country gave him." A number of people asked me if I wanted to run for the township council and eventually become the mayor. No, I said, enough was enough.

One reason why I stopped some of my social and community activities was a couple of comments I heard or overheard from friends who thought I was directly or indirectly profiting from these activities. For sure, a few people do profit from membership in service organizations, but generally the people in there are unselfish, and they do a lot of altruistic work purely from the goodness of their hearts. They donate their time, energy, and money. In return they get inner happiness, pure joy. At least that was my only motivation. Two friends, one Indian and the other Italian American, asked me casually on separate occasions how much

I was making under the table from being the vice president of our board of health. Surely these are misguided people, but I wonder how many others think that way.

The leadership skills I learned from my friends in the Kiwanis Club came in handy for a number of other endeavors I've undertaken. I started Diwali Day in my hospital. It was later dubbed India Day. Once a year we doctors and employees dressed up in Indian clothes, had a festival of Indian music and dance, and served Indian food to the whole hospital. Years later, I helped start Eid Day in the hospital to commemorate the Muslim heritage. I also started an annual India Day in my town, and for the county. After getting encouragement, we had similar annual programs for our Hindu temple and for other associations.

✦

One Sunday in 1985, Dr. Rajinder Kapila and his wife, Bina, had invited some old classmates from our medical school. We were sitting in their backyard, chatting and reminiscing about the good old days of Maulana Azad Medical College in Delhi. Somebody brought up the topic of starting an alumni association in America, and meeting for a reunion. The whole thought was far-fetched. Altogether, we knew fewer than twenty Maulanians in America. Various ideas were being tossed around in a totally nonchalant way. Maybe if we wrote to these few people we knew, they could contact other people from the college, and the association would grow. "Jagdish has the power of the pen, and he can bring us all together," said Bina Kapila. I was given the task of looking into it.

That was the birth of MAMCOAANA, Maulana Azad Medical College Alumni Association of North America.

I wrote a letter to a few people, maybe seventeen. Soon my second letter was sent to thirty-five. And then to fifty-five. The letters were getting longer and more flowery, with old tidbits about the college life, and in 1985 I planned our first reunion in Mount Airy Lodge, about two hours from my house. About seventeen families came to attend for the weekend; some flew from long distances. We had a good time. The rest, as they say, is history. We have had reunions every year, in every corner of America and Canada. The newsletters are regular and longer, there are more than a thousand life members, and up to two hundred families come together for a long weekend for the annual reunion. A lot of fun and frolic. It now continues under the leadership of younger Maulanians. During these reunions I often talk about how miserable my life was during those five years of medical college. They ask me, then, how come I was so enthusiastic in starting the association. I don't know. Blame the Kiwanis Club; they infuse enthusiasm into you, for anything. Blame my penchant for writing.

⚜

During the late 1980s the department of psychiatry at Barnert Hospital was having a morale problem. The chairman was no help; he had actually created the problem by micromanaging and offering severe criticism of everybody. The social worker, the nursing supervisor, and some other key staff members were leaving. The president and CEO, Fred Lang, asked me to take over the

267

chairmanship. He was persistent, and I took the job on a part-time basis "until we find the regular chairman." That was nearly twenty years ago, and I remained the part-time chairman until 2008. Slowly I reduced my involvement in private practice and started taking interest in the larger affairs of the hospital. I was a board member and was active in every important committee of the hospital. No wonder I never made the kind of money I could have: I was busy with administrative tasks of the hospital and the department of psychiatry.

Like every other doctor, I used to hate meetings . . . when I was a doctor. Then I became more a teacher and an administrator, and I started liking those "damn" meetings.

Becoming the president of the medical staff was costly in many ways. My private practice suffered, and my family saw less of me. I also became less actively involved in community service. A few doctors were quite vocal; they had never seen a psychiatrist in the position of the chief of "real doctors." Also, when I was instrumental in bringing action against a couple of bad doctors, they went ballistic and insulted me publicly. Some of the Indian doctors were my worst critics. I did what I had to do and stuck to my guns. Action was taken against impaired physicians and some who ignored the quality of patient care. I became a real leader, popular in some circles and hated in others.

⚜

I started some innovative programs in hospitals and nursing homes, for which I was generously rewarded—and awarded. The

Home Health Assembly of New Jersey honored me as its home health physician of the year, and the Passaic County Medical Society honored me as its physician of the year. A surprise came when I was the only honoree at Barnert Hospital's black-tie gala in 2002. It was a festive affair attended by several hundred people, and my whole family and I were flying high. Later, the New Bridge Mental Health Center honored me in its gala, and I didn't even work there; I was becoming universal. The National Alliance of Mental Illness (NAMI) honored me several times. Now that I am old, and a has-been, the Mental Health Association in Passaic County gave me its Growth Award, which felt like a lifetime achievement award, and an invitation to start thinking about retirement.

I have been asked to take some very coveted state and national positions in my profession which I declined; I never thought I deserved all those honors or positions, but it felt good to be offered them. At times I also felt that the state and the country were not ready to accept a foreign-looking person in those high positions. Maybe it is just my paranoia, but there is no dearth of hypocrites who would encourage you to get to the top and then make your life miserable. Yes, I have witnessed it myself. Also, I believe I lacked the ambition and drive to go higher than I did.

I consider myself a kingmaker, not a king. I have some sort of complex; I believe I am not worth it, or that I cannot fulfill the responsibility of high office. I even refused to take the presidency of my small Hindu temple. I believe I have had more importance in my life than I deserve, and I am scared of more. (I must need a good psychiatrist to analyze me!)

❧

I have had a mission to help people, in my own way. Quietly. I have helped so many psychiatrists start their private practice. I often invite young doctors for lunch and discuss with them their options in terms of an office practice, job, or hospital practice. They love it because I pay for lunch and give free advice; it's a hobby. I discuss where they should have an office, what kind of patients to expect initially, how many, and when. I tell them which hospitals to join, where the money is, where they will get more name and fame. In the beginning I let them use my office address and my answering service, so they don't incur any expenses before they start earning some dough. I tell them not to depend only on their practice until they are established, but to have a part-time job to bring home the bacon. I remember my mistakes and remind young doctors not to repeat them. My wife and some of my close friends have warned me time and again that the same people I give advice to will turn around and stab me in the back, take away my job or my patients, or talk bad about me to others. But I don't listen. And as far as I know, nobody really has stabbed me in the back in any major way.

I give the Kiwanis Club of Montville and my friends there much of the credit for bringing out the leadership in me, a person who suffered from an inferiority complex for the first half of his life.

36

My Perspective on the American Health-Care Crisis

The other day a conservative radio talk-show host was proclaiming, "We have the best health-care system in the world." I don't know what he was smoking, but I submit that he was dead wrong. Our health-care system in America is not just leaking, it is broken. Most Americans agree that it is in crisis, and something needs to be done NOW.

No one profession is to blame. The whole system has run amok. Ever-advancing medical procedures, politicians, lawyers, health-care workers, hospitals, health maintenance organizations (HMOs), and clergy—all have played a role in the dizzying spiral of costs. There have been great strides in some surgical procedures, in reducing strokes with some marvelous medication interventions, in treating cancer and in psychiatric drugs, but in my opinion, the high cost of health care cannot take credit for that.

I have been practicing medicine in this country for more than forty years. I have been a clinician, a teacher, and an administrator.

I have chaired bioethics committees and all the important committees in hospitals and nursing homes. I have been on the policy-making end of some very important organizations, and have seen how difficult it is to bring about reform. I have known unethical health-care workers and administrators and have known of deals being made behind the scenes in medical and psychiatric societies. I don't have all the answers, but I have some insight into the complexity of the problems.

⚜

According to the National Coalition on Health Care, the cost of health care in the United States was $2.3 trillion in 2007, or 16 percent of our gross domestic product (GDP). It is projected to be $4.3 trillion in 2016, or 20 percent of GDP. More than half of Medicare dollars are spent on patients who die within two months. One percent of the population accounts for 25 percent of the nation's health-care expenses, and 45 percent of all the health-care expenses are paid by government sources. Our per capita spending on health care is double that of France, Australia, or Canada, and two and a half times that of England or Japan. Granted, our life expectancy has increased, but not more than in other peer countries. Our life expectancy and freedom from misery are no better than in other developed countries. The administrative costs of health care in the United States are six times more than some other countries. Much of that is attributable to burdensome government regulations.

I submit that a significant reason why we like to prolong life and misery is greed and self-motivation. The hospitals, long-term-care facilities, doctors, lawyers, religious organizations, pharmaceutical companies, medical appliance manufacturers, and even the families (the government pays for health care of terminally sick patients) are all trying to prolong life and prolong miserable existence for financial reasons, directly or indirectly.

⚜

I have seen firsthand that unnecessary procedures and tests, and unscrupulous hospitalizations, are disturbingly common. Hospitals pay the doctors to bring more and more patients to the hospital. It is illegal and unethical, but there are loopholes. Hospitals need more patients in order to survive. In the 1980s hospitals kept expanding, building more beds. Now they have empty beds, and many hospitals have closed or consolidated. To attract more patients they start newer, fancier programs, bringing better and more advanced technology as doctors demand it: heart surgeries, cancer specialization, gastric bypasses, and so on. These specialized services need fancy and expensive equipment, and marketing. Health-care costs keep rising.

Mammography has become routine for women and endoscopy for everyone; so many people are having angioplasty. We don't know how much morbidity or mortality has been reduced by that, or *increased* by that. One study indicated that all those angioplasties had no effect on the final outcome. Yet they are still being performed in large numbers. As a matter of fact, as soon as doctors see problems, they don't advise waiting even for a day; who knows what may happen between now and tomorrow. (On the other hand, if the doctor has to go to his child's Little League game or all the operating rooms are occupied, the procedure can be postponed until tomorrow, or Monday.) Procedures bring money. And if the procedure is not done in a timely manner, you may hear from the lawyer. I wonder how many angioplasties would not be needed if the insurance company refused to pay for them. We are a procedure-happy society; we don't like it if a doctor says that the procedure is not necessary—so the doctor usually doesn't say that.

It is common for a doctor to order several consultations, and then for those consultants to call that doctor in return when they need his or her specialty. I am not saying all the consultations are unnecessary, but I believe that many could be avoided. Some of the reason may be because we practice defensive medicine, but the other is simple greed. More consultations cause an increase in the length of stay in the hospital, more tests, more procedures, more medicines, more side effects, and more complications. The health-care costs keep rising. Please note that there is no mention of the patient's wishes or true best interests in this equation.

❧

Some time ago, the recommended upper limit of blood cholesterol was 250. Then it was lowered to 200. Now they talk about 150. How much was that influenced by the pharmaceutical companies and availability of newer anticholesterol drugs? We will never know. They will also bring up triglycerides, A, B, C, whatever. Almost half of my elderly patients are on anticholesterol drugs. Why? In a recent, hugely attended national conference, the speaker was saying that all diabetics should be on anticholesterol drugs even if their cholesterol tests and all other tests are normal. The conference gave doctors CME (continued medical education) credits for free and was sponsored by pharmaceutical companies. I have been saying for years that most of this ever-increasing cholesterol hype is a fraud, and I believe someday the medical community (and the pharmaceutical companies) will agree with that—when insurance companies stop paying for those drugs or when the patents of those drugs run out.

Somebody decided to raise the bar on anemia too. Now more people are considered anemic with the same amount of hemoglobin that they had a year ago because the drug companies have new, expensive drugs for anemia they are promoting extensively.

By the way, this CME system for doctors is another scam in the health-care system, motivated by greed. In New Jersey you need fifty CME credits each year just to renew your medical license, and some companies are making a bundle by giving the credits for money for attending "educational" activities of doubtful value. In addition, in 2008–2009 you will not be able to renew your New Jersey medical license unless you do some extra hours of CME in "diversity" training. I wonder who lobbied for that, and who is going to profit by teaching diversity sensitivity to doctors.

It is now becoming increasingly clear that pharmaceutical

companies are sponsoring and supporting much of the medical research, and paying the doctors involved in the research, on the side. They pay doctors to attend their presentations, sometimes at exotic resorts, where they wine them and dine them to the hilt. They call them their consultants, or speakers, or associates, or thought leaders, or whatever. This practice has decreased quite a bit since the pharmaceutical companies made a new code of ethics. However, it is still going on with sugarcoated names. I believe that if a drug company invites fifteen doctors to a posh restaurant for dinner and pays good money for food and drinks and a speaker and trinkets, it recoups all that if just one doctor writes two extra prescriptions the next day for the drug company's antipsychotic or antidepressant medication. The return on investment is probably much higher in the case of medicines for high blood pressure, high cholesterol, gastric acidity, fibromyalgia, or glaucoma.

Recently another scheme came to light in which manufacturers of prosthetics for knee and hip replacement were paying up to half a million dollars a year to orthopedists using their product. The more procedures a doctor performed, the more he or she would get from the prosthetic manufacturer. In the good old USA, a major research project on CT scans for lung cancer can be sponsored by the tobacco industry and the CT scan machine manufacturer, published in the peer review journals, and become a state-of-the-art treatment model for lung cancer.

⚜

The popularity of a new, expensive drug does not necessarily depend on its efficacy or lack of side effects. More often than not, it is due to the quality of marketing. A drug was approved for a seizure type of condition. It is being used for a host of neurological, psychiatric, and pain conditions. The pharmaceutical company is reaping the benefits. Most doctors do not know its mode of action or approved indication, but they are prescribing it anyway, for conditions ranging from headache to bipolar disorder. I believe the company paid a major fine (mere pocket change for the large company) for promoting it for unapproved conditions. That did not matter really, because the doctors' habits had already formed; the company did not need to promote it anymore. And to make it a bigger coup, the company made the pill only in 100-milligram dose, and the usual dose was from 900 to 3,000 milligrams a day.

Numerous medications come in several doses—for example, 25-milligram tablets all the way up to 500-milligram tablets. The company will promote it to start at 25 milligrams twice a day, and slowly keep increasing it to 500 milligrams to 800 milligrams a day. The FDA insists on starting low. The 25-milligram tablet costs just slightly less than the 200-milligram tablet. You do the math, and calculate the profits of the drug companies. There are so many examples in psychiatric medications; there must be many more in other specialties.

In nursing homes, tremendous abuse of medications is prevalent. An eighty-year-old patient is started on an antacid, twice a day, and it continues forever, at twelve dollars a day—just because he had heartburn one night and the nurse woke up the doctor. Who has not had heartburn in his life? I once asked that question, and was reminded that if the doctor stopped the medicine and patient got stomach bleeding, no lawyer would defend him.

If a patient takes too many medicines, that increases not only the cost but also the side effects and bad reactions. It is said that if you take six medications, chances are that you will end up in the emergency room within six months. An average patient in a nursing home takes more than that every day.

Newer psychiatric medications are approximately ten times more expensive than the old ones. The drug companies say they have fewer side effects. Do they really? If you use the older medication and the patient gets side effects, get ready to defend yourself in a court of law; you may not get malpractice insurance next year. New medicines are "the standard of care."

⁂

A while ago the medical staff at my hospital was discussing a new designer antibiotic, which could be given only in cases of sepsis when at least one body system had failed. It had to be started within three hours of diagnosis, and the drug company was pleased to supply the drug within that time period. The survival rate was 6 percent more than with our older, considerably cheaper antibiotics. The cost: $36,000 for three days. The argument was put forth that usually the doctor did not even see the patient in a community hospital within that time frame, and if one system had already failed, the patient's quality of life would be very poor even

278

if he or she survived. Doctors objected; they insisted that we had to have access to that antibiotic; what about the liability?

Patients are being kept alive in the name of "dignity of human life." At this time "quality of life" has lost all meaning; it is the *quantity* of life we care for. We talk some gibberish of "culture of life" and "culture of death" in the same breath and want to prolong the dying and increase the suffering. A prematurely born one-pound baby kept alive makes a big headline. A patient may be in a deep coma, have contractures and bedsores, and have tubes in every orifice of the body for artificial breathing and feeding and waste removal, but be kept "alive" nonetheless for months or even years. We physicians have made people believe that everything can be cured with modern technology; we don't have to die. And if we die, our loved ones should hire a lawyer and sue. Many times we doctors care more about how we write the chart than how the patient is doing. After all, the attorneys, the health insurance companies, family members, and state inspectors are going to look at our notes, not the patient. In my circles there is a popular saying, "If you didn't document, you didn't do it." So if you documented good care, you provided it. Right?

I have been called to see a forty-two-year-old stockbroker who is quadriplegic. She has been unable to move any limb for several years, has her neck extended, has a urinary catheter and a feeding tube, keeps her eyes open even when sleeping, and has no speech. Yet when she was found tearing, her physician called me to rule out depression and see if she needed antidepressant medication. I had to see the patient but could not communicate with her. I saw no evidence of depression, and she did not need antidepressants (at the cost of fourteen dollars a day) which might compromise her metabolism further. If the primary physician had not called me or I had not seen the patient promptly, we might have heard from the family or their attorney.

Once our bioethics committee met with the family of an eighty-four-year-old, brain-dead woman to discuss the possibility of discontinuing artificial life supports. Two children were there in the room; a third was on the speakerphone from California. They started arguing with one another about whether the tubes should be taken out. They had not seen each other for many years, and at least one had not had a relationship with the mother since he was in his twenties. The primary physician walked out of the meeting after fifteen minutes because he had a procedure to perform. We ended up doing nothing until God decided for us, and she died in three days.

Hospitals try not to let you pull the plug. Their excuse: lawyers. Another comatose patient had a valid advance directive (a living will saying she did not want to be kept alive artificially), but the primary doctor refused to let her "die" for reason of his religious beliefs. It took weeks to find another doctor to take over the case, and for the hospital lawyer to review it and give his permission to go ahead. We in America care for each human life, not the costs; we extended her life and her coma for weeks.

Another family consisting of three siblings in a similar case was urging us to hurry up and pull the plug. A little investigation showed that there were millions of dollars involved, being eaten up in their mother's care in the hospital.

Some families call me to inquire how come their relative in the hospital or in the nursing home is not on antidepressant medication. They also suggest that I am withholding the medicine because the government (Medicaid) does not want to pay for it. They even remind me that if I don't prescribe an antidepressant, I will hear from their lawyer.

I have a patient in her eighties, obese and diabetic. I have been seeing her for depression and insomnia. She had pain in her abdomen, went to the emergency room, saw her physician, and had an extensive workup done, including a CT scan. At her next appointment with me she asked if she had a case to sue her doctor because he did not order an MRI.

I suggest that a main reason for our ever-increasing health-care costs is that we are getting *too much* health care. According to a recent article by Shannon Brownlee ("Why Does Health Care Cost So Much?" *AARP Magazine*, July–August 2008), Americans spend $500 billion to $700 billion annually on unnecessary care, largely because doctors are afraid of being sued if they don't order all those tests. Furthermore, according to Elliott Fisher, MD, a noted Dartmouth researcher, unnecessary care leads to the deaths of as many as 30,000 Medicare recipients annually. We spend more than $16 billion a year on spinal fusion for acute back pain, even though there has never been a rigorous government-funded clinical trial showing that the surgery is superior to other methods of relieving back pain. According to some reliable sources, a whopping 50 percent of surgeries, tests, and procedures are not backed by scientific evidence.

⚜

Corporations are trying to refuse to give medical insurance or are charging exorbitant amounts in premiums and co-pays. More and more people in the country are uninsured. They go to the emergency rooms, which cannot refuse treatment because of the government regulation, thus usurping resources—and legitimate emergencies get neglected, or their treatment is delayed. Government regulations, the Joint Commission on the Accreditation of Healthcare Organizations (JCAHO), and other agencies increase expenses exponentially in the name of quality of care.

An individual who wants "good" health insurance pays more than $10,000 a year, in addition to all the deductibles, the co-pays, and many other expenses. God help him if he needs insurance for the whole family. How many working-class Americans can afford to have personal health insurance? And how many people are stuck in jobs that make them miserable (which, by the way, is not good for their mental or physical health) because that is the only way to get reasonable health insurance?

Poonam fell and broke the lower end of her femur. The orthopedic surgeon was with the patient for a total of less than three hours during the whole procedure. (Follow-up was done at the hospital by residents.) His fee: over $25,000. Thank God, the hospital was in our network, or we might have lost our house. Yet for some strange reason, preoperative doctors at the hospital got paid separately and were out of our network. How come? We ended up paying for part of the emergency-room services, fees for several doctors and other professionals, and co-pays and deductibles. What a system! And we had insurance; imagine if we hadn't.

A hospital may send a bill for $50,000 and accept $9,000 from an insurance company as full payment. If the patient had no insurance and had a house, the hospital collection agency would place a lien on the house. Why does a doctor send a bill for $5,000 when he knows that the insurance is going to pay $1,000 or less?

❧

Recently I was giving a lecture, and in answer to a question I reminded the audience that Medicaid paid me $19 for half an hour of work when I started practice in 1972. It still pays me the same amount for half an hour of work. Then I spent four-fifths of the time in seeing the patient and one-fifth in charting; now it is the other way around. Of course, I chose the example of the insurance company that pays the least. It has not increased the fee in more than thirty-five years.

My ophthalmologist friend was examining my eyes and lamenting at the same time. He had recently installed another high-tech machine in his office at a cost of more than a million dollars, and an HMO had just informed him that it was going to pay only $350 for a cataract operation. He pointed toward four or five young women working in his office, very expensive. He was planning to stop doing any cataract surgery; it didn't pay anymore to do that. There was a time when he was getting paid $1,500 for the same work. Then HMOs came, and Medicare clamped down on the fees, and the payment was reduced to $1,000, later to $750, and now to $450, which was okay, but the new rate of $350 was intolerable. HMO companies are making millions; their CEOs get annual compensation of millions of dollars. The more they reject the procedures for reimbursement or deny days of hospitalization, the more their compensation becomes. I ask, if a $450 fee is acceptable, then was the $1,500 a rip-off of the system?

Malpractice insurance premiums are out of sight. My friend the ear, nose, and throat specialist came in to see me one day and announced that he was retiring the next day. He had had a couple of malpractice suits, and his annual malpractice insurance premium was going to rise to $210,000, so he had decided to quit. He would have worked for three or more years but he would have to make at least a million dollars a year to keep his office open and pay his malpractice insurance. What a waste of talent and experience!

❦

I have been doing competency evaluations for guardianship for more than twenty years. It started with an occasional call from the Passaic County Adult Protective Services. When their dedicated social workers got stymied in their work by a senile or behaviorally difficult client who had no family or needed placement in a nursing home for his or her own safety, they would call me to go with them, examine the client, and certify whether he or she (let's call it a he) was competent to handle his own affairs. Then they would go in front of a judge and get a guardian appointed for him, for safety and placement of the demented person. Sometimes judges were satisfied with one doctor's affidavit; other times they wanted two. Usually they wanted the doctor to appear before them in the court and give testimony. Later they started relying on testimony by telephone. Now they generally just need the two doctors' certificates, no discussion with the doctor. The process has changed in many ways since those days.

It was a rare occurrence; I was doing it for fun. My fee was minimal; I believe I charged $200 for this service. It involved several telephone calls, visiting the patient at home (sometimes far-off places in Passaic County), typing an affidavit, notarizing it, and mailing it within a certain period of time. I enjoyed it; I was making friends with the social workers. It was also an excuse to make new contacts for referral. Also, it felt like I was doing community service. For the last few years, though, competencies have become a big and lucrative business. Sometimes it seems like there is an epidemic of Alzheimer's disease. Even though I do less than half of what some other psychiatrists do, it still keeps me quite busy. Lawyers in the area have discovered me, and I get calls from them frequently. My fee is anywhere from $500 to $850. I keep raising it every year. (Greed!) About one in six attorneys does not pay. I don't send the bills to the collection agency; I don't complain to the bar association. I do nothing. I know one psychiatrist who charges from $1,800 to $3,500 and collects her fee in advance before she will go to a patient's home for evaluation.

There is another psychiatrist who claims to be a forensic specialist and charges by the hour, $500 per hour. If these figures are horrifying you, let me mention here that psychiatrists make the lowest annual wages of all the medical specialties. I hire board-certified psychiatrists in the clinic at $80 an hour, sometimes a little more. And plenty of them are available at that rate. On the other hand, when we have to hire other specialists, wages are much higher, almost unmentionable, especially for those doctors who do surgical, endoscopic, or any other procedures. HMOs and government insurance companies pay for procedures, not for evaluations and medication prescriptions. Because the "procedure" doctors make more money, lawyers are always looking for cases to sue them, and their malpractice insurance premiums are sky high. And the health-care costs keep going up.

In my home-visit business I have witnessed many interesting cases. Elder abuse by families and children is not uncommon; it may be physical abuse, or emotional or financial abuse or just total neglect. Then there is the self-neglect, especially in demented patients. A frail woman was living in a shack in a remote area, with no running water or electricity. She owned several acres of premium land surrounding her house, worth at least 2 million dollars. Another elderly woman had more than thirty cats she was feeding, and the neighboring kids were buying cat food for her; she probably ate some of that food herself. She gave the kids large sums of money for the cat food. She was senile and did not know her age but could name most of her cats. The visiting social worker had discovered large amounts of cash hidden around the house. I have seen old people living in houses where not an inch of floor or their body was visible because of cockroaches. I have seen stale, maggot-infested food being eaten.

Once a retired doctor called the police on me, and I had to go through the interrogation of policemen to prove that I was not trespassing, that I was there merely to evaluate his competency, on advice of a lawyer. A social worker was with me to vouch for that, thank God. An old man had his large, expensive house full of old magazines and newspapers, almost five feet high; he insisted that one day he was going to read them and then throw them away. A woman had sent all her savings to an offshore lottery outfit because she was convinced that she had won a million dollars, and was eagerly waiting for the mail; she had no money left to buy food.

Sometimes when I see a patient on request of an attorney and tell him that in my opinion the patient is competent, the attorney gets so mad at me that he either does not pay for my services or needs three reminders before he does. In other instances, when I call a lawyer and tell him that in my opinion the patient is competent, he tells me not to send in the report and not to bill him; he will send me my fee. Presumably this attorney hopes to find another psychiatrist who will agree with him and call the patient incompetent. I believe he will find somebody.

᳀᳀᳀

Many years ago, our local medical society had invited a prominent television personality to train our officers on how to give interviews on radio and television. With a lot of fuss, he was telling us some do's and don'ts. At last he asked us to say one important sentence, to impress the viewers. He liked mine; I was the sole foreign-looking officer in the studio. I said something like, "If I had to get a serious illness, I would rather get it in the United States than anywhere else." That was then and it was probably true; now we are behind many countries, even some of the developing nations.

Discussion of universal health care or national health insurance was a taboo until recently. If it is discussed, doctors and lawyers and all the concerned parties vehemently object. Why? The fear that their incomes would go down to the levels of doctors and lawyers in England and Canada.

Is universal health care the answer? Is it feasible in America? Some sort of universal health care has to happen here if we are going to make any sense of health care in this country. Not necessarily the British type or Canadian type, but maybe a unique American style of universal health care—market driven, whatever that means. In my opinion a single-payer system of universal health care may also work here. It will probably bring in two-tier care (where the very rich will go abroad for care, maybe to India or Thailand), but that would be better than the present many-tier care system (where everybody is doing his own thing).

Universal health care and government-supported care bring something like socialism to mind, and that word is a taboo for us Americans. We forget that our government is already messing up the health-care system with Medicare, Medicaid, and numerous regulations. Every time I bring up the topic of possible universal health care, somebody in the audience says, "It will never happen in this country; pharmaceutical companies and lawyers spend too much money on lobbyists." H. L. Mencken said that under democracy, a good politician is as unthinkable as an honest burglar. It is probably much worse in nondemocratic societies, so let's not blame democracy.

We Americans are spoiled when it comes to health care. We want the best care, we want it now, and we want it free. Yet some measured rationing of health care is not necessarily a bad thing if it can help prevent some of the egregious inequities of the system we have now.

37

How Not to Kill
Medical Institutions

In this chapter I would like to give two specific examples of the decline of once-thriving medical institutions: Passaic County Medical Society and Barnert Hospital. Both cases were unnecessary, both were a loss to the community, and both illustrate some of the problems that bedevil our health-care system as a whole.

꩜

Passaic County Medical Society (PCMS) is an important component of the Medical Society of New Jersey (MSNJ), the oldest state medical society in the United States, founded in 1766. I joined PCMS in 1972 and never quit.

When I started private practice, it was mandatory to belong to the local medical society before you could apply for privileges in a hospital. So the medical societies were a thriving business. Some time later, this requirement was ruled unconstitutional, and membership in medical societies started dwindling. Indians in general, and Indian medical doctors in particular, did not voluntarily join organizations and societies; they just did not see any return for their membership fee. I myself was always questioning why I was continuing the membership when not too many other Indians stayed for long. As a psychiatrist, I was probably making the least amount of money compared to other "real" doctors, and the membership was expensive. Also, like the hospitals, medical societies treated psychiatrists as stepchildren. But I continued. I even became a county delegate and attended their annual meetings at steep cost. There was a time when I was the only Indian in a sea of delegates. And, of course, I was thoroughly ignored.

It was much later that Indians understood the need to become part of the system of organized medicine. Curiously, either they would not join a particular association, or if they joined they wanted to know how soon they would be elevated to its presidency. In the 1960s and 1970s Indian doctors had no chance of reaching the top in almost any national association, or even in a state society. The high positions were being passed around from one white man to another. It was the same with residencies in desired specialties, or professorships and tenures. The situation has not changed much even now.

In the 1980s the New York/New Jersey/Philadelphia area had an influx of Indian doctors—just by sheer number they were being counted in local circles. They looked different, and some of them were becoming activists. They were making demands and at times were being heard. In some parts of the country, conditions for their acceptance were really bad. It is only recently that they are being recognized as almost equal.

In the 1990s there was a revolt by Indian doctors in the Northeast. They started throwing their weight around, looking for the chairmanship of departments and important committees in the hospitals, and in medical societies. They did make some inroads, especially in small community hospitals, but generally they did not gain the recognition they felt they deserved. One fateful day they decided that they had to take over PCMS. There were enough Indian doctor members, and nobody cared about them. More of them joined. One Indian doctor ran for the presidency, and all the Indians showed up for voting. Many saw the office of the society for the first time. More and more of them kept coming and voting; the society offices looked different that day. The Indian doctors won a hard-fought battle.

As a side effect of this victory, however, the energetic white doctors withdrew their support, resigned from important committee positions, and stopped coming to meetings—and some actually resigned—thus hurting the pocketbook of the society. Now their revolt was almost as visible as that of the Indians. Attendance at the meetings and the infectious enthusiasm of the meetings before the new Indian president sank lower and lower. There were other reasons too for the slide of the society, but I believe that was a momentous day. As the years went by, more Indian and Middle Eastern doctors took up important positions. PCMS almost declared bankruptcy, and I watched. I was a member of the executive committee during the whole time, becoming vice president and then refusing to become its president. The struggling organization is now trying to regain its clout, but the glorious days of the past are over.

⤜⦿⤛

Barnert Hospital opened in 1908 as a small clinic in the then-thriving city of Paterson, New Jersey, as a sanctuary for Jewish doctors who were denied privileges in some other hospitals only on the basis of their religion. Jewish patients also had difficulty getting admission into the hospitals existing at the time. Barnert continued to cater mostly to Jewish doctors and patients, thriving and expanding until the 1970s. Until recently, it was the only kosher hospital in North Jersey.

In 1991 I gave a lecture at Wayne General Hospital. After the talk, a well-known old-time gynecologist came to me and asked, "Did I hear correctly, Dr. Dang, that you are the chairman of psychiatry at Barnert Hospital?"

"Yes, Dr. Giannini, you heard it right; I became the chairman about two years ago."

"Hey, I have heard that Barnert is a totally Jewish hospital; they don't even give privileges to non-Jews. And you don't look like a Jew to me."

I smiled. "They are experimenting on me." The truth is that by 1990, fewer than 20 percent of Barnert's active doctors were Jewish.

The other hospital in Paterson, St. Joseph's, is much larger than Barnert. It is Catholic in name and in spirit but has very few

293

Catholic doctors and patients anymore. These two Paterson hospitals had a long-term rivalry going on, partly religious and partly financial. As described earlier, when I set up my private practice in 1972, I got admitting privileges at both these hospitals, but later my supervisor at St. Joseph's told me that I could not belong to both; I had to give one up. He gave me several flimsy reasons. That is why there is a hiatus in my Barnert Hospital privileges, when I left it for a while to stay at the bigger institution. Major hospitals in North Jersey kept Indian doctors out as long as they could. As I found when I was struggling to start a practice, they made excuses like board certification, office within three miles of the hospital, department closed for new members, and so on. It was especially true for prestigious departments like orthopedics and cardiac surgery. However, small community hospitals could not make those excuses, they needed doctors and patients, and Indian doctors came in droves. And the white doctors started leaving. I watched with horror. Then the Middle Eastern doctors arrived. Cliques formed. Cross-consultations increased, as did hospital length of stay.

In the 1970s the Paterson demographic landscape changed. Jewish families kept leaving, replaced by African Americans and Hispanics. Jewish doctors also started quitting at Barnert. In addition to the foreign doctors coming and white doctors leaving, the mix of patients changed too. Uninsured patients became the norm rather than the exception. Most of the patients were Medicaid, Medicare, and charity. The state refused to pay reasonable dollars for charity care even though it passed laws requiring hospitals to care for patients who could not pay. In addition, the billing practices of the administration left a lot to be desired. The board of trustees fell asleep at the switch. St. Joseph's was not happy with the competition and kept pulling its strings with the state regulators.

Meanwhile, as described earlier, hospitals all over the country had overexpanded in the 1980s and now had excessive beds; the state decided that some hospitals had to close. In the 1990s, when other hospitals were consolidating and merging, we looked for a buyer. Somehow nothing happened. The board decided to change the administration. CEOs came and CEOs left, and the hospital kept getting into the hole, which grew deeper with each passing year. Each administration blamed the previous one for its problems; and that administration blamed the doctors, who in turn decided that it was all the fault of the board. Barnert Hospital declared bankruptcy in August 2007. Suddenly one Friday we were told that the hospital was closing the following Monday. The same evening the state said it had made a mistake; the hospital would close in two months. But people read big headlines in the newspapers about the hospital closing, so the damage had been done. Employees started looking for other jobs, patients were reluctant to come to the hospital, and doctors were afraid to bring in new patients.

The hospital stayed open for almost six more months, but it was always touch-and-go. It was a farce. Expensive consultants, accountants, and lawyers kept giving conflicting messages; every Monday there was a new rumor of the institution closing that

Friday. Every day the newspapers were filled with news of the hospital closing or not closing—even partial closing was a possibility. The state made it clear that it was not ready to help, the Housing and Urban Development Corporation wanted to cash in its loans and bonds, the bankruptcy judge was getting confusing reports from the attorneys, and the other hospital across town wanted to take over the hospital, but for free. Skirmishes among the medical executive board, the administration, and the hospital board were becoming openly hostile. This drama went on for months. I was in the thick of it, one of two doctors in the so-called turnaround committee, made up of consultants, accountants, and lawyers. The turnaround never happened, and Barnert Hospital closed its doors on February 1, 2008.

A true community institution died that day, and residents of Paterson mourned.

38

With Justice or
Litigiousness for All?

Many people have asked me why I am always making fun of lawyers in my writings. Have I been really hurt by lawyers? No, I say I have been hurt by doctors, construction workers, financial advisors, insurance agents, but never by lawyers—so far, anyway. Then why?

One reason may be because they are so easy to make fun of. Everybody else does; why shouldn't I? I have worked with patients, families, doctors, lawyers, judges, police officers, and child protection agencies. I have inspected jails, state institutions, juvenile lockups, and group homes of various kinds. I know a little bit about the system.

My patients over the years have told me horror stories about the legal profession in America. Angus once said the American empire would be buried by lawyers, insurance companies, and paperwork; that was even before these three problems haunted the doctors. Maybe he had great foresight.

❦

A patient had an automobile-accident case. His attorney told him to take an extended leave from work, and later to go on permanent disability, physical and mental, to strengthen his case. He went to the offices of doctors, lawyers, physical therapists, psychiatrists; he made depositions, went to court hearings, and ultimately "won" his case. He brought me a newspaper clipping with the big news of his victory; he won about $500,000.

He actually got less than $80,000, however. The doctors, chiropractors, physical therapists—and his attorneys, who congratulated him on his "victory"—took the rest. This was after almost two years of following the legal profession's advice. After not working for a long time, he was not able to go back into the full-time job market and became a permanent cripple. Nevertheless, he won the case, yet he seemed to have lost everything. In my opinion his attorneys prolonged the case for many months, for the wrong reasons.

❦

Almost thirty years ago when I was working in a mental-health clinic, I went to appear in a court in Sussex County as an expert witness in a rape case. The girl who was allegedly raped was my patient. The courthouse was in the boondocks of New Jersey. After being sworn in, I was raked over the coals. It seemed like both the lawyers and the judge were against the girl who was raped, and against me, her psychiatrist. One of the lawyers picked

298

up a large book of psychiatry from his desk and asked me if I had read that book. Yes, I had; it was the standard textbook. "Now, doctor, can you tell me what is written on page 872?"

"No, sir, I don't know what chapter you are talking about."

"It deals with hallucinations."

"What about hallucinations?"

"Can you define hallucinations for me, doctor?"

After I defined the word, he said, "That's not what it says here."

That's it, he did not let me explain, just moved on to another question. He did not say it, but he was insinuating that the girl was hallucinating that she was raped.

My lawyer was trying to outdo the defense lawyer, and both were outdoing me. And they were outright insulting my patient, who was sitting there. I felt she was going through the process of rape again and again. Every time I looked toward the judge for help, she said, "Answer the question, doctor." After all, the judge was a lawyer too.

I was asked to come back after the lunch recess. I was exhausted and anxious. There were no cell phones back then, of course, so I asked around for a pay phone to cancel my afternoon appointments. I was directed toward the cafeteria. I entered the phone booth and was dialing my office when I saw the same two lawyers eating lunch, laughing with each other, toasting each other, like close friends; inside the court they looked like mortal enemies. I felt as if they were laughing at me and the poor girl who got caught in their legal web.

Recently I was in a court of law for a competency and guardian-ship proceeding. A homeless man had been hospitalized several times. I was called by a social-service agency to examine him in the hospital, and when I saw him he was in bad shape. Another psychiatrist and I certified that he was incapacitated. Many months later they discovered that he had inherited more than a million dollars, had the money, but chose to live like a home-less derelict. With money came newfound relatives, and so the case ended up in court. I was representing the social-service agency, and the homeless man was being represented by a court-appointed attorney who is a friend of mine. The man's family had a third set of attorneys. I was given an hour's notice to appear in court.

My lawyer friend came out of the courthouse and shook hands with me, saying, "It's always good to see you, Dr. Dang." She had frequently called me for her cases that needed guardian-ship examination.

Yet during cross-examination she asked me questions to try to discredit me, my qualifications, and my testimony, all at once. "You saw him in the hospital and drew your conclusions. Didn't you think it was important to visit his house and see its condition? Did you actually see him drunk? Did you think that seeing him once was enough?" It felt like my sister was asking me how come I was lying about my name and my religion. This attorney would never want me to visit the house of her client if I saw him in the hospital. And she would not want to pay for a second visit. She knows my credentials by heart.

A few days later I heard from the social worker, who asked the attorney why she was beating the hell out of me. She was told that my friend was just doing her job as an adversarial attorney, nothing against me. The attorney had to put some doubt in the mind of the judge so that the patient could be judged competent and could get hold of his money. Doubt about me, that is: my integrity and my testimony. Me, her friend and her associate. Some profession!

❧

Several times my patients have asked me to increase their disability on the advice of their counsel. If I refuse, their attorney tells them to change their psychiatrist, or refers them to his own. Ambulance chasing is not just fictional; I have actually met some ambulance chasers.

I was seeing a couple in therapy who had decided to divorce. They wanted a friendly divorce and had amicably decided this in terms of their substantial assets and custody of their son. That was until they saw their attorneys. Then it became a very ugly affair. At least three of their properties were sold, and they bought separate condos. Their child was tossed around among them and the grandparents. My guess is that at least nine attorneys made a small fortune in that process, and there was enormous psychosocial damage to the family during those tumultuous three years. Sadly, this is not an unusual case.

So many medical tests are being done because we are afraid of being sued. So much time and money is being spent in emergency rooms just to ward off lawsuits. So many children are being taken away from their families by the Division of Youth and Family Services (DYFS), not always because the children are truly in danger of abuse or neglect, but too often for fear of lawyers and judges. DYFS was instituted with good intentions and has prevented a lot of misery in children, but like so many other systems and organizations, it is crippled by regulations and a litigious society.

⚜

Most of the purposes for which psychiatric medications are being dispensed are illegal. It seems like the Food and Drug Administration (FDA) is somehow mixed up with the trial lawyers and the drug companies. Most of the drug studies are sponsored by the manufacturers of those drugs, and the FDA is aware of that. They approve or disapprove drugs, and indications for their use, as dictated by those companies. For example, the most prevalent symptom of psychiatric illness is agitation, and not a single drug has been approved for that symptom. If a drug is prescribed for agitation, it is called an off-label use; the trial lawyer will grill you unmercifully if you prescribe a drug for an off-label use for the most common psychiatric symptom and anything goes wrong.

Almost every drug for psychosis carries a black-box warning for use in the elderly and the demented, and every antidepressant has a black-box warning that it may trigger suicidal thoughts, even though its main use is in depressed and suicidal patients, and it usually alleviates depression rather than increases it. If I give an antipsychotic medication to a demented patient, I have to tell the patient and relatives that I am prescribing something that may cause stroke or death, and they are supposed to give me permission in writing to use it, and I have to document this exchange of information in detail, or I could get sued. The FDA quickly writes black-box warnings and gives trial lawyers a go-ahead to sue whoever is prescribing the medication for a patient's health and well-being. The procedures for approval of new drugs are so cumbersome and expensive that new drugs are unaffordable. Pharmaceutical companies don't even test most new drugs in children and pregnant women for fear of lawsuits and prohibitive costs of research in the present litigious conditions.

I can talk about psychiatric medications only; I am sure it is the same or worse with other, more expensive drugs. Just as a hair dryer must carry a warning not to use it in the shower, and a cup of takeout coffee has to warn the consumer that it is very hot, in the same way doctors have to do extra tests and write reams of papers cautioning patients about anything we do, for fear of lawyers, and in the name of protecting patients' rights. I am all for protecting the rights of the patient, but this too is going too far. Everything I do for the welfare of the patient, every word I write in the chart, has to be based on the fear that I might be sued, and this cannot help but influence my opinion of the legal profession.

A society cannot function if every thought and every deed of the doctors, patients, manufacturers, and professionals has to be directed by the lawyers.

❧

We are quick to point out corruption in the third-world countries. We forget that it happens in a major way in the good old USA. A burglar with a good lawyer could probably win a suit against a homeowner because there was no light on when he broke into the house and fell and got hurt. A murderer would probably be advised by his counsel to sue the gun manufacturer for making an accurate gun. One of these days all American newborns will be informed of their bill of rights, including the right to sue their parents for bringing them into this wretched world. . . .

❧

While Barnert Hospital declared bankruptcy and searched for a buyer, the case dragged on in the courts for months, as described in the last chapter. During this time we struggled to keep the hospital open while strapped for money. However, during the whole process we were paying an overwhelming number of lawyers: our bankruptcy lawyers, our buyer's lawyers for due diligence, lawyers for the lenders, lawyers for the heirs of Nathan Barnert (who started the community hospital a hundred years ago), lawyers for the secured and unsecured creditors, lawyers for the court-appointed ombudsman, and other unspecified lawyers.

❧

Once I called the attorney who had made my will; I had a question or two. He started asking me about my children and grandchildren and told me about his two "brats"—his sons whom he sometimes wanted to choke—and whether it was wise to take them to a psychiatrist. Suddenly I realized that the telephone call was getting very long. I asked him whether I was being charged for the time I was spending with him on the telephone. Of course, he said; the clocks in his office were synchronized with the telephones, and for every six minutes of call I was paying the firm one-tenth of their hourly rate. And I was discussing his "brats" and giving him psychiatric advice during that time.

My examples don't even come close to the horror stories I have heard from people in various other professions, and from nonprofessionals, who are being tormented by the need for legal compliance.

When you go to court even to pay for a minor traffic violation, you are treated like a career criminal. They have devised ways to reduce your charge if you pay an extra fee to the court, *through an attorney*. The attorneys all seem stressed out to keep the decorum of the court and to keep the cases moving. In spite of that, most Americans, including me, believe it is impossible to get swift justice in our courts. Inordinate prolonging of the cases smacks of greed. We need tort reform and some modification to the class-action suits. Most judges are political appointees cleared by the bar association, and many are, were, or will be partners in law firms representing big business in the court. Hardly anyone is representing the interests of the little guy. Many of the politicians are attorneys. There are too many lawyers; their ethics committee consists of lawyers, while there is not one doctor on the ethics committee of the New Jersey State Board of Medical Examiners.

❧

I have nothing against lawyers. By and large they are good people, and they have expenses too, like everybody else. They have to pay for their ex-spouses alimony, their children's college education, and their own yachts and small planes. And they have to pay their psychiatrists.

According to John Grisham, "Politics has always been a dirty game. Now justice is, too."

PART NINE

Indian and American

39

Exploring the
Vast American Landscape

I have always loved driving. Most people shun driving at night, but I truly enjoy it. In the early years most of us immigrants drove a lot, I more than others. I had more time than most doctors, and I did not mind spending money. As a matter of fact, spending excessively has been one of my weaknesses. I have never denied my immediate or extended family any reasonable request. During the oil crisis of 1970s, I often heard other doctors joking that the way I spent money, it looked like I had some oil wells back in India. During Kiwanis Club meetings, and the Fourth of July parade meetings, Irwin Pastor often remarked that I spent the club money as if I were spending my own. This notoriety followed me to my family too. Once my uncle Puran sat beside me and gave me a serious piece of advice that I should save some for a rainy day. I assured him not to worry; I had enough for emergencies.

When we lived in Massachusetts, Poonam and I took trips north to Canada and south all the way to Florida. Nearly every weekend we would go to New York, or Maine, or some place in between. From New Jersey we went to Boston or Washington, D.C., or Niagara Falls. We took many trips out West. We would fly to Colorado, rent a car, stay with the Glassmans for a day or two, and then drive north, south, or west. We planned trips each time in a different direction, booking motels (and later, hotels) and seeing the sights. We took a lot of pictures and made a lot of albums.

❧

The vastness of the American West fascinated me. One morning we left the motel carrying the sleeping children, settled them into the car, and started driving. They woke up around eight o'clock and were hungry. Unlike most Indians, we did not carry food with us during our travels. We drove and drove on the flat roads with no sign of a living being around, until we saw what looked like a dusty, lonely gasoline pump and a dusty, lonely man standing near it. We stopped the car and asked him if there was a coffee shop nearby. "Yup, eighty miles ahead."

"Suppose we go back?" I asked.

"Fifty miles."

Another time, we were driving through the desert under the early-afternoon sun when suddenly a cop appeared on the roadside and waved me to stop. "You were going seventy-two miles an hour in a fifty-five-mile speed zone." He was right, I was.

"I am sorry, officer. It is a rented car, and I may have lost track of the speed limit."

"There's a speed limit of fifty-five miles an hour all over the country, mate. You owe me thirty-two dollars: seventeen miles over the limit plus a fifteen-dollar fine. Only cash. I will give you the receipt."

"I am not so sure about that. For one thing, I have not seen another car for hours, and nobody here would drive less than seventy-two on these flat, wide-open roads."

"You're right. Everybody here drives fast, and I give a ticket to every car that passes by. If you want to fight the ticket, you can come to town with me and talk to the judge."

Looking at this cowboy in a uniform, I thought of the western movies I had seen. "Is it one of those towns where you are also the judge?"

"Absolutely. You can come with me in my plane and see for yourself." He pointed to a small plane that was parked behind a barren bush that I had missed. It is an unbelievable story, but true. I gave him the thirty-two dollars, got a receipt, and kept driving.

❧

When our children were a little older, we involved them in planning our trips. They were very fond of Barbara Auntie and Irwin Uncle (that is what they called them, following the Indian way of calling all elders uncles and aunties), so we ended up going to Colorado first on most of our trips. Once, when they were about fifteen and thirteen years old, while we were watching home movies and looking at the albums, it suddenly occurred to them that we should plan a trip retracing the path of another family trip we had made about eleven years before that. I loved that idea, pulled out the old travel documents and photographs, and started planning.

Well, we made the trip, but our path could not be retraced. Some of the motels did not exist, and others we went to did not conform to our taste; we had graduated to higher standards. Now we wanted a hotel with air conditioning, a pool, and a nice place to eat. Overall we enjoyed the trip because the sights and natural beauty had not changed. The canyons still looked the same as they had in our old pictures; Disneyland had most of the same rides and exhibits that we remembered. Even the flat, dusty roads still stretched for miles without any sign of human habitation. Once we got lost and ended up on top of a mountain, where the road ended. We were contemplating our next move when it started snowing hard. It was July; the kids were wearing shorts and play-ing with snowballs, and Poonam and I were shooting pictures—almost duplicating a similar experience from many years ago. It was a memorable trip.

We went on a few trips abroad, and we visited India every two to three years. (More about those visits in the next chapter.) The Glassmans got us into cruises—Barbara's father loved cruising—and we took many cruises, with and without the Glassmans. Nita loved a cruise, any cruise, and later went on one with her friends. For a while she even considered working on a cruise ship.

Poonam and the children did not care, but I needed Indian food after every few days of steaks, hamburgers, and pizza. During one of our first trips to Los Angeles, I had this urge. I started looking in the Yellow Pages. Nothing. Then I started calling strangers from the telephone directory, common Indian last names like Shah or Gupta or Sharma. Not too many people were home; it was a workday, and only we were on vacation. Well, I finally found a lonely soul at home and asked if there were any Indian food places around. Yes, there was a sort of an Indian food stall, about fifteen miles out of Los Angeles. We drove there and were disappointed to see that it was a fast-food place owned by an Indian, serving hamburgers, and chicken curry and rice, and some very Americanized Indian dishes. We were not looking for any such thing and showed our dismay to the owner. He graciously took us upstairs, where his mother was cooking real Indian food for her own family, and invited us to join them for a luncheon.

Similarly, halfway through a cruise to the Caribbean Islands, we ended up going to the back of a store of an Indian and sharing his lunch with him. In those days we were the only Indians taking cruises.

We continue traveling, vacationing, and cruising, sometimes with our children and grandchildren. Most immigrants do. We generally choose destinations within America; it is so vast and tourist-oriented. I enjoy thinking, feeling, and acting like a tourist when on vacation.

40

The New India: Blossoming, Affluent, Materialistic

Poonam and I have visited India more than fifteen times, for any-where from two weeks to two months at a clip. Most Indians do that if they can afford it, some more often than that. We took our children with us until they grew big enough to refuse to go any-more. While Poonam enjoyed shopping for Indian clothes and jewelry, I never felt at home. I was afraid to eat or drink there for fear of Delhi Belly, and in fact got sick with gastric symptoms for a couple of days during each trip. Poonam, on the other hand, ate everything and was able to digest everything; she took an anti-biotic here and there (not a course of antibiotics for a whole week!) as a precautionary measure. We always went during the Christmas holidays even though airfare was more expensive during that season, because children needed fewer days off from school during the Christmas holidays. Also, winter is the best time to visit India, because Delhi heat can be brutal in summer.

During the first few visits I just stayed home, tucked in bed with several blankets. I talked with the family members and ate home-cooked meals. Central heating was unknown there, and room heaters were not considered safe. Windows were seldom closed, and the temperature inside the house was virtually the same as outside, cold enough for a jacket or a sweater in December. I enjoyed making small talk with my parents, greeting visitors, and drinking tea all day long. After a few trips we started taking a week's vacation to other parts of the country, like Jaipur, Madurai, Kerala, Varanasi, or wherever. Of course we took the children to various tourist spots in Delhi and Agra, and we went to Poonam's parents in Aligarh. India is so vast and so awesome.

As mentioned earlier, the small house where I had grown up in Rajinder Nagar had changed hands: my parents were now living there with my two youngest brothers and my sister. My uncle Khushiram had built another house in Ashok Vihar, another area of Delhi, and moved there. By my second visit, in 1971, the Rajinder Nagar house had undergone some renovations. By my third visit, in 1974, it had been razed and completely rebuilt. It was now three stories high and had some amenities, but after a few visits I became unhappy with the creature comforts and opted to stay in a hotel within walking distance of my house. This was unheard of in that culture and did not sit well with my family. "What will other people say? Here is a big house named Vic Villa after your son, and you are staying next door in a hotel? Is our family dysfunctional? Are we having problems with each other?" Despite all these valid inquiries from the community there, I kept my American ways. After questioning me a few times, they reconciled themselves to the fact that I was going to be stubborn on some aspects of my life, and so I stayed in hotels. What a rebel!

Even though our house had three stories, it still looked small in that neighborhood because all the other houses now had seven stories or more! They looked as if they were made of Legos. My father once said all that construction was illegal. I told him I had read that come of the construction in New York was illegal. In my small town in New Jersey, though, the inspectors were sticklers about the rules.

Every time I went there, I saw a different India. It was blossoming. It was affluent, industrialized, mechanized, and capitalistic. There were cars and elevators, hot water in the faucets, and air conditioners in the windows. There were five-star hotels and fast-running, timely trains. Air travel was becoming a commonplace. There was more food, and of different varieties; people were eating out and had even started refrigerating foods. The number of televisions and television channels was mind-boggling. Common people talked about the stock market and gold and diamond businesses. On the other hand, houses had high walls and fences around their perimeter, with glass or barbed wire on top, and even guard dogs. Windows had bars, and many houses had armed guards. People looked old; hunched backs, gray hair, and missing teeth were common. Most of the small talk revolved around big money. Many of my classmates were retired around age sixty. There was more population, more pollution, more corruption (almost like New Jersey).

The Rajinder Nagar market where I had spent my childhood could not be recognized. There was hustle and bustle everywhere, and choking crowds, and no place to walk or to sit. Each store had been divided into two to five busy shops. There was so much traffic that crossing the street was difficult and time-consuming. Karol Bagh was a sprawling shopping center near Rajinder Nagar. When we were in Delhi, we walked there practically every day: to Roshan's to eat *kulfi* (ice cream) and *samosas* (small fried pastries filled with spiced vegetables), or pizza at Narula. We shopped for saris at Zohra and spices at Roopak's. We went to various stores for gold and silver jewelry and ornaments. There were thousands of stores, some as small as sixteen square feet, where every inch was crammed full of merchandise and the owner stood outside the store screaming and hawking his goods. There were also large, fancy jewelry stores, where an armed guard was standing outside. Inside, a model-like hostess welcomed you, and if you were a mon-eyed customer (she knew it by your looks), she took you into a special private room to offer you snacks and tea, and showed you specially decorated showcases of diamonds and gold jewelry. All these stores, large and small, were full of people who were shopping extensively. Indians have remarkable buying power.

I was amazed that in that market where twenty thousand people worked and half a million people passed through every day, there was not one reasonably clean lavatory. Where did people go to relieve themselves? One wooden telephone pole had at least fifty open wires going in every direction—I guessed more than half were illegal, stealing electricity—and to me it seemed like a major fire hazard. But as they say, "Everything goes in India." And India is springing forward, day by day.

When Victor and Nita went to India with us, they enjoyed the love and the warmth of the people there. They were especially surprised to see that there were servants in almost every house they went to; chauffeurs, cooks, gardeners, and porters were everywhere. But our children were dismayed to see that it was common to have ten and eleven-year-old boys and girls working full-time as domestic and store help.

Once, when Victor was in high school, I took him to my medical school. He was fascinated to see the dissection hall, the laboratories, and the auditorium. Encouraged by that, I made the mistake of taking him to my high school. The building was in severe disrepair. The desks and chairs and windowpanes were all broken down. The chemistry lab had reagents so old that I thought maybe they had not been replaced since I was studying there, almost twenty years ago. I could not gauge how he felt because, witnessing that scene, even I had tears in my eyes.

What upset me more was the social change. People were more materialistic, more crude, more sarcastic, and more angry. They were becoming westernized too quickly. The mix was confusing: they were shedding old Indian traditions, yet at the same time singing praises for their old system. Religious orthodoxy and provincial and nationalistic dogma were becoming a norm. Maybe these are the traits that keep a diverse country like India united as a nation—and a democracy at that.

41

To Be an Indian in America

To be an Indian here should not be any different from being any other kind of immigrant, but it is. We are neither white nor black. We are not even yellow. Most of us don't look Spanish. Most of us speak English when we come here. We are generally well educated and earn a good living. Many Indian women wear saris and other different-looking clothes, at least for the first few years after their coming here, and some men, Sikhs, wear beards and turbans. We are a small minority in numbers but highly visible, especially in the Northeast and the West. We generally do not live in enclaves and are spread out. We are loved and we are loathed, sometimes simultaneously.

When I came in the 1960s, we were an anomaly here. There were very few Indians to identify with. Most of us were men, and students or interns. Many of us married Americans, in a sort of assimilation process, and got lost to both the Indian community and the Americans. Others started their own identities and affiliations. Sometimes we sacrificed our identity on the altar of success. Did we ever become a full part of the white culture and its social quilt? Will we ever? Should we? We struggled, but our struggle was probably less than that of some other minorities in America. Some of us will disagree; they think our struggle has been more than others'. Reasons cited are the same for either argument, same as I have mentioned already. Some of my friends have horrifying stories of discrimination experienced here during their earlier years, or throughout their entire life. Are these stories real or exaggerated? It doesn't really matter; they perceive it that way. My stories are not so bad, or it may just be my perception. American history shows that all immigrants were discriminated against when they came here. Irish, Italian, Jewish, Japanese, Hispanic—everybody has those stories. We have to accept that reality, and keep going, keep struggling.

Another trait: many minorities in this country have rivalry with other minorities, but in my opinion, Indians are less vulnerable to this. Do we ever enter the American elite? Yes, we do. In many spheres we have. Again, that can be disputed. We "show off" our American friends and colleagues, proudly inviting as many of them to our social and family functions as we can. This is the Indian American dream.

Not all of our behaviors are driven by conscious and unconscious needs, wants, and defenses. Several other factors play a role. For example, our children bring us close to or take us away from certain ethnic groups. Or a child may get married into a white family or one of another ethnicity. Love is a forceful emotion. We try hard to steer our children away from any such "unscrupulous" action, but ultimately relent. We are afraid to lose our children after we have shown our liberalism in sending them to Ivy League schools, and getting them into respected professions, and when they fall in love we wring our hands. The extent of our "American-ness" also changes if we start a business with a non-Indian. Or if we live in certain parts of the country, depending on how united or not united Indians are in that area. Our social, cultural, and family background is sometimes a deciding factor in our becoming assimilated into different ethnic groups.

❧

During my five years in Boston area, most of my friends were Indian. Of course, I had that very white New Zealander, Angus. And I was showing him off. Poonam and I were also very friendly with my white colleagues and supervisors in the hospital, more than were other Indians. When we moved to New Jersey, Fair Lawn was a hub of middle-class Jews, and we made friends with them. And there were the Glassmans, who were with us all the time. We did not have one Indian friend. Five years later we bought a big house in Morris County, in an old, conservative, Republican town. I got involved in local affairs and made several American friends. But by this time there were many Indians in New Jersey—and Poonam, friendly person that she is, made many Indian friends too. Most of my friends were American when I was active in the community. Later, when medical and family responsibilities increased, I slowly gave up those activities and lost track of those associations. Poonam continued building her base of friends, and eventually we ended up with Indian friends entirely.

I am reminded of an incident that pinpoints our thinking, at least my thinking. One evening I came home and started complaining that the house reeked of Indian food. I was also talking about Indian pictures on the walls and Indian artifacts lying around in the house. My father-in-law, who lived with us at that time, asked me what was so wrong about it. "Papaji, suppose an American friend comes in. How uncomfortable is he going to feel?" He calmly reminded me that in the ten years he had been with us, he had not seen one American friend of mine in the house. He was right. Even though I was meeting many of them at work and in clubs and restaurants, I did not really have an American friend close enough to come to my house.

⚜

We keep trying to find our place in this world, in this community, and even in the Indian community, here and in India. We Indian Americans often discuss whether we are more accepted here or in India. Mostly the conclusion is that we have lost our space in India. Indians in India consider us pompous, snobbish, rich, AIDS-ridden, war-mongering Americans who have lost all our original values. We, on the other hand, think we are following more Indian traditions and have more of our value system intact than they have back home. This is because Indians in India are copying Americans in everything, and overdoing it. Every Indian in India criticizes America at every chance he gets, yet every Indian has an inner desire to move to America someday. I believe this attitude prevails almost all over the world, this love-hate relationship with America.

Once we were visiting Tirupati Temple in South India. I had to buy a *dhoti* (a loin cloth) and wear it, with no other clothes on me, and all the men were sitting on the floor, in *dhotis*, waiting for the prayers to begin; women were not allowed in that session. The man sitting next to me asked me if I was from America. (In India they all notice if you are from America; we may talk their language but our accent and mannerisms give us away). When I told him yes I was, he wasted no time in blasting America in several ways, including that "every" child in the streets of New York was carrying a gun. (There had been a well-publicized incident of a child shooting another, a few days before.) Less than five minutes later he was describing how his son was going to high school and he would like him to go to America for further studies, and was saving for the trip. If the prayer hadn't started just then, he would have asked my address and whether I could send him a support letter for his son when the time came for him to go to America.

❧

What is our comfort level with Americans, or with Indians here and in India? Jordan and I were good friends. We met in the club once a week and met at least a few times more here and there, for playing cards, for community service, or just to shoot the breeze over a cup of coffee in a restaurant. Once there was a twenty-four-hour benefit volleyball game marathon in the high school, and I opted to chaperone from three to six in the morning, mainly because I had chronic insomnia and was accustomed to being up at night for hospital calls. Jordan also chose that shift. We ate, drank coffee, talked, laughed, and played cards most of the three hours, sitting on the bleachers while the kids played volleyball. We had great fun. Suddenly I realized that maybe I was pretending most of the time. I was holding cards differently, the American way, playing differently, swearing differently; I was hiding behind a facade. I don't think Jordan had any idea of my feelings. But I did feel that way!

I am aware of occasionally speaking a sentence in British English or Indian English rather than American English, or holding a knife and fork differently from my companion. I become quite self-conscious at such times, somewhat anxious. The more we associate with Americans, the more we become aware of our "Indian-ness," and the more we feel we are just visitors. We get attracted to other Indians. We want to build temples and start our alumni associations. We want to "belong" to other Indians. We go and build hospitals and clinics in our little towns in India, vie to get awards in India and be recognized there. My brother Harish started a radio program of Indian music and community news in Boston almost thirty years ago. I believe most Indian households in New England are tuned to his program every Sunday for a couple of hours. We are still looking for our identity; maybe we always will be. We need to prove something; there is so much guilt in us.

⚜

I may mention here another aspect of our life in America: hospitality is in our blood. Most Indians like to give lavish parties, but perhaps Poonam and I go a little overboard with parties for family and friends. I have also initiated and arranged parties for hospitals, drug companies, alumni associations, and others.

Diwali is the biggest festival in India, sort of the Hindu New Year. Big celebrations. Here too we celebrate *Diwali*, some more, others less. In our house, we do a little bit of that ritual too. However, our big day is Thanksgiving Day, a uniquely American holiday. We prepare for it for days and weeks and have almost all the relatives and a few close friends at our place. As the immediate and extended family increased, the list of invitees has changed over the years. I remember past Thanksgiving dinners when there were as many as fifty men, women, and children standing around the dinner table—which held two large steaming turkeys, all the traditional trimmings, and Indian foods for the vegetarians among us. We go through the rituals of saying grace and thanking God for bringing us to a bountiful country, of carving the turkey, and so on. The festivities go on for several days of special breakfasts, lunches, and dinners; of watching the parade and the football on television; and of drinking, playing cards, and singing. Many of our out-of-state relatives stay with us for the whole weekend.

What about Christmas? A few Indians are loath even to talk about it, while others have the tallest Christmas tree in the neighborhood. We belong to the second category. If Poonam had her say, we would have a small tree in a corner, a sort of a symbolic gesture, but in the family discussion I and our children (especially our daughter-in-law, Shilpa), and now our grandchildren won out, so we have all the excitement of Christmas in our house. Some Indians go out of their way to look for the cards that say "Season's Greetings" or "Happy New Year" rather than "Merry Christmas," but I don't. I also used to be an enthusiastic participant with other Kiwanians when we went Christmas caroling to various nursing homes. Interestingly, one of the other ardent participants was Jewish.

Though it was many years ago, people still remember our twenty-fifth wedding anniversary party at Moghul banquet hall in Morristown, and before that the party for my parents' fiftieth anniversary in New York at the Tandoor. Moghul was not even fully renovated when we signed up for our party. Sneh and Satish Mehtani went out of their way to make it a successful event, and then their restaurant took off. After the party, when I went to pay the bill, Sneh said she did not have a count of the people who came, and since we had not decided on the price beforehand, she asked me to pay whatever I wanted to. I kept insisting on paying her a reasonable amount. The stalemate continued, so I left a blank signed check for her to fill in any amount she wanted. I hear that she told the story of the blank check to a lot of people. A friend later gave an anniversary party, and when I complimented him, he lamented, "You raised the bar for all of us."

Since then Satish and Sneh have been good friends and have done a number of fabulous parties for us, even helping arrange our son's engagement party in India. (More about that later.)

﹏

What about American politics? As the saying goes, when we are poor, young, and students, we are Democrats. As we mature, have some hard-knock experiences, and become wealthy, we tend to become Republicans. For this reason, most of us first-generation Indians (and other immigrants) are Democrats at heart. As time goes on, we turn Republican. (Our children will probably lean more toward Republicans.) When I retire and get active in community affairs again, I may switch parties again. Who knows?

We are against guns. We strongly believe in social welfare and reforms, but we don't like taxes. We generally favor legal abortion. I am a registered Republican. I registered because of peer pressure; all the club members, and it seemed like all the townsfolk, were Republican. I felt like I almost had to declare my alliance. At that time, I didn't even know the difference between the two parties, if there is much difference. I strongly favor legal abortion because I work in a town where children are giving birth to children, and children are being neglected and abused by their mothers and their mothers' boyfriends, and also by their adoptive or surrogate parents. Substance abuse is a major problem. The fewer children born to those young mothers, the better they would be treated, I hope.

That reminds me of an incident. Many years ago I was seeing a twenty-five-year-old patient in the hospital. She had a history of mental illness and drug abuse, had five children from five different fathers, and was pregnant again. While taking her history and going into the details of her problems, I happened to ask whether she had considered family planning. She started screaming, accused me of promoting abortion, called me an anti-Christian, and threatened to sue me.

Most Indians like to criticize America. I believe most immigrants do, as do most Americans. We disapprove of the way Americans bring up their children and treat their elderly. We talk about their capitalism and their social systems: the health-care and legal fiascos, the insurance rip-offs, the education system and the political corruption. I usually bring up the other point of view and start defending American systems. But I am careful not to antagonize the leaders of my group too much and not to emphasize my point. I don't want to be ostracized by the community. Usually I am dismissed as "that crazy psychiatrist" anyway. It is somewhat bizarre that I am the only nonwhite person during the annual function of the Montville Township Chamber of Commerce. To belabor another point, I am also the shortest man in that gathering. And I attend it every year—a certifiable masochist. Then again, I am the only nonwhite person they have honored as the Citizen of the Year.

※

We try to change our value system, but some of our values are deeply rooted. Even now when I meet somebody for the first time and his name sounds Punjabi, I ask him if he is from Punjab.

I know I am never going to see him again and it does not even matter to me whether he is a Punjabi, or even an Indian. The question is almost a reflex action from me.

Wives of a couple of my Indian friends have confided in me about physical abuse, and I get into a major dilemma there. Are they asking for help from a friend or from a psychiatrist who can steer their husbands in the right direction? They even come to my office and sit in the patient's chair and cry. At the cost of losing the friends, I have called in their husbands and reminded them that this is not India, and that any kind of abuse here can lead to their arrest, suspension of their professional license, losing their job, even jail time.

Many parents have brought their teenage or college-age children to see me because they don't "obey" them as they should, and the children in turn tell me about the suffocating conditions at home, like eight p.m. curfews, having to call home every half hour, their room being searched frequently by their parents, and them being slapped for bringing home grades below their parents' expectations. All parents deny their child's substance-abuse problems; Indian-American and immigrant parents in general take the denial to an extreme. We have severe guilt if our children don't grow up the way we think they should, leading to depression, family discord, or worse.

I have also treated people from other countries who came to me because they thought I could understand them better, "being from the same culture." Sometimes I have helped them and at other times I had to leave them to their own defenses. I can't reform the whole world. Some people just will not change their thinking, feeling, or actions after having moved eight thousand miles away and lived here for many more years than they lived in India, or in another part of the world.

As a psychiatrist you learn to more or less detach yourself from your patients, but it becomes hard when you can actually see yourself in them. A second-year resident in psychiatry was overly protective of his wife and child, allowing them little freedom. He was abusive to them, physically and mentally. He had been a doctor in India, and after several years of practicing surgery there, he had come here in his forties. He could not get settled or get a residency in surgery, so he ended up in psychiatry, which he did not like. He was suspicious of his wife, accusing her of having an affair, and was becoming paranoid and overly religious. We all felt that he should not be doing psychiatry, but none of us was willing to say it openly. I was quite troubled by his plight. Then one day he just disappeared. We were told he had left his residency and returned to India. I felt very sad after that, maybe we all did. We never talked about it again, but I still sometimes feel bad about the whole episode. Maybe we could have helped him.

⁂

I once treated a young Indian woman who was a homemaker and a paranoid schizophrenic. She stayed home and hallucinated all day, refusing to take medications. One time her husband, who was a factory worker, beat her up—badly. A neighbor called the police.

330

He was handcuffed and taken to the police station. The wife did not speak English. She kept crying and screaming, and wanted her husband released. An interpreter was involved, which was expensive. The husband told the police to call me, her treating psychiatrist. This became a three-way conversation on a speaker-phone, with a judge. They wanted to get rid of the case, but they could not let the wife go on her own, and they needed an excuse. The judge asked, "Is it possible, Dr. Dang, that Shanti (not her real name) imagined the beating up?"

What would you do in this case?

"Yes, your honor, but—"

"Oh good, case dismissed. Shanti is directed to see Dr. Dang in his office within one week."

About three months later, the husband wanted a letter from me that his wife was dangerous to their son and that he should be granted an immediate divorce and she should be sent back to Bombay. I declined to write the letter, probably not on clinical grounds, but for moral and personal reasons. Even though she was somewhat controlled, Shanti was a sick woman. A mental patient would be unaccepted by her in-laws and maligned by her parents in India. She would end up in a public mental institution with horrible conditions and die of dehydration or malnutrition.

Did I do the right thing? I still wonder.

✦

As the Indian population has increased here, especially in New Jersey, so has the population of Indian senior citizens and the natural problems accompanying them. Our parents, who come here in later life after having led fairly normal lives in India, find themselves lonely, bored, and useless. They come here for the love of their children, who are busy at work and building their own lives. Most don't get driver's licenses here and are virtually shut-ins. Their children take them to parties on weekends, where they feel lost in the younger crowd. Back home the houses were close by. People visited friends without calling them beforehand, just walking over to see them and talking for hours, mostly politics. Here there is none of that. Some parents are being used as baby-sitters, cooks, and house sitters. Yes, they see their children prospering and quasi-happy, but their own lives are practically over; they start thinking they are a burden on the family. The concept of assisted-living facilities or nursing homes does not exist in their minds, and there are virtually no suitable nursing facilities where they can get their kind of lifestyle and vegetarian food.

With the help of NAMI (the National Alliance on Mental Illness) and Anu Singh, I developed a program of dance and song that I present to day-care programs for Indian seniors. I start a dialogue about old Bollywood movies, their stories, actors, singers, joys and sorrows, depression and suicides. Then I tell them that it is a mistake to think that mental illness and depression happen only in America. We Indians are not as "pure" a society as we think we are. We have depression; we have suicides—just think of these songs and dances from the movies. We should recognize these problems and get help. I tell them that modern antidepressants are wonderful, with virtually no side effects, and Medicare pays for psychiatric treatment. Before I end my talk, I start the tape of the song again and invite them to the floor to dance with me. From all indications the program has been successful and entertaining, and has been able to bring the point home to seniors and their children about psychiatric problems in our community.

Even though I am generally a bit critical about our Indian sociocultural traditions, I do recognize and discuss some of their virtues as well. I believe I have been able to help many of my countrymen adjust during various phases of their life in America.

42

American Born,
Yet Our Children

When I came to the United States, I had to feel my way around as an infant does. I had very little guidance and had to improvise at every step. At that time most of us immigrants had to mold our own personalities and attitudes. We formed our opinions and acted in our own unique ways.

It was the same with bringing up our children. I had read about American culture and heard stories from my patients and their families. I liked what I heard and I liked the concept of a melting pot. Poonam and I discussed that a lot, and we talked extensively about bringing up our children. She had few opinions and deferred most of those decisions to me. I did not want our children to look different, sound different, or behave differently from their peers. They were surrounded by all American friends and families; there were no Indian enclaves then. So we spoke English to them and adopted American foods, habits, and mannerisms. When we were building our house and our children were six and eight years old, we had a separate telephone line installed in their

334

rooms. We were rebels to some extent; most Indians did not think the way we did.

Years later, long after our children were grown and independent, I was giving a lecture to about five hundred teachers and other officials from schools in Paterson. The topic was related to racial and ethnic issues and the mental health of children. Paterson's population is almost equally divided among whites, African Americans, Hispanics, and "others" (mostly Middle Eastern and Asian). In the question-and-answer period a teacher asked me whether I regretted depriving my children of learning my native language and thus losing some of their rich Indian heritage in the process. Good question. I don't know the answer. I think she was right that there was a loss involved, but I can also justify my actions with various intellectual and rational (and irrational) explanations.

⚜

One of the first words that my daughter Nita spoke was "coffee." At home we did not drink coffee, but we often ate out, another non-Indian trait at that time, taking our young children to restaurants and diners, a non-American trait then. So when we were wandering through the mall and Nita saw a restaurant, she naturally pointed and said "coffee."

Do I think there is anything wrong with this? No, I do not. But an average Indian American would be ashamed to admit that his daughter's first word was something so mundane and materialistic. He would be proud to report that her first word was "*om*" or

"God" or *"Dadi"* (Grandmother). If I said publicly that my daughter's first spoken word was "coffee," Indians around me would cringe, and my mother would hush me up by saying, "Okay, but you don't have to advertise it." This is just a minuscule example of the big picture of our culture; it is not bad or good, it's just different.

In the late 1970s some of us friends, all Indian, were sitting and chatting in the basement of one of our houses. We had had a few drinks already. The topic turned to our children, who were growing up in America and now approaching their adolescence. The parents were all of the opinion that we must give them the total Indian makeover. I was the only holdout. I felt we could try, but that we had to be ready to deal with some acculturation.

"What would you do if your teenage son came home drunk at three in the morning?" I asked.

"I would take off my shoe and beat the crap out of him," was the response of one friend. (We do not have the concept of a belt.)

"You would do no such thing. He could get you arrested, you know," I said. "And it wouldn't help the situation anyway."

Then I asked an even more provocative question. "What if your unmarried daughter got pregnant?"

You can never, ever, fathom this kind of dialogue in India.

"I'd kill myself," was one answer.

I know everybody was smirking and thinking, "A crazy psychiatrist. How could our children turn out to be so rotten?"

It turned into a raging social and cultural debate. I sat back and quietly listened. The two cultures have good and bad components; a comfortable medium is hard to find.

To complete the story, the same friend, in front of many of the same people, said to me many years later, "You were right, Jagdish, when you talked ten years ago about children coming home drunk and young girls getting pregnant and parents having very little say in children becoming Americanized." Everyone in the room grew silent; you could cut the tension in there with a knife. At that time we all had teenagers and were facing the problems of their growing up.

I feel that there is nothing wrong with parents instilling their value system in their children. My problem is that some people like to give sermons about their views a little too much. Indians are very quick to criticize any minor deviation from their thinking, especially on social and political issues. It is interesting that the parents who practice religion devoutly and try to instill Indian values in their children have just as many problems with the next generation as those who don't.

꧁꧂

Because my family members—and later Poonam's—were coming here one by one and staying with us, our children had to learn some of those Indian values that the new arrivals were so proud of. Victor became very much Indian but he abandoned everything Indian after college. Nita, on the other hand, was an all-American kid. She detested the Indian habit of walking around barefoot, and every time somebody entered her room barefoot, she cleaned it thoroughly afterward. Even we could not understand her American accent at times. Later, in her adulthood, she started learning and following quite a few Indian customs. Poonam and I find it strange. Recently an old friend said, "You and Poonam were so liberal in your views that we thought your kids would be the most spoiled children, and also that they would certainly marry non-Indians. And look at them now. They both are the ideal examples to follow, and both married Indians. Wow!" I was startled to realize that this friend, and indeed many Indians, believe that marrying within your own culture and religion is the biggest yardstick in grading one's upbringing!

I predicted a long time ago that of our first-generation kids, one-third would marry Americans, one-third would marry Indian Americans from their parents' background in India, and the last third would marry Indian Americans from other regions and religions. (Of course I would not talk about the ones who might stay single, or gays or lesbians; I would never be invited to that house again.) Whenever I said that, most Indians would feel shocked and dismayed; they could not imagine their children even marrying out of their caste. How could they think of them going out of their ethnicity and religion? Many parents did not prepare themselves for this eventuality and became depressed when it happened, and many have tried to block it, losing their children in the process.

Another thing that we Indians are unprepared for is that not every child is going to become a doctor, a lawyer, or an engineer, nor will every child enroll in an Ivy League school. We keep pushing them to excel in studies, to reach for the moon, the way my uncle Khushiram wanted so badly for me to get a gold medal in medical school. Sometimes we push them too hard. It is detrimental to the psyche of the child. We are comparing him or her to another child who did so well. In India it may be tolerable—everyone does it—but in the United States it becomes an anomaly. This leads to complexes and causes conflicts. When the child does not attain our expectations, we are ready to criticize him or feel guilty to the point of becoming depressed. Dr. Allan Strand, former headmaster of the Newark Academy, used to say we should practice "benign neglect" in bringing up our children. I wish we Indians did that.

Victor and Nita were sent to private schools from a young age. I did not want to do so, but Poonam insisted on it. She said that she had always wanted her children to go to private schools since she herself could not. She thought private schools made them smart and mannered. In those days I was quite involved in my township, schools, politics, and community organizations. I knew that our town had good schools and our children would do fine. Money considerations were not brought into discussion; I don't remember ever making too much of a fuss on how she spent money. The stock market was doing fine. She prevailed and they went to private schools. I often wonder whether this was a wise decision and will never know the answer. If Poonam has her say, our grandchildren will go to private schools as well.

Our children did not have too many toys. (Maybe we didn't know about all the American toys, and there were not so many back then.) Our children did not make us run from one after-school activity to another. They did join Little League baseball and the YMCA, and took piano lessons and attended dance school, and whatever, but not as much as I see kids doing nowadays. At least part of the reason was that we did not know any better. Also, I was working odd hours. It is possible too that fewer extracurricular activities were available then.

❧

Our beliefs change as we grow older, and we sometimes wonder how we would have changed raising our children if we had known then what we know now. When I was young and idealistic, I had some altruistic leanings. Many of them were fulfilled. Any discussion of money was a taboo. Now I find that I was wrong. Money is very important, sometimes maybe the most important attribute in one's life. I have seen wealthy people with no other human quality being worshipped and pandered to. In any social function you can see where more people are congregating, not around the most intellectual or the nicest person, but around the richest person. In medical societies and community organizations too, money talks and begets the most respect. Strangely, almost anybody you talk to says, "Money isn't everything," or "You can't take it with you," or some such phrase. But I now think that is a smoke screen. I believe, maybe too late, that money is more important than we let people believe. I also believe that money can buy happiness in many cases, contrary to the popular belief and indoctrination of young minds today.

Profession matters too. Maybe in some cultures what you do is not so important, but in the two cultures that I know, Indian and American, after asking your name, everyone asks next what you do, and your respect goes up or down with that answer. I now cringe when people say, "As long as it makes him happy" about their child who is delivering pizza after his college education. I used to like that phrase and thought it was a unique quality of Americans, but I just don't think it's true anymore. "Dignity of labor" is okay but to a limited degree.

Another thing that bothers me is that we in America often say, "Family comes first." We don't really mean this either. If we believed in it, there would not be so many family breakups and so much marital discord. More often than not, instant gratification, wealth, status, career, religion, friendships, and even sports come before family.

So many books have been written about how best to bring up children. I believe the jury is still out in deciding the right and the wrong practices in raising children of immigrants.

43

The Next Generation
Comes of Age

Victor and Nita went to high school at Newark Academy in Livingston. Victor seldom did much homework, but Nita was always busy with her books. It was the same school, the same teachers, so we always wondered why the difference. He got interested in baseball cards at a very early age, and by high school he was so obsessed with them that he opened a business of buying, selling, and trading cards. He went to flea markets and shows to buy and sell. At one time we were receiving baseball cards by mail or UPS almost every week, sometimes very large shipments. He made thousands of dollars, but at the same time started neglecting his schoolwork. Poonam and I worried that this did not bode well. After all, we are Indian parents, liberal or not. But there was little we could do, since our children are American children.

Still, his grades and SAT scores were good, and he was admitted to the engineering college at Boston University. Then he suddenly lost interest in his business and baseball cards in general. We still have hundreds of boxes filled with baseball cards in our basement. It is possible that one or more of those cards are very valuable. Poonam reminds Victor every chance she gets that one of these days she is going to throw all those boxes out. He only smiles, points to his son, and says, "Those cards now belong to Dhruv; you would never do that to your grandson."

⚜

During his school years, Victor went through the usual dating, prom, and other coming-of-age rituals in America. This was all unfamiliar territory for Poonam and me, but we went with the flow. Unbeknownst to us, he was getting serious with an Indian girl who lived with her parents and brother across the street from us. Shilpa was going to Rutgers University in New Jersey, and they were visiting each other regularly. He came home from Boston frequently, and we thought it was to see us . . . but probably it was to meet Shilpa. Now we know that she was visiting him in Boston as well.

After finishing college, they both started working. By this time Shilpa's parents and Poonam and I knew what was happening, although we were still not officially brought into the loop by the children. Then one day he proposed to her by kneeling down and presenting her with a ring attached to a baseball card specially embossed with the message that he wanted to marry her. She consented. That was when they decided to tell their parents.

It was rare in India for a boy to select his own spouse, let alone propose to her, without telling his parents—or, more accurately, asking their permission. But we accepted this American custom.

❦

You might think any two Indian families in the United States would be instantly delighted that their children had chosen each other, but it's a bit more complicated than that. India is a large country with many languages, religions, customs, and cultures. There is another curious phenomenon involved: provincialism. I don't understand it much, and even scholars on India have had difficulty analyzing it. Let me try to explain this as a layman, in a somewhat crude manner.

Each region has its own identity. Even people in the same region and same town may have different systems of living, probably dictated by their language more than any other difference. For example, they may have moved from one region to the other years ago, but still may have maintained different food habits, different clothes, different music, different holidays, and so on. In America, it would be like North Carolinians speaking a completely different language and having significant cultural differences from New Jerseyans, and North Jerseyans from South Jerseyans. That's not all; people from midtown Manhattan might have a total dislike, bordering on hatred, for those from downtown. South Indians generally dislike North Indians (at least they used to) and vice versa, but people from Madras (now Chennai) also have negative feelings about those from Bangalore, both in South India. The quality and intensity of their dislike may differ from state to state and region to region. They live, work, and play together but do not feel the same toward one another inside their hearts, and any infraction of their separateness can result in a major community upheaval, even a riot. Intermarriage can be one such infraction. Indian history is full of incidents of bloodbaths and even wars as a result of marriages between different castes, religions, or systems.

When Indians are in a foreign country, these feelings are diminished but do not disappear completely.

⚜

At the time Shilpa and Victor brought up the topic of marriage to their respective parents, it was immediately apparent that her parents were from Gujarat and we were from Punjab. The consolation was that we were both from India and both were Hindus. But it wasn't much consolation—we felt that we did not have much in common with them. Nevertheless, I was overjoyed at the news; Poonam was shocked in the beginning but quickly reconciled. Shilpa's parents were somewhat upset but relented in no time, and we started having meetings for preparations for the "union of two families." That is how we define a marriage.

Poonam wanted to have their wedding done in a totally Indian way, with full seven-star merriment. Shilpa's parents would have been happy with a simple celebration but would go along with whatever we wanted, and I didn't care either way. Even though we lived across from each other, most of the communication between the sets of parents was done through Shilpa, at least in the beginning, with Poonam organizing on behalf of the Dang family and Shilpa for the Shukla family.

We realized right away that my mother could not attend the wedding because she was bedridden with cancer in India. Victor got this idea that we could all go to India and let her witness the engagement party. Even though he and Shilpa were already engaged by the American custom, they still needed a full ceremony to be recognized as "engaged" by Indian standards.

A little engagement party kept mushrooming into a huge bonanza. Shilpa's parents had earlier gone to India and had engaged their son, Samir—a sort of "arranged engagement" to an Indian girl in their home district in Gujarat. They were planning to go back to get him married there anyway, and welcomed the thought of getting Shilpa and Victor engaged in India during that time. Poonam called India and asked my parents to go to a Hindu priest and find an auspicious day in November 1994 for their engagement in India, and we decided to have the wedding in the United States in July of the following year.

⚜

We called my brother Sanjiv in India and discussed the plans, including all that he would have to do there and what we would be doing here. Various functions had to be arranged. Victor asked Sanjiv if it was possible to have something special like an elephant during the engagement ceremony, or fireworks, things that could not be done here in America. "A piece of cake," said Sanjiv. We were also in touch with our friend Sneh Mehtani of the Moghul Restaurant in Morristown, who knew all about planning weddings and had connections with hoteliers in India.

The Shuklas departed for Ahmedabad, Gujarat, and we went to Delhi. All the arrangements had to be made and we had limited time. Fortunately, just as you didn't need to give people in India several months' notice for a wedding, you didn't need years or months to arrange a wedding there. Even though this was going to be an engagement, almost everything was done like a wedding.

About twenty people from the Shukla family came by train from Ahmedabad to Delhi. When they arrived, a large contingent of the Dangs was waiting at the train station to receive them and greet them and escort them to their hotel. To a non-Indian, the hugs and kisses between virtual strangers would have been overwhelming. But to the Dangs and Shuklas, each family member was trying to outdo the next with the outward show of affection; soon two families were going to be one.

We had several functions. Day One: a religious ceremony to ask for blessings as we began the "joining" of Victor and Shilpa. Day Two: musical entertainment in a hotel with a live band, elephants to greet the visitors, dancing and eating, and fireworks at the end of the evening. (The fireworks were done on the street in front of the banquet hall.) Day Three: a reception for more than two hundred people at Taj Palace in Delhi, a five-star hotel. A lot of food, drinks, flowers, bands, and dancing. Sneh Mehtani showed up in person to attend the final party, in a two-day whirlwind trip to India. One interesting note: word spread quickly that we were serving real Black Label scotch brought in from the United States; the party became raucous and a lot more fun.

Miraculously, my mother was temporarily rejuvenated and

was able to participate in the celebrations, even dancing a little with Victor and Shilpa. She passed away, a happy lady, a few weeks after our visit.

⁂

I may mention here the *janeu* ceremony, a rite of passage for Hindu boys, similar to the bar mitzvah for Jews or the Holy Communion for Catholics. It is considered one of the thirteen *sanskaras,* or rites of passage, in the cycle of life for Hindus, along with others such as birth, marriage, and death. It is a centuries-old tradition and is commemorated by wearing a white knotted thread around your neck and shoulder, to be worn for rest of your life. Historically, it was an important aspect of religion, but many Indians don't practice it anymore, and most boys take the thread off after a few hours or a few days. In my family, the tradition is to have two boys get *janeu* together. In my case, my brother Harish and I went through the ritual together, on the morning of my wedding. Similarly, the morning before Victor's engagement we went to a temple with our immediate family, and a priest did the honors of making Victor and his cousin Gaurav, son of my brother Girish, wear the *janeu*. We had a small celebration afterward.

The day after the engagement festivities, the Shuklas took the train back to Ahmedabad, where they began the preparations for their son's wedding. Victor, Poonam, and I flew to Ahmedabad and participated in the wedding ceremonies of Samir. Shilpa came to Delhi with us, and we went on vacation for a few days to Jaipur, and sightseeing in Rajasthan, staying in marvelous hotels con-

348

verted from pre-partition castles or forts, each one at least a couple of hundred years old. This was also a first in my family—that we went around openly with our son and future daughter-in-law. (I broke a lot of social barriers among Indians.) Upon our return to Delhi, Shilpa went to Ahmedabad, and the two families flew separately back to New Jersey.

❦

That was when Poonam and Shilpa went into high gear with the wedding preparations.

There were many problems. We had never arranged a wedding here or in India. We had never even seen an Indian wedding in America, being one of the first Indian families to come here. We were groping in the dark, and what made it even more difficult was Poonam's insistence that it had to be big, and Indian. Many family meetings were held, many plans made, and just as many changed. Nowadays you can go to an Indian wedding show to pick and choose which clothes you want, which jewelry, which color horse, which band or DJ, which videographer, photographer, caterer, decorator, helper, hotel, priest, and so on. Fifteen years ago none of this was readily available, even with money, and we had to do a lot of research and legwork.

Although we felt that a trip to India was necessary, I did not want to go. Poonam decided to go alone and make the arrangements. (She enjoys visits to India more than I do.) She rented a car with a chauffeur and drove around in the hot sun for three weeks. Wedding cards were printed—large, fancy, silken cards with inserts for the four ceremonies. She bought the best and most expensive wedding *lehnga* (three-piece long dress) for Shilpa after visiting a dozen stores and meeting with even more tailors. She bought several outfits for Nita, Victor, herself, and me, as well as some clothes for the extended family, and for friends of Victor and Shilpa. On the music night we wanted even the men to wear Indian clothes, so she had to buy *kurta-pajamas* (knee-length decorated tunics over loose-fitting pants) for our American friends. This was no small task, as almost everything in India is small. I have often said that whatever you buy in India looks smaller when brought back to the United States. When it came to clothes, she could not even find clothes in the large and extra large sizes required by our American friends. Nevertheless, Poonam made it work by getting those clothes custom-stitched. She also bought jewelry, make-up, more than seven hundred wedding favors—small sterling silver bowls engraved with the names of Victor and Shilpa and the wedding date, in decorative boxes—and the numerous "props" needed for the various Indian rituals (dozens of artificial flower garlands, silver rings for the girls, and on and on and on).

In those days, there were not many banquet halls around that could accommodate more than 500 people and have a large dance floor too; most weddings here were done for between 200 and 300 people. And not too many hotels allowed Indian food catering by an outside vendor. Now the large banquet halls abound and even the fanciest hotels vie for Indian weddings and let you serve Indian food; they have discovered the financial power of Indian

Americans. Our friends Sneh and Satish Mehtani were instrumental in effecting this cultural change in New Jersey.

Another big problem was that we knew too many people. The hotel ballroom would not hold more than 550 people. The Shuklas were going to invite about 250 of those. With all the people we knew, and our large family here in the United States by this time, it would have been impossible to reduce the number to a mere 300. All the people we knew expected to be invited and would really feel offended if they were not; it was the first big wedding of the second generation among our acquaintances.

Victor came to our rescue. He put his foot down: no children except from the immediate family. Until then children always came with the parents to an Indian wedding. He also shortened the list by saying no friends of his parents whom he had never met. Still, it was a hardship to reduce the list to the required number. Some people reminded us for years that they were not invited. Making table assignments was another difficult task as we Indians were not yet accustomed to table seating at parties—it was all random seating to that point. We pulled an all-nighter with our friends Rajan and Shashi Sang figuring that out.

❦

The prewedding festivities consisted of a day of religious ceremonies at our house; an evening of henna painting on the hands of the women while they sang and the men drank and chatted (the Shuklas across the street were having similar celebrations); and an evening of food, drinks, music, and dance at the Moghul

Restaurant in Morristown. The real wedding ceremony and evening reception were held at the Marriott in East Hanover the next day, July 15, 1995. We had all the male members of the family and close friends wear tuxedos for the reception, and of course the women wore colorful, ornate Indian outfits for every function. Shilpa wore the silk *lehnga* that Poonam had brought from India, rust color with extensive gold embroidery, and Victor wore a tuxedo with a bow tie and vest made of the same silk as her *lehnga*. Finally, on Sunday, we wrapped up with a brunch at the Marriott. We went all out.

For the wedding ceremony, Victor was decorated with flowers and a gold crown in customary fashion, and he rode on a decorated horse around the parking lot of the hotel. A drum player beat on his *dhol* (loud Indian drum) and marched alongside Victor, while the entire groom's party danced around the groom and horse in a frenzied, celebratory manner. Everyone, from the youngest child to the oldest grandmother, was dancing and jumping. It was a spectacle, a show of the elation that the groom's party feels in the knowledge that they will soon be "gaining a daughter-in-law" into their family. The tradition stems from the notion, as described earlier, that the bride leaves her family and joins the family of her husband.

My father had come from India for the wedding and was in his glory, dancing with the groom's party in the parking lot. It was hot—one of the hottest days of that summer—and he was perspiring profusely. When I tried to stop him, he said, "We are accustomed to more heat than this in India. Do you understand how happy I feel that my American-born grandson is marrying an Indian girl?"

⁕

As is customary, when the groom's party reached the hotel doors from one end of the parking lot to the other (the bride's home, symbolically), the Shuklas welcomed us with open arms, and the two families met in *milni*: they hugged and got "united." The father of the groom hugged the father of the bride, dancing with each other; each uncle met uncle, grandfather met grandfather, and so on, while the drum sound was growing louder and louder. We broke another tradition: we had even the mother meeting the mother, and a loud cheer went up from the audience. Every time somebody was meeting, the drum player got a tip from groom's party and bride's party, and the sounds of his drum were becoming ear-shattering. It seemed like this *milni* went on forever, until the priest intervened and asked that the bride be brought from inside her "home" (a room upstairs in the hotel, in this case). Shilpa was beautifully adorned Indian style and brought down by her brother Samir and her friends. Victor and Shilpa exchanged ceremonial garlands and received blessings from their parents, a very poignant moment.

In a decorated hall the priest performed various rituals, and the couple was pronounced husband and wife. Lunch was served and everybody dispersed to rest and come back in the evening for the reception. The bride and groom sat in a *doli* (decorated car) and went to our house; now Shilpa was a member of our family. The Shukla family cried. They were losing a member of their family, even though we still lived on the same street.

⚜

It was a bit different with Nita. Poonam lost sleep for days before Nita's first prom. She was a junior, going to the prom with a very nice Indian boy from her school. We knew his parents, but still Poonam kept pacing for the whole evening until she came home.

Nita started dating late and shunned advances from young men for a long time. Her sporadic dates were always Americans, mostly Jewish. After finishing her studies at the University of Pennsylvania and her MBA at the Stern School of Business at New York University, she was living in Hoboken and visiting us frequently. Once she mentioned she was dating a man named Frank. We didn't know if he was an Italian or an Indian, as she said. We thought nothing of it until they started going together seriously and she found out that his real first name was Pankaj and his family was Punjabi, even though all his friends were Italian and everybody called him Frank. The similarity between the two families did not end there. When we met his parents—in a hotel lobby in Bridgewater, a meeting arranged by our children—we found out that they were from Rajinder Nagar in Delhi, only a couple of blocks from where I lived as a child. His mother might have gone to the same school as I, at the same time. They too had come to

354

Rajinder Nagar as refugees from Pakistan. (Marriages *are* made in heaven!)

Eventually Pankaj Khurana proposed to Nita, and they were engaged to be married in June 2005. By this time Indian weddings had come of age in America, and planning one was not such a difficult project. Of course, Nita and Pankaj and his parents were involved in every decision we made. We had attended many Indian weddings by then, some even more elaborate than Victor and Shilpa's several years earlier. Many chores had to be accomplished in India, like buying outfits for men and women, jewelry, wedding favors, and so on. (Nita wanted all her American girlfriends to wear Indian clothes on the night of the music program).

So Nita, Poonam, and I decided to go to India for three weeks. Pankaj had not been to India since he came to the United States as a toddler, and showed some interest in joining us. But how would society there look at us with him accompanying us, and not yet married to our daughter, not even formally engaged? We decided it was okay. I, the prodigal son, was going to defy social norms once again, and he went to India with us.

We had a delightful trip. We did all the shopping and went sightseeing in Delhi, Agra, and Rajasthan. We even attended a couple of weddings among the family and friends there. In my experience the grandeur and luxury of Indian hotels is unmatched anywhere in the world. And there is so much history in Rajasthan that three or four days there were really not enough, especially with Pankaj's interest in old architecture. The Taj Mahal, of course, cannot be described; it has to be witnessed and experienced. I expected a lot of snickers and raised eyebrows on us bringing our future son-in-law to the wedding of my cousin Anjali's son Ruchit, but to my surprise everyone was hospitable and welcoming.

⁂

Nita and Pankaj were married on June 11, 2005, with as many elaborate, carefully planned functions as any we had seen, at the Sheraton in Mahwah, New Jersey. They wanted the wedding to be performed outdoors and had beautiful ceremonies with fountains as the backdrop. In the *doli* ceremony, Pankaj took Nita in the decorated car, and her brother and cousins symbolically pushed the car to send her away. All the bride's party cried during that moment. Yes, I cried too; I was losing my little girl.

At the reception the same evening, there were 550 guests dancing and singing, eating and drinking, giving toasts and roasts. Nita wore an exquisite blue *lehnga* with silver embroidery, and Pankaj wore a matching custom-made tuxedo.

Nita and Pankaj now live in Princeton and have two young twin boys (with very non-Indian names: Shane and Devon). Victor and Shilpa live in Montville and have three children (with very Indian names: Dhruv Jagdish, Avani Maya, and Sarina Laxmi). Did our children take our suggestion for their children's names? Nope. We often attend our grandchildren's Little League games, soccer practices, dance recitals, and school functions.

Poonam and I feel very lucky to have our daughter-in-law, son-in-law, and grandchildren in our lives. We took a cruise, all of us together, a year ago and enjoyed it thoroughly. And now our children are planning a cruise for all of us next year, for our fortieth wedding anniversary. Poonam loves these family reunions and vacations; she lives for them.

⚜

During the wedding ceremonies of my children I couldn't help but reflect on the arranged marriage of my parents seventy years ago, then my early experiences in America, and going back and marrying Indira (now Poonam) after having had just a glance at her—and spending forty great years together. Our children found their own mates, American style, getting wed in Indian-American elegance. The contrasts between each generation and the next are just a microcosm of how social changes are happening around us, particularly for immigrant families. The next generation will have its own unique trials and tribulations, successes and failures.

Indians and Americans have their own particular social, political, and economic challenges, and they will resolve them in their own way. Despite the many problems facing both countries, and the world, I am hopeful about the future.

Acknowledgments

I have been blessed with three of the most wonderful women in the world: my wife, Poonam; my daughter, Nita; and my daughter-in-law, Shilpa. They read my drafts of the manuscript and gave suggestions. My greatest inspiration came from Nita, who kept asking me when I was going to write a book, any book. Then she said I should write my memoirs for the sake of my grandchildren and future generations. I agreed.

My brother Harish and his wife, my Bini *Bhabi*, made corrections, and I incorporated some of their ideas.

It was not completely a family affair. My friend Steve Clark read the manuscript, reread it, and Americanized the book. I am grateful for his invaluable help.

I would like to thank Janet Frick for her careful professional editing; she had to deal with my idiosyncrasies and my writing style. Also, I was pressing her to rush the project. I am grateful to Saija Autrand for her elegant cover and interior design, and everyone at Trafford Publishing who worked on this book.

Finally, a large number of people over the years have encouraged me to write my memoirs. They have my gratitude.

ISBN 142518512-6